# Praise for *How to Mellify a Corpse*

"Vicki León's *How to Mellify a Corpse* is a scintillating compendium of ancient beliefs and practices, from magical thinking to proto-scientific inklings."
—ADRIENNE MAYOR, author of *The Poison King* and *The First Fossil Hunters*

"León returns with another volume of fascinating miscellany, this time about the thought-world of the Greeks and Romans. Her lively anecdotes range from Stoics to stargazers, from ceremonial scapegoats to (mostly pseudo) scientists. In a world still poised between superstition and reason, León shows us that the examples of the ancients are more pertinent than you might think."
—STEVEN SAYLOR, author of *Empire: The Novel of Imperial Rome*

"Like a literary time machine, Vicki León's book plunks readers into the sandals of antiquity's greatest sages, soldiers, and kings. A captivating read from start to finish."
—ALAN HIRSHFELD, astrophysicist and author of *Eureka Man: The Life and Legacy of Archimedes*

"Vicki León's penetrating account of the Greco-Roman world ranges from forward-looking science, technology, and philosophy to mind-boggling superstition. All of it brought to life through a huge cast of real people, from the renowned to the deservedly obscure, and told with style, humor, and energy. It's a perfect combination: the ancient world seen through perceptive modern eyes."
—DR. STEPHEN MOORBATH, professor emeritus at the University of Oxford

"Vicki León has done it again, turning a litany of ancient names into warts-and-all portraits of real philosophers, early scientists, and architects. With acerbic wit, she makes accessible the complex teachings of our icons from the deep past."
—DR. JACQUELINE WALDREN, Institute of Social and Cultural Anthropology and International Gender Studies at the University of Oxford

"An endlessly fascinating book, full of things that are shocking, unsettling, and, of course, just plain weird."
—*Booklist*

## Praise for *Working IX to V*

"Vicki León has the rare gift of being able to conjure sharp prose from serious study. *Working IX to V* is a delight: a richly entertaining romp through the everyday lives of people whose world was, in their own eyes, not ancient at all."
—RUTH DOWNIE, author of *Semper Fidelis: A Novel of the Roman Empire*

"What I really like about *Working IX to V* are its fascinating portraits of a remarkable range of people in the ancient past. They are funny, they are outlandish, as people often are, but the portraits are authentic and they bring the past to life. Beyond the belly laughs, Vicki León reveals herself as a researcher and writer of immense curiosity and considerable erudition whose enjoyment of the classical world is lovingly and wittily presented to her readers in this book."
—MICHAEL HAAG, author of *Alexandria: City of Memory*

"Move over, Plato, Caesar, and Cicero! Make way for the down-and-dirty lifeblood of ancient Greece and Rome. The classical world has never been such a hoot as it is under the deft quill of Vicki León. One would expect an author of such impeccable scholarship to be dry as a bone. Instead she tickles our funny bone, finding a way to indelibly stamp the weird and fascinating details of ancient Greece and Rome into our brains."
—ROBIN MAXWELL, author of *Jane: The Woman Who Loved Tarzan* and
  *The Secret Diary of Anne Boleyn*

"Drawing on the same outrageous sense of humor that's made her Uppity Women series so popular, León demonstrates how uncannily similar the workaday experiences of the ancient world are to ours."
—*Publishers Weekly*

# THE JOY OF SEXUS

## LUST, LOVE, & LONGING IN THE ANCIENT WORLD

## VICKI LEÓN

Walker & Company
New York

Published by Walker Publishing Company, Inc., New York

A Division of Bloomsbury Publishing

All papers used by Walker & Company are natural, recyclable products
made from wood grown in well-managed forests. The manufacturing processes
conform to the environmental regulations of the country of origin.

LIBRARY OF CONGRESS CATALOGING-IN-PUBLICATION DATA
HAS BEEN APPLIED FOR.

ISBN: 978-0-8027-1997-3

Visit Walker & Company's website at www.walkerbooks.com

First U.S. edition 2013

1 3 5 7 9 10 8 6 4 2

Designed and typeset by Suzanne Albertson

Printed in the U.S.A.

# CONTENTS

꘎꘎꘎꘎꘎꘎꘎

## SECTION III

# Legendary Loves & Sometimes-Real Romances 65

## SECTION IV

# Love Hurts. But Changing Gender Really Smarts 97

## SECTION V

# Red-Letter Days & Red-Hot Nights 129

## SECTION VI

# Love Is a Many-Splendored Thing 157

## SECTION VII

# For the Love of It—Pure Passions 191

## SECTION VIII

# Demon Lovers & Gods Dark & Light  223

## SECTION IX

# Love Dilemmas & Lust at the Crossroads  249

# INTRODUCTION

Y ou've read the clichés about platonic love, heard about Sappho and lesbian relationships, seen the Roman orgy movies. But what was sexuality really like in ancient times? Did the Greeks and Romans get married only to have procreative sex, or was erotic pleasure part of the bargain? What about romantic love, and who shared it? Did anyone call themselves transgendered? And what was the true status of gays?

Scientists, wildlife researchers, and religious leaders have declared for centuries that human homosexuality must be an aberration or a choice, because it does not occur in the natural world. Wrong. In our times, to the

*Orgies might look chaotic but an emcee directed activities.*
*No last-minute walk-ins, either; members only.*

surprise and delight of many, biologists and researchers in the field have observed more than 450 different species engaging in same-gender mating activities, including bighorn sheep, albatrosses, beetles, bison, bonobos, ostriches, guppies, warthogs, flamingos, and various species of butterflies.

Their hijinks have been noted in the *New York Times* and elsewhere, with piquant details such as these: "A female koala might force another female against a tree and mount her . . . releasing what one scientist described as 'exhalated belchlike sounds.'" And further: "Male Amazon river dolphins have been known to penetrate each other in the blowhole."

With these discoveries, the whole paradigm of sexuality has changed. Instead of just the Darwinian imperative to pass on our genes, it appears that a certain saucy broad called Mother Nature might also just like to have fun. As yet, we don't know how these same-sex activities among creatures other than humans impact reproductive strategies. Who knows—we may find they create indirect ways of survival in a whole host of species, including our own.

Another factor besides evolution is in play here: biological exuberance. The jaw-dropping variety of animal and plant life covering this planet carries out its sexual mission in countless complex ways. None of it is aberrant. All of it demonstrates the lavish way in which life exhibits its rainbow of options.

As author Bruce Bagemihl argues in his book *Biological Exuberance*, given the apparent "purposelessness" of so much mating activity in the wild, scientists have had to rethink their basic models of what sex is all about. His take on it? "Sex is life's celebration of its own gaudy excess.

*Most centaurs were half-male, half-horse, but who's to say there weren't mythical chick centaurs among them?*

It's an affirmation of life's vitality and infinite possibilities; a worldview that is at once primordial and futuristic, in which gender is kaleidoscopic, sexualities are multiple, and the categories of male and female are fluid and transmutable."

In countless ways, the ancient Greeks and Romans would agree with his theory—and confirm it. Although some were sophisticated thinkers, most were plainspoken, earthy folk. They treasured physicality. Knowing early death too well, they lived in the moment. They absorbed life through their pores.

Although Greek and Latin words and roots were used to create such terms as *heterosexual*, *bisexual*, *homosexual*, and *lesbian*, both cultures would have looked askance at these labels. To them, all manifestations of love and erotic behavior were somehow connected, all part of a whole. Men and women alike craved love but also feared its power; they called it the thunderbolt, that love-at-first-look feeling. To them, love could have claws. Passion—fulfilled or unrequited—could be as bitter as myrrh.

With trepidation, they entered the game with joy nonetheless. And they played it in a dizzying variety of ways—female-to-female relationships, male-to-younger-male courtships, same-sex wedded couples, male-female marriages, short-term liaisons, dynastic incest, bonded military lovers, and still other combinations you'll get to know in this book.

As in today's world, love took many forms, from maternal to altruistic, from hard-hearted to passionate. No one has a definitive answer as to why the Greeks and Romans of both genders handled their sexual urges and love imperatives in the complex

*As the Greeks knew, Cupid's arrows stung, often randomly scoring a bull's-eye.*

way they did, but several aspects of those cultures offer provocative clues.

First of all, neither the Greeks nor the Romans thought about sinfulness and guilt in the Judeo-Christian sense. The idea of mankind's fall from grace never occurred to them. Even women, despite having to endure a lifetime of domineering males, would laugh incredulously at the thought of sex being a sin. Adultery could be a crime, as could rape, but for reasons other than sinfulness. A tangle of laws eventually would seek—not always successfully—to control some sexual behaviors and criminalize others.

In their polytheistic societies that we call pagan, there were no churches or congregations as we know them, no priests to lecture or act as middlemen to a deity. They believed in a celestial place, jam-packed with gods and goddesses who were divine yet flawed. In them, Greeks and Romans saw themselves, at once perfect and imperfect. Some of their supreme beings were lifelong virgins: Artemis, Athena, and Vesta. Other deities were sex addicts, troublemakers who rarely paid a penalty for their misbehavior. Sex, love, jealousy, and revenge were integral parts of the gods' lives, and thus it seemed right that human lives should echo them.

*She's awfully short, but I could still get aroused.*

As John Clarke, author of *Looking at Lovemaking: Constructions of Sexuality in Rome Art*, says: "The Romans are not at all like us in their sexuality . . . Here was a world before Christianity, before the Puritan ethic, before the association of shame and guilt with sexual acts. And it is a world that had many more voices than the ones we hear in the ancient texts that have survived."

Both Greeks and Romans felt the urgent need to have more than one deity on the job to handle the myriad aspects of love and sexual activity. Not only that, but both cultures freely borrowed deities from one another or created parallel ones: the Greek Aphrodite and Eros paralleled the Roman Venus and Cupid, for instance. Since marriage therapists, daytime television, chat rooms, and self-help books were not yet on tap, the love deities eventually amassed an entourage of minor gods devoted to different aspects of passion, from seduction to unrequited love. The same applied to deities of sexuality, fertility, marriage, and childbirth. They were equally important in the everyday lives of long-ago people, who routinely sought their advice and asked them to intercede in their personal lives.

Diane Ackerman, author of *A Natural History of Love* and many other books, has recently written about interpersonal neurobiology and the discovery that the brain is constantly rewiring itself based on daily life. As she eloquently puts it, "as a wealth of imaging studies highlight, the neural alchemy continues throughout life as we mature and forge friendships, dabble in affairs, succumb to romantic love, choose a soul mate."

That continual growth and flexibility was something that the Greeks and Romans came by organically. They expressed it through ecstatic and transformative experiences, such as being initiated into the Eleusinian Mysteries or the Bacchic rites; or by taking part in females-only retreats, such as the Thesmophoria festivals held in fifty parts of Greece. They sought it through all-night symposium sessions with the guys, arguing over the meanings of love and its relation to goodness; or by watching and weeping at Greek dramas or at ceremonies conducted by Rome's vestal virgins. In their ardent drive to feel love and achieve sexual connection, the Greeks and Romans were irrepressible.

*The love goddess is in; please take a number.*

Unstoppable. But realistic. With a smile, they said in Latin, *Amantes sunt amentes*—lovers are lunatics.

Within these pages, you'll meet a wildly diverse crowd, whose outspoken and at times baldly X-rated language and actions may shock you. These are men and women in the raw. In the flesh. Some in love, hotly glowing. Others in longing or betrayal, darkly poisonous. Most are Greeks and Romans, but entries also incorporate other cultures and nationalities who became part of the Roman Empire. To add richness, Greco-Roman views and customs are compared with those of Persians, Jews, ancient Egyptians, Etruscans, and more.

You'll meet familiar faces—including Socrates and the men and women who adored him; Ankhesenamun, Egyptian pharaoh Tut's young wife, a serial victim of incest, although she wouldn't have called herself a victim; and the outrageous sister-in-law of famed poet Sappho. And unfamiliar faces as well, including the busy women and men who produced the first porn books and the first *Joy of Sex* how-to manuals—some of them illustrated! Plus the sex-addicted daughter of emperor Octavian Augustus, who single-handedly shattered his plans for a more moralistic Roman society.

You'll explore other love fixations and sexual obsessions, from dolphin adoration to beautiful buttocks, from fears about hermaphrodites to fears about garden thievery. Plus examples of selfless love, one being the unusual tale of the real-life Amazon who loved and fought alongside Mithradates, the rebellious king who defied the Romans for decades.

In addition, I've included the best myths and legendary tales of love and sexual surrender within these pages, from Helen of Troy's real career to the musical love story of Orpheus and Eurydice.

*Mark Antony went wild on Lupercalia but didn't do badly the rest of the year, either. He had five marriages and countless liaisons.*

The mechanics and body parts of biology and love also get their due, from long-ago kissing to the important role played by masturbation in ancient myth; from foreskin meddling to Hymen, the god of maidenheads. Since much of Greco-Roman sexuality was celebrated through traditional festivals, you'll eavesdrop on snake handlers, follow the phallic processions, and attend Lupercalia, the wild and wolfish celebration that preceded our Valentine's Day.

Over the decades that I've spent in the sunburnt corners of Greece and Italy and the lands circling the Mediterranean Sea, I've searched for clues about the flesh-and-blood people who once lived and loved there. And I've studied those who live and love there still.

Over time, I've come to understand what mattered to them: Their rootedness to their family homes, to their village or city. Philoxenia, their hospitable love of strangers. Their sensual awareness, their way of living in the moment. Their rough, bawdy humor. The way in which they lived their music in their bones. Their awareness of posterity, procreation, and the importance of their children. Above all, their fearlessness when it came to expressing emotion and to boldly courting that which gives life meaning.

I've also glimpsed the casual brutality of those long-ago times—the darkly punitive aspects of enslaved societies, and how sharply they contrasted with the desperate lengths to which the privileged sometimes went to stave off sexual boredom. To feel truly alive.

To help you see, feel, and grasp what I've found, I've drawn from a huge well of often contradictory pieces of evidence, written and pictorial, highbrow and lowbrow, from philosophical musings to lewd graffiti, from love charms to personal letters, from secondhand gossip to respected archaeological sources.

*Stone statuettes*

*Since earliest times, humans have admired the fecund female and worshipped her miraculous ability to bring new life.*

Countless people, places, events, and topics in this book intertwine in interesting ways, so you'll find them cross-referenced within entries and also in the index.

As the Greeks would urge: drink deeply!

*Let's get this drunken revel on the road—*
*I'm getting goosebumps!*

# The Birds, the Bees,
# & the Body Parts

# APHRODISIACS:

## Love solutions from Aphrodite

When it came to intimacy readiness, Greek and Roman lovers were perennially inventive. They set store by a wide spectrum of aphrodisiacs, some still in hopeful use today, including raw oysters, the fleshy symbol of the goddess Aphrodite (Venus among the Romans). Aphrodite emerged from the foamy crest of ocean waves, which the Greeks saw as a type of marine semen. Some adventurous thinkers also believed that women discharged semen—but naturally the male variety was the only starter that counted.

These pioneers on the frontiers of sexual virility wandered far beyond oysters, however. Pomegranate juice from Aphrodite's favorite tree, mixed with wine, scored high with ancient Egyptians and other males in the Middle East. So did lettuce. Although toxic, mandrake root was an evergreen. So was opium as a wine additive.

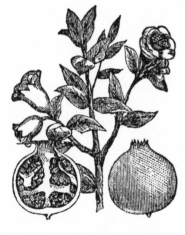

Many ardent souls preferred lotions applied directly to the male organ—one provocative but now-mysterious favorite was called "the deadly carrot." Some approaches, however, such as the honey-pepper mix, the tissue-irritating nettle oil, and the cantharides beetle (Spanish fly), gave painful new meaning to the expression "All fired up and ready to go."

An everyday erotic helper was olive oil, with or without additives such as coriander. It was invariably slathered on before lovemaking. Greek wives kept an earthenware container of it by the bed, since they were expected to personally anoint their husbands' members.

*As an aphrodisiac, the pomegranate wine cooler had an enthusiastic following around the ancient world.*

The medicine cabinet of the average Roman male held an array of herbal plants and potions, an aromatic ointment made from spikenard being very popular. Other aids to Venus were added to wine, a social lubricant that provided a one-two punch: among them, gentian and a red-leafed root in the orchid family called satyrion, named for the randy prowess of the mythical satyrs. Roman emperor Tiberius, on the other hand, swore by another exotic tuber called skirret.

Some aphrodisiacs (including the roots of mandrake and satyrion) were thought powerful enough to work by being handheld, although that might have presented its own problems in the boudoir. Other potency objects, from red coral to wormwood, could simply be placed under the bed to be efficacious.

The "like attracts like" theory of sympathetic magic played a big part. Men routinely wore amulets resembling male and female genitalia. Beyond the items to be worn, ingested, held, or rubbed on, women and men alike had steadfast belief in the power of love potions and binding spells. Such spells got extra vigor by using nail clippings, hair, or excretions of one sort or another from the beloved, the object of desire, or the one who'd done the dumping.

Given the staggering variety of nostrums, modern readers may long to know: Did any of these measures actually put steel into the male organ, and/or make the ladies more inclined?

Like our verbally aroused websites and spam e-mails today, there were testimonials and stories aplenty; then as now, evidence was more anecdotal than scientific. In imperial Roman times, however, at least one court trial did revolve around apparent aphrodisiac success.

The defendant? Apuleius of Madauros, today remembered chiefly as the author of *The Golden Ass*. A glib orator, Apuleius was quite a successful social climber from a more modest family background than his girlfriend, Pudentilla, a wealthy widow. In A.D. 158 he was sued by her irate family for seducing her into marriage. How did he do it? According to his own defense speech, which has survived the millennia, he merely fed her a splendid dinner of oysters, sea urchins, cuttlefish, and lobster. An aphrodisiac blue-plate special, loaded with zinc—maybe Apuleius was onto something.

## ANTI-APHRODISIACS:
### Reverse Viagra or face-saver?

Roman and Greek males of yore thought of themselves as raging bulls of desire, whose drive at times might be overwhelming. Their wives, lovers, concubines, and household slaves, male and female, no doubt agreed, but for different reasons. Fortunately, men had already discovered the solution for the too-potent Latin libido: loading up on anti-aphrodisiacs, the reverse Viagra of ancient times.

What were these Cupid controllers that could dampen physical urges? Consuming cress, purslane, cannabis seeds, nasturtium flowers, or the ashes of the chaste tree would do the trick. So would that horrific, erection-withering substance, fresh lettuce. In order to *maintain* sexual vigor, Greek and Roman male diners were careful to combine lettuce with aphrodisiacally active arugula to neutralize it. Or just avoid lettuce like the plague. (On the other hand, lettuce was considered highly lascivious among the Egyptians, as you'll learn in section II of this book.)

Mouse dung, applied as a liniment, was a favorite anti-aphrodisiac. So was rue boiled with rose oil and aloes. Drinking wine in which a mullet fish had drowned and sipping male urine in which a lizard had expired both had their loyal adherents.

Nevertheless, taming truly terrific potency required strong measures, like nymphaea, an herb guaranteed to "relax" the phallus for a few days. One writer even boasted that it would "take away desire and even sex dreams for forty days!"

Consumers and healers alike put powerful faith in certain animal parts, including those of the hippopotamus, the exotic wonder drug of the age. Hippo parts were believed to have multiple curative powers. For snakebite, victims simply choked down a coin-sized piece of hippo testicle in water. If troubled by mange, they burned hippo hide until reduced to ash, then applied it. For the hippo's vital role in temporarily inhibiting sexual desire, users were instructed to take the hide from the left side of a hippo's forehead, then attach it firmly to the groin. The woman's groin, that is. (After studying the matter, I'm convinced that the struggle to attach the device, much less wearing it, would make both partners give up sex—perhaps forever.)

That recipe, among many others, comes from Pliny the Elder's multivolume book *Natural History*. He goes on to say: "A most powerful medicament is obtained by reducing to ashes the nails of a lynx, together with the hide ... these ashes, taken in drink, have the effect of checking abominable desires in men ... and if they are sprinkled upon women, all libidinous thoughts will be restrained."

We long to know more than Pliny and other writers offhandedly tell us about hippos' foreheads, ashes of lynx, lizards drowned in male urine, and the blood from the ticks

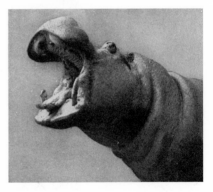

*We'll never know why, but a hippo's forehead was considered just the thing to rein in those hyperactive sex drives in males.*

taken from a wild black bull. Where did one obtain these rare and exotic substances? Didn't they smell to high heaven? Was stench the active ingredient? How on earth did they strap these things on? Ancient recipes tantalize. Being free of details, they leave us to imagine the startling lengths to which Greeks and Romans tried to manipulate their sex lives.

Equally ingenious was the face-saving marketing involved. As their libidos waxed and waned, men told each other that anti-aphrodisiacs were essential to control their otherwise overpowering sexual drives. Long-ago women, always on the lookout for ways to control conception and flatter at the same time, wisely kept mum.

## SPONTANEOUS GENERATION:
### Birds, bees, wind in the trees

When it came to reproductive matters in the natural world, most Greeks had myopia. Granted, it's easy to miss the mating antics of insects and worms, and watery species from eels to shellfish. Instead of supposing that their methods of reproduction took place far from prying human eyes, natural scientists of that time preferred to believe that certain species had the knack for spontaneous generation. No parents needed.

Aristotle, for instance, announced that caterpillars reproduced from dew, grubs came from dung or fig trees, gnats from timber, and worms from snow or putrefying sap. Furthermore, he taught that bugs emerged from dried sweat, flies from vinegar slime, and certain winged insects from fire. He wasn't alone, either.

It was widely believed that the common cicada sprang from the spittle of cuckoo birds—and that bees never mated, instead buzzing to life from putrefying matter. While the wild bee population quietly went about reproducing itself, honey-gatherers and beekeepers in every corner of the Greek world wasted a lot of time slaughtering oxen, leaving them to rot, and anxiously awaiting a new batch of bees to form in the stinking carcasses.

Aristotle was far from being a theoretical intellectual. Unlike Plato, he enjoyed empirical field research; he even spent his honeymoon grubbing around the tidepools on the island of Lesbos. (This may say more about his marriage than his vocation.) He took copious notes on his work, insisting later that eels grew spontaneously from mud. He also claimed that mussels, oysters, hermit crabs, and the murex (a nearshore mollusk valued for its purple dye) grew out of the slimy gunk that formed on the bottoms of ships.

Even when observing mammals and larger creatures, the Greeks utterly failed to spot any X-rated action, giving rise to widespread beliefs that mice reproduced by licking salt—or, in a pinch, by licking themselves. Fantastical theories abounded. As Pliny the encyclopedist confidently wrote, "We have it from many authorities that a snake may be born from the spinal marrow of a human being."

The generative powers of the wind were blamed for the conception of some animals. Breezes, especially the wayward one called "the fecundating spirit of the world," could impregnate mares, sheep, and tigers. Fowl too could produce what were called "wind eggs."

When Christianity really got rolling in the second and third centuries A.D., church leaders often used the widespread belief in spontaneous generation and wind impregnation to defend the virgin birth of Christ. Church father Augustine helpfully pointed out that Noah didn't have to stock the ark with two of every species, since insects and other creatures could do their own generating.

*Although Greeks and Romans adored honey and kept bees, they also subscribed to the mad belief that new bees sprang from the rotting corpses of livestock.*

## HYMEN:

### A god, a song, a membrane

Known in Latin as *hymen vaginae*, throughout history this elastic little membrane over the vaginal opening has caused a world of trouble for women. It's a pretty standard part of reproductive systems, one that human females share with elephants, manatees, whales, horses, and chimps. But don't get too proud—the hymen is also standard equipment in slugs and several other humble species.

Some human females are born without hymens; some tear the membrane in childhood—and in still other cases, the darn thing entirely covers the opening, which usually requires surgery in order for a girl to menstruate without pain.

For these reasons and more, ten out of ten doctors today will tell you that it is impossible to confirm virginity by hymen examination. Nothwithstanding, various cultures around the globe have made—and continue to make—life hell for their women by insisting that you cannot have the former without the latter.

How did the hymen get its name? Oddly enough, Hymen (or Hymenaeus) was a minor male deity, the god of marriage ceremonies. In ancient Greece, members of the wedding party would call his name aloud, to make sure that Hymen attended; it meant rotten luck for brides and grooms if he didn't show. In his Greek tragedies, playwright Euripides called Hymen "the god of hot desire!" which makes him sound more like a male stripper.

The deity Hymen was sometimes thought to be a mortal youth who looked very feminine; by other accounts, he was the son of the god Apollo.

Hymen was also pictured as a pretty child with wings, usually carrying a torch in his hand to escort the bride. In Greco-Roman art, his image is easily mistaken for one of the Erotes, the winged love godlings who were part of Aphrodite's entourage, discussed elsewhere in this book.

As in today's world, weddings were big business in ancient times. A great many Greek poets, from Hesiod and Alcman to the great Sappho, earned fat commissions by composing beautiful melodies and verses to Hymen the marriage god. They were called *hymenaios*. Sappho and company also cleaned up by writing poetic lyrics that were sung outside the wedding chamber itself, called *epithalamia*.

At Roman weddings, on the other hand, guests belted out obscene lyrics to the tunes that were traditionally called *fescennines*.

Dancing through the streets with torches lit, the members of a typical Greek wedding procession followed the carriage of the bride and groom, singing the *hymenaios*. Male and female members of the wedding party sang alternating verses to each other, filled with happy, flirtatious, often bawdy words, many of them double entendres about the frightening size of the groom and the purity of the bride. Each verse ended in the words "O Hymenaeus Hymen, O Hymen Hymenaeus."

Once the newlywed couple entered the flower-adorned nuptial chamber, with the best man guarding the door, the wedding party stood outside and all of the young women sang the *epithalamia*. Accompanied by flutes and lyre, they warbled verse after verse. Why such noisy, lengthy entertainment outside the chamber? According to an ancient commentary on the wedding poetry of Theocritus, "The epithalamia is sung, in order that the cries of the young bride, while she is offered violence by her husband, may not be heard, but may be drowned in the song of the girls."

Curiously enough, among Romans, maidenheads were sometimes broken beforehand for a religious reason, the belief in divine impregnation. According to author Barbara Walker's *Women's Encyclopedia of Myths and Secrets*, "Roman brides routinely deflowered themselves on the wooden or stone phalluses of Hermes, Priapus, Tutunus, or some other 'anointed' god before lying with their bridegrooms, so that their firstborn children would be god-begotten."

In earliest Roman times, a life-size phallus of Tutunus, the ithyphallic god of fertility, was present at the ceremony itself. Two long-ago authors noted that brides were obliged to sit on it to promote their fertility while chasing away evil.

Since time immemorial, brides-to-be have sought help with hymeneal restoration in those cultures where to be lacking meant an unpleasant death. Long-ago Greek brides who'd already lost their virginity often stuffed small sponges soaked in blood in the appropriate aperture. Another traditional solution was the deft use of leeches in the hours prior to the wedding-night consummation, a method used with some success since ancient times and into the modern era, by groups as diverse as medieval Italians and nineteenth-century brothel workers in London. Hymenoplasty surgery to repair maidenheads routinely takes place in many parts of the world today, including in Muslim communities. In Japan, the procedure is poetically called "virginity rebirth."

Hymen, that ancient deity, would no doubt get a chuckle out of all that premarital skullduggery.

## CLITORIS:

### From a verb to a deformity

Back in the B.C. era, the Greek medical community smugly "discovered" that a certain nubby little organ possessed by women was the feminine equivalent of the penis, or so they thought. They called it *clitoris*, from the Greek word meaning "to shut." Their other name for it was *nymphi*, meaning "bride" or "lovely young woman." (In our time, the plural *nymphae* still refers to the labia minora, although the term is usually employed only by physicians.)

Since long-ago masculine ideas about sex and satisfaction could be boiled down to the simple equation: "males—active; females—passive," a feminine organ that looked and acted a bit like a would-be phallus, in miniature, was repugnant to the average Greek male, who wanted no part of feminine sexual aggression.

This was especially true when it came to size. Any clitoris bigger than petite was thought to be excess baggage. What better course of action than to get rid of it in cosmetic surgery fashion? Is this starting to sound like the epidemic of female circumcision and genital mutilation in today's world? It should.

Grotesque as it sounds, medical advice in the first century B.C. and the first few A.D. centuries, even from the likes of leading practitioner Soranos, author of *Gynaikeia*, and his colleagues, was: cut it off. Here is a verbatim quote from a primary source entitled "Concerning an immensely great clitoris." (This isn't praise, trust me.) "An uncouth size is present in certain clitorises and brings women into disorder by the deformity of the private parts. As most people say, these same women, affected by the lust (or erection) typical of men, take on a similar desire, and they approach sexual intercourse (with men) only under duress. If it comes to that [i.e., an operation], the women is to be placed lying on her back and with thighs closed, lest the viscera of the feminine cavity become distended. Then the excess part is to be held in place with a small forceps and cut back with a scalpel in proportion to its unnatural size."

The writer cautions against whacking too much of it off, since "it produces an excessively harmful effect on the patient by the copious discharge of the cutting back." As in bleeding to death, I suspect.

Paulus of Aegina, a later Greek writer, agrees but also claims that such women are eager for sex. As he puts it, "An immensely great clitoris occurs

*As Rome's political schemer Fulvia found out, it wasn't easy being a hell-raiser.*
*She gained such a reputation for belligerence that soldiers wrote*
*naughty words about her clitoris on their slingstones.*

in some women; the presenting problem is shameful impropriety. According to what some people report, some even have erections similar to men on account of the [bodily] part and are eager for sexual intercourse."

The Romans felt equally daunted by an aggressive, too-large clitoris, called *landica* in Latin. On the stones and lead projectiles they made for warfare, soldiers and slingers often wrote obscenities and vile messages aimed at the enemy. Archaeologists have found at least one lead projectile on which is scrawled *Fulviae landicam peto*, "I'm aimed at the clitoris of Fulvia."

Fulvia was a real person, a detested political spitfire who jumped in and led an army into civil war because her husband at the time, Mark Antony, was busy committing bigamy with Queen Cleopatra VII of Egypt. Hey, perhaps Fulvia had her own lead projectiles with obscene suggestions about Cleopatra on them. You'll read more about Mark, Cleo, and fascinating Fulvia elsewhere in this book.

## CIRCUMCISION:
### Foreskin meddling

When it came to genital modification, males in the ancient world suffered more extensively than females. Whenever the Egyptians went to war and captured POWs, they weeded out the uncircumcised men and snipped off their genitals. The circumcised prisoners did not fare much better, I regret to say; they kept their jewels but lost their hands!

Archaeologists have found mummies with indications of circumcision, and estimate that the practice had been going on in Egypt since the twenty-third century B.C. In their culture, circumcision took place at puberty.

Although the Egyptians had sharp knives of copper, and medications to stop the bleeding (made from honey, cuttlebone, and sycamore), the operation clearly stung. A well-preserved wall relief from an Egyptian tomb shows two teens getting circumcised; it includes dialogue between those operating, which says: "Hold him, do not let him faint!"

In contrast to the ancient Egyptians, who made a V-shaped cut and left the foreskin to dangle on either side, the Jews removed the entire prepuce. The Old Testament contains some terrifying tales of circumcision. King David, instead of giving his new father-in-law the bride-price in gold, or a nice box of cigars, was forced to fork over one hundred foreskins taken from their traditional enemies, those foreskin-flaunting Philistines.

*Some long-ago cultures circumcised male newborns; others, such as the Egyptians, inflicted it on their teenagers.*

What scholars (and everyday Bible readers) call the Old Testament's most baffling verse is Exodus 4:25–26. In it, Zipporah, the wife of Moses, uses a flint and circumcises their son Gershom herself, then declares, "You're a bridegroom of blood to me."

Although the Canaanites, Phoenicians, and other groups practiced circumcision, some neighboring tribes did not. As told in Genesis, it so happened the prince of the Shechemites sneakily had illicit sex with Dinah, the daughter of Jacob. What made it so heinous in Jewish eyes was the fact that the prince sported a foreskin. The two families consulted; because the prince loved Dinah, his father suggested that the two tribes intermarry—to which the sons of Jacob agreed, if all the Shechemite males first got circumcised. The prince and his people duly went for it. On the third day, however, when all

Shechemite males were still clutching their crotches in agony, the Israelites massacred them.

One of the key reasons for the Jewish uprising called the revolt of the Maccabees was due to the banning of traditional Jewish practices by Seleucid ruler Antiochus IV. He outlawed circumcision with the death penalty.

During Greco-Roman times, male Jews sometimes drew unwelcome attention in the public baths and gymnasia because men used the facilities primarily in the nude. To be able to participate or possibly just blend in with uncircumcised males, some Jews actually had prepuce reconstruction surgery in Judaea.

The Greeks abhorred cutting but did meddle with male penises in other ways. At gym workouts and in competitive sports, such as running, men took part in the nude but insisted on covering the glans or tip of the penis. To do so, they pulled the stretchy foreskin over the tip, concealing and then tying it with what they called a "dog leash" knot. At times, they used a thin leather lace to secure the knot.

Although it would seem a question of personal choice, male circumcision—its benefits and drawbacks, its place in Jewish and Islamic traditions, and current accusations about children's rights and infant mutilation—is again making news around the world today.

## CONTRACEPTION:
### Birth control, alpha to omega

Long-ago women tried a vast number of inconceivable approaches to contraception and birth control.

A great many of them were alarming, worthless, magical, and/or harmful strategies to prevent pregnancy. Among the plethora of bad choices? Drinking iron rust. Consuming mint, parsley, or asparagus juice. Extracting worms from a certain big spider, fixing them onto deerskin, then attaching them to a woman's body.

There were two old favorites that would be known in family planning circles today as "closing the barn door after the cows get out." The first instructed the user to rub male and/or female private parts with cedar oil or honey—*after* coitus. The second advised inserting a pepper-covered pessary (an early "tampon" made of lint or wool) once sexual intercourse had already been accomplished.

Back in the time of Hippocrates and his disciples, the fifth century B.C., doctors and healers from the Holy Land to Greece suspected that something from both male and female humans had to unite in order to cause conception. A disciple-written Hippocratic essay called "On the Nature of Women" says: "After coitus, if a woman ought not to conceive, she makes it a custom for the semen to fall outside when she wishes this." This could have been coitus interruptus, using fingers to wipe out the vagina, or expelling the semen by deliberate sneezing or douching.

One of the humblest birth control methods may have been fairly effective. Women employed olive oil, usually as a pessary inserted into the vagina. The oil's viscosity did a darned good job of decreasing sperm motility. Other effective methods included alum; gum resin from the acacia tree (its lactic acid is a good spermicide); vinegar (its acid kills sperm); honey (sticky as olive oil) on wool plugs or other objects to block the entrance to the vagina. A recipe found in the Kahun Papyrus, the world's earliest known contraceptive advice, suggests a paste made of milk and crocodile dung. While high in the "ick" factor, the paste would have been absorbent and entrance-plugging as well.

Aristotle also recommended olive oil, albeit failing to keep toxic lead out of the picture. As he put it, "Anoint that part of the womb on which the seed falls with oil of cedar, ointment of lead, or frankincense mingled with olive oil."

Ancient Egyptians and Jews followed a similar train of thought, using olive oil on a sponge as a vaginal insert—thousands of years before Dr. Marie Stopes lobbied for a more advanced version on behalf of England's poor women. The oily sponge was an invaluable innovation, since it made insertion and removal much easier and more reliable. Some Jewish authorities also insisted that women use the sponge *during* pregnancy to prevent injury to the fetus or a second fertilization (which they thought possible).

There were hundreds of plants and herbs whose active ingredients were thought to be contraceptive in nature. Many of these substances would (theoretically) act as birth control agents in smaller doses, and as abortifacients in larger ones; thus, those who prescribed them—and those who took them—really had to know what they were doing.

What, if anything, was the most effective contraceptive in Greco-Roman times? No contest: the remarkable plant called laser or silphion (in Latin, silphium), a relative of asafoetida or giant fennel. Depending on the amount and the time of month it was taken, silphium could serve as a reliable birth control agent or a menstrual cycle regulator. Most accounts agreed that it was a relatively harmless abortifacient if used correctly. Women

*Unlike the unlovely body parts of the hippo, the silphium plant gave results, being the closest thing to a reliable birth control agent.*

would drink a tea made from its large leaves, or take it in wine containing a small amount of the plant's sap. Silphium juice was also made into a pessary; possibly this was the method most frequently used to bring on a miscarriage.

Silphium was rare; the wild plant only grew within a restricted area on the plateau of the Greek city-state of Cyrene (present-day Libya) and resisted all attempts to domesticate it. After its discovery in the seventh century B.C., silphium became exceedingly popular, and not just for female reproductive use. Its sharp juice served as a key flavor enhancer in cooking. It was also touted as an antidote for poison and a panacea for everything from warts to leprosy.

By the middle of the first century A.D., silphium was worth its weight in silver denarii. In fact, the plant itself appeared on the beautiful coins of Cyrene. Importer-exporters made fortunes, filling the ever-growing demand. Around A.D. 55, however, disaster struck. Terrible weather occurred that year, as did overgrazing by local sheep in Cyrene. But the last straw was a dispute between the natives who harvested the wild silphium and the Cyrenaic city officials. When a meeting of the minds failed, the angry harvesters ripped out all the plants they could find.

A Roman importer managed to obtain a stalk of the last wild specimen. Hoping to score big financially, he delivered it in person to the current emperor—who happened to be Nero. After paying for it, Nero callously consumed the plant, down to the last bite. Why? Because, as Roman emperor, he could.

# PREGNANCY AND CHILDBIRTH:
## Tattoos, prayers, & birthing bricks

Pregnancy and childbirth in long-ago cultures were chancy situations, rites of passage that women devoutly prayed for and desperately feared at the same time.

Prenatal care, vitamin intake, baby showers, and other pastimes? Not bloody likely. Mesopotamian, Egyptian, Greek, and Roman women were more apt to wear protective amulets and spend time on their knees, praying to an array of goddesses who concerned themselves with pregnancy and safe delivery. Egyptian mothers-to-be asked for help from Hathor, goddess of fertility, and from the hippo goddess Tawaret, who guarded newborns and women in labor. They also made offerings to Bes, a dwarf god who warded off evil spirits. As reported by the *Smithsonian* magazine, some researchers now believe that pregnant women in predynastic Egypt wore tattoos as protective amulets on their abdomens, thighs, and breasts. They cite certain tattoos that have been found solely on female mummies, which range from patterns of dots and diamond shapes to small images of the god Bes.

Pregnant Greek women were pretty much stuck with one goddess, called Eileithyia, for prenatal guidance and childbirth protection. Roman women, however, called on a number of specialized deities. To ask for the help of Candelifera or Lucina, expectant moms lit a candle. Carmentis had a childbirth festival to observe, and she was invoked in one of two ways as the baby came into the world: Postverta, meaning "feet first," and

*Although children were longed for and childless couples often adopted, pregnancy was a high-risk gamble way back when.*

Prorsa, meaning "head first." Diana and Di Nixi were also major goddesses of childbirth.

Not to overlook the help of male gods, women also prayed to brother deities named Pilumnus and Picumnus who kept newborns from evil spirits and doubled as gods of happy matrimony. Mater Matuta, goddess of growth and childbirth, had famous temples in Rome that dated from Etruscan times. Her festival, the Matralia on June 11, involved mysterious rites and sacred cakes. Lastly, Juno, queen mother of the gods, presided over various aspects of fertility and offspring; Juno Opigena guarded women in labor, whereas Juno Sororia protected girls at puberty and Juno Caprotina was in charge of fertility in general.

To make labor easier, women also relied on sympathetic magic. They carefully untied any knots in their clothing and unbound their hair to remove any symbolic obstacle to safe delivery.

Despite heavenly help, high anxiety reigned, and understandably so. Working from human remains and from the tattered historical record, archaeologists and historians have guesstimated that in the pregnancies of long-ago Egyptians, one child in three births might have died as newborns. During Greco-Roman centuries, it's estimated that 5 to 8 percent of newborns died at birth or within one month. The mortality among new mothers was grievously high as well, most of these deaths being due to germs and infection, it's thought.

Methods to ease and speed labor ranged from the helpful (drinking lots of liquids) to the merely bizarre (putting a vulture's feather under the mother's feet, or placing a sloughed snakeskin on the mother's thigh). More dubious aids included the ingestion of truly nauseating materials, such as fat from hyena loins.

On the plus side, women gave birth with the help of midwives, among female friends and relatives, and in a warm and supportive environment— usually at home, since hospitals and birthing centers as we know them did not exist. Among the Greeks and Romans, a low birthing chair or stool with a crescent-shaped hole in it was the main "equipment."

While in labor, Egyptian women preferred squatting or kneeling on birthing bricks, which left just enough room for a deft-handed attendant to catch the baby. In 2001, a southern archaeological dig in Abydos turned up an actual birthing brick. It was covered with still-colorful paintings of the new mom, her attendants, and her newborn son. It may have been used by a princess named Renseneb some 3,700 years ago.

During labor, she and her helpers might have chanted certain incantations to speed a safe delivery. One such chant began, "Come down, placenta, come down!" and continued with elaborate pleas to the goddess Hathor and to Horus, the falcon-headed sky god.

Childbirth was such a huge risk that midwives always kept certain tools at hand in case labor proved difficult—or impossible. This included a long, slender saw, used in extremis to cut a baby to bits to extract it from the womb.

## WOMBS:
### Hysterical wanderers

Gals two thousand years ago were plagued by a variety of female disorders, not the least of which was that vagabond organ, the womb. This impertinent piece of tissue, according to most Greek and Roman medical professionals, behaved more like a garden mole than a proper organ. If a woman weren't careful, her womb was apt to burrow into her chest, causing feelings of suffocation and breathlessness. When womb wanderlust hit, sometimes the gadabout would head south. When that happened, female patients complained of nervous tension, hot spells, and crying jags.

This syndrome began back in the misty past, long before Hippocrates showed up. Healers of that day called this condition "hysteria," from the Greek word *hysteron* or womb. Then, during a eureka! moment, Hippocrates and his followers figured out the cause: if a woman was careless enough to let her womb dry out, it would soon take to the open road, looking for a moister organ to attach to.

After devoting much thought and discussion to the topic, the medicos arrived at a general consensus: that wombs could only be made to return to their proper sites through fear. Some practitioners tried straightforward magic to quell the hysterical wanderers. Curse tablets written on lead or papyrus became a popular prescription. A typical one contained execrations such as, "Womb, I invoke you, stay in your place! I adjure you by Iao, and by Saboa and by Adona, not to hold onto the side but stay in your place." Tablets and amulets inscribed with this and other scolding messages have been found from Roman Britain to Roman Egypt.

More serious treatments for hysteria were action-oriented. Doctors believed that the nature of the uterus was to run away from bad smells. Thus medicos would surround the afflicted woman with a variety of stenches, from burned wool to squashed bedbugs. If that didn't terrify the womb into submission and back into position, the patient was subjected to loud noises. The doctor might accompany his yells with a symphony on metal plates. Blowing vinegar through the patient's nose was another of the milder therapies.

A dislocated womb called for even sterner measures. One recommended treatment began with a garlic and ewe's milk dinner, followed by a fumigation of the womb with fennel, absinthe, and a good purge, and finishing up with vaginal suppositories of opium poppies, almond oil, and rose oil.

Hysteria was a stubborn ailment; over the centuries, a significant number of chronic cases proved to be hardcore. Finally, however, there was a true medical breakthrough of sorts. This remedy, deployed only when all other options had been explored, was a type of physical therapy that involved external (and sometimes internal) massage of the pelvis. Euphemisms aside, what that actually meant was doctor-enabled masturbation!

Female patients did seem to get relief, doctors noted approvingly. Some of them even appeared to pass out during therapy. The only dilemma? Massage therapy was but a temporary cure. The problem kept returning, as did the patients. Not that a lot of long-ago Greek and Roman healers complained, mind you.

You may be chortling, but the same nonsensical beliefs persisted well into modern times. In fact, during two hysteria-prone centuries from the 1700s into the early 1900s, so many women on so many continents flooded medical offices with their complaints that a number of physicians developed an early but virulent form of carpal tunnel disorder.

Although doctors knew a bit more about female anatomy than their counterparts had two millennia prior, the whole idea of female orgasm and sexual pleasure was terra incognita. They called the relief experienced by women receiving genital massage "hysterical paroxysm."

*Wombs had a nasty habit of wandering about women's bodies. To remedy that, medicos used bad smells, loud noises, and milder cures, such as the fennel plant.*

Physician-assisted healing manipulations came to occupy so much time that an emergency program, an all-out War on Wandering Wombs, was launched to find mechanical aids to carry out such therapy. Thus in 1869 was born the prototype of the mechanical vibrator and its revolving, ever-evolving versions. Doctors Taylor and Granville invented the first ones, followed by a flood of imitators. Most devices were powered by steam, water, or batteries; when electricity came into consumers' lives, so did the plug-in vibrator.

Doctors and midwives continued to service women patients who were not do-it-yourselfers. Vibrating machinery in doctors' offices got ever more impressive, culminating in such devices as the four-foot-tall Chattanooga Vibrator. Little-known technology factoid: in the United States circa 1905, there were only five household appliances considered "essential" enough to electrify. And the vibrator was one of them!

In other sections of this book, you'll find more details on orgasm, masturbation, and on the ingenious sex toys of long ago.

## ABORTION & INFANTICIDE:
### The sad arithmetic of babies

"If she is bled, a woman will miscarry." That quote comes from the pen of Soranus, the leading gynecologist in the early part of the second century A.D., who was quoting Hippocrates, who probably flourished around 420 B.C. Their advice about early-stage abortions suggested bleeding the pregnant female, administering sitz baths, using vaginal suppositories, or giving her effective herbals such as silphium or more dangerous drugs.

The Athenian philosopher Socrates, whose own mother was a midwife, remarks in Plato's *Theaetetus*, "The midwives, by means of drugs and incantations, are able to arouse the pangs of labor and, if they wish, to make them milder, and to cause those to bear who have difficulty in bearing. And they [the midwives] cause abortions at an early stage if they think them desirable."

About now, perhaps you're wondering: what about that blasted Hippocratic Oath? Didn't long-ago medical practitioners swear that they would never do abortions? Actually, no. The Greek has often been mistranslated (sometimes deliberately) to suggest a wider prohibition of abortion. Here's what it did say, verbatim: "I will not give a [vaginal] suppository (called a pessary in ancient times) to cause an abortion." Other abortion measures, including drugs, bleeding, and manipulation of the woman's body, were allowed, however.

About five centuries after the original Hippocratic writings, a Stoic writer physician named Scribonius interpreted the oath to mean that Hippocrates was antiabortion and possibly anticontraception. Scribonius's writings in turn influenced many others, even though a third-century A.D. papyrus text of the Hippocratic Oath confirms the "suppository only" reading.

These "lost in translation" issues might seem to be quibbles, but they are supremely relevant in our day and age. John Riddle, in his book *Contraception and Abortion from the Ancient World to the Renaissance*, notes their relevance, "when so many states have passed anti-abortion laws based in part on a misreading of the oath and thus of a doctor's sacred obligations."

Infant exposure and infanticide were other difficult alternatives for females unable or unwilling to keep the child. (The number could have been substantial, keeping in mind that female slaves during their fertile years were often the unwilling sex objects of owners, pimps, and customers.)

In our century, much has been made of a papyrus letter found in an ancient Egyptian rubbish heap, written by a Greek man to his expectant wife. The document is a mix of husbandly affection and casual brutality. It ends: "If it's a boy, let it be. If it's a girl, expose it." The letter provokes urgent questions. Were all female babies considered throwaways? Was infanticide of either sex a crime?

Here is another not-so-amusing example, written by an Athenian comic poet named Posidippus: "Everyone, even a poor man, raises a son. Everyone, even a rich man, exposes a daughter."

Numerous scholars have done population studies by gender, and their opinions are far from unanimous. Laws in ancient times generally did not protect newborns or fetuses. Depending on time and place, certain cultures did not even consider a fetus or newborn fully human yet; Romans required the father to publicly accept the child first. Thus such children might lawfully be buried in the garden of the household. That said, female infanticide, based on studies of ancient gravesites and skeletal remains, does not seem to have been extensive enough to skew the ratio of males to females.

Nearly everyone has heard about the ghastly doings of the Carthaginians, the onetime superpower of the Mediterranean on the north coast of Africa, whose worship of the god Baal and the goddess of love and war Astarte required regular sacrifices of infants. For nearly six hundred years, babies were supposedly incinerated in small batches—and during a crisis, in huge offerings of five hundred or more. The motive for such

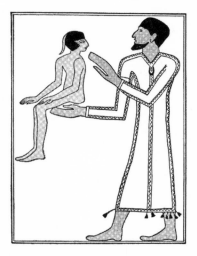

*In slave-holding societies, unwanted pregnancies were terminated via abortion or infant exposure. Ritual sacrifice of children, however, now appears to have been quite rare.*

mayhem? These sacrifices were thought to confer blessings on the parents who offered up their children.

That grim picture may not be true, however, as a painstaking, long-term archaeological study is revealing. A University of Pittsburgh team has for decades studied the cremated remains of 540 children in 348 burial urns in the Tophet cemetery near Carthage. As reported in a recent issue of *Archaeology* magazine, "[they] determined that about half the children were prenatal or would not have survived more than a few days after birth, and the rest died between one month and several years after birth." The bottom line? As the article notes, "Their findings suggest a credible and biologically consistent explanation of the Tophet burials that offers an alternative to sacrifice."

# Sexual Pioneers Around
the Mediterranean

## EGYPTIAN FERTILITY:
### Lettuce love & lust

Many millennia ago in Egypt, a nation that extravagantly admired fertile women, adored its children, and celebrated lovemaking, stumbled on a discovery with deep implications for deity worship, family planning, and personal intimacy.

In a word, lettuce. To be specific, *Lactuca serriola* and *Lactuca sativa*, a prickly variety found on Egyptian soil that was a dynamite aphrodisiac. (To the Egyptians, anyway; the Greeks thought otherwise and viewed lettuce with horror, as you'll learn from the entry in this book on anti-aphrodisiacs.)

The lettuce discovery occurred in conjunction with the early worship of a god called Min, whose fertility cult was in full swing even before human pharaohs started to reign in 3150 B.C. As the lead deity of male sexual potency, Min carried a harvesting flail in one hand and his upright organ in the other. His festivals were spectacular, at times orgiastic.

Just before the harvest began, the statue of Min was taken from the temple and brought into the fields lining both banks of the Nile River so that he could bless the crops. Folks at the festival played games in the nude, the climax of the shindig being a maypole-climbing competition.

Naturally, the festival food revolved around lettuce. This particular variety was romainelike in appearance, tall and straight-leafed. When squeezed or rubbed, the lettuce gave off a milky substance that looked a lot like semen to the Egyptians. Since this type of lettuce

*Although the Greeks condemned lettuce as a virility killer, the Egyptians drew the opposite conclusion. Lettuce played a prominent role in their fertility festivals.*

was described as having opiate and aphrodisiac properties, those festivals must have been memorable.

Being a relaxed and sensuous society even after the rigid, top-down pharaoh system of governance was instituted, Egyptians continued to worship Min. In fact, whenever a new pharaoh came to power, he was obliged to honor Min in a special way. At his coronation ceremonies, the new pharaoh had to sow his seeds. Literally. Some experts and wishful thinkers take this to mean that he hunkered down in the dirt and planted some brussels sprouts. But ancient accounts hint that the incoming ruler had to demonstrate his virility by manfully cuffing the camel, shall we say, then ejaculating into the Nile River. Only then could the annual flooding of the Nile be assured, a phenomenon that all of Egypt depended on for life to thrive.

The Egyptians had additional myths in which lettuce took a leading role, including the hot competition as to who would reign over Egypt, the sky god Horus or his uncle Seth.

These gods being extravagantly sexual beings, Uncle Seth greets his nephew by attempting an anal probe, which misses, spattering semen between the legs of Horus. The quick-witted Horus wipes up some of his uncle's sperm sample and tosses it into the Nile.

Somewhat later, Horus collects a sperm sample of his own, then invites his uncle over for lunch. He serves Seth his favorite food, lettuce, made with a white "dressing" of his own invention. Seth apparently enjoys his lunch, after which the two go down to the river to ask the rest of the gods to help settle their rivalry.

The end result? Horus wins the wank-off. He becomes Egypt's leading god, thanks to his quick wit and clearly superior procreative juices.

## MASTURBATION:
### Solo sex can be divine

For those times when a person is depressed, distressed, or just can't be bothered to get dressed, masturbation has always offered a modicum of comfort.

In the United States, masturbation has gone through long periods of being utterly reviled and/or hysterically forbidden. Today it seems to be looked at uneasily but without revulsion, a private, slightly embarrassing pleasure that barely qualifies as a transgression in the Catholic Church.

In ancient times, however, masturbation was a necessary and celebrated act that gods around the world performed. Men and women of long-ago

*To maintain the rivers upon which all life depended, folks in Egypt and Mesopotamia believed that their male gods routinely fired sperm samples into the waters.*

civilizations whose lives and livelihoods depended on river water—such as the Nile and the Tigris-Euphrates—believed that their gods supplied their own ejaculate to keep those fresh waters flowing.

Sumerians, among the earliest of literate cultures, wrote about their god Enki, who used to fondle himself to keep the Tigris River topped up. The Egyptian god Hapy did the same for the Nile River, to maintain its yearly flooding. (Read the prior entry to see the additional help given the Nile by its pharaohs and other gods.)

One Egyptian creation myth has the god Atum appear out of the void—and then, since voids are generally empty and boring, he masturbates, which brings him a nice surprise in the form of Shu and Tefnut, the first human beings, who set to work creating humans in a more gregarious fashion. But the highly imaginative Egyptian story-spinners didn't stop there. Their god Osiris performed even more astonishing feats with his own semen by resurrecting *himself* through sacred masturbation. He also conceived his own son Horus using his semen alone.

When the gods engaged in masturbation, it was perceived as a magical, creative act. Many cultures around the Mediterranean Sea also regarded its use by humans as natural and a healthy substitute for other sexual experiences.

Greek mythology pointed to the god Hermes (Mercury among the Romans) as an early adopter. He then taught it to the goatish god Pan, an ancient Arcadian deity of shepherds, forests, and animals tame and wild. This was an act of kindness, since shaggy, loud-voiced Pan had great difficulty getting any girlfriends in human form—or goat form, for that matter. He once had the hots for a nymph named Echo, but she'd rebuffed him. Newly inspired by masturbator techniques, Pan went on to teach solo sex to shepherds and others.

On the less exalted human plane, Greeks and Romans alike approved of masturbation as well. Poets such as Martial mentioned the common practice of fondling oneself while reading erotic material and gazing at pornographic art. Masturbation was also a popular subject on Greek vase paintings—including drinking cups.

Mark Twain once gave an impudent speech called "Some Thoughts on the Science of Onanism." In it, he quoted none other than Julius Caesar, who appeared to have been a real fan: "To the lonely it is company; to the forsaken it is a friend; to the aged and impotent it is a benefactor; they that are penniless are yet rich, in that they still have this majestic diversion." To that statement he adds, possibly in jest: "There are times when I prefer it to sodomy."

Speaking of Onan; remember that poor guy in the Old Testament's Genesis 38:8–10, who took a lot of flak for refusing to inseminate the wife of his recently deceased brother? Maybe he just hated being rushed into something that personal. No small talk, no engagement ring, just God ordering him to procreate with his sister-in-law Tamar, since his brother had died before producing a son and heir. Unenthused, Onan nevertheless had dutiful sex with Tamar, although afterward he spilled his seed on the ground. Deeply displeased, God promptly put Onan to death.

Although modern students on the subject are pretty sure that what Onan did was coitus interruptus or pulling out before ejaculating, Jewish rabbis from about 100 B.C. took the passage to mean that Onan wasted his seed, a type of birth control. Very sinful. The early Christian fathers took a different tack: since Onan's copulation wasn't for procreation, it must have been for pleasure. And thus was immoral.

Eventually Onan's name and his activity became a synonym for masturbation: onanism. From the earliest Christians onward, a variety of religions came down heavily on masturbation, calling it one of the four "unnatural vices." (The other three vices: homosexuality, bestiality, and sex in anything other than the missionary position.) Some Early American colonists went them one better, making it a death penalty crime.

In the mid-1700s, thanks to a flood of avidly read "dangers of onanism" books and pamphlets written by English crank S. A. D. Tissot and other quacks, Onan's deed newly panicked the English-speaking world about masturbation. And boy, did the Victorians run with it. Manual manipulation was life-threatening and would cause blindness, spinal consumption, polio, suicide. "Experts" selling potions and weird devices abounded. Some educators lobbied for schoolboys to wear skirts instead of tight trousers. Onanism-phobia and bizarre masturbation-quelling diets ruled until well into the twentieth century, possibly until the cathartic year of 1969, when Philip Roth's hilarious, revelatory *Portnoy's Complaint* came out.

## PORNOGRAPHERS:
### A gender-friendly occupation

The word *pornography* was created by cobbling together the Greek word *porne*, "prostitute," and the Greco-Latin root *-graphy*, "writing."

But porn, explicit sex manuals, and very graphic graphics were around much earlier than Greco-Roman times.

So far, the record for the oldest how-to on love couplings is the five-thousand-year-old *Chinese Handbook of Sex*, written by an emperor with time on his hands, evidently. (Sorry to disappoint, but the often-cited *Kama Sutra* from India is not only a Ravi-come-lately for sex advice, having been composed between the second and fourth centuries A.D., but only a fraction of it is on sex.)

Judging by what has come to light, the ancient Egyptians were the first to produce X-rated graphic novels. Or at least one. In early 1897, as British archaeologists Bernard Grenfell and Arthur Hunt drearily plowed through thousands of papyrus fragments they'd found in the ancient rubbish heaps of Oxyrhynthus, Egypt, they stumbled upon a lascivious picture book. On the sadly damaged eight-and-a-half-foot scroll, the erotic connection between music and sex was explored, illustrated with twelve panels of satirical, eye-popping graphics covering a wide range of Egyptian ideas on smutty fun.

One vignette shows a "sexual Olympics" sort of challenge; an aroused man attempts sex with a nearly naked woman who is standing above him in a chariot! The whole thing may be a parody, expensively carried out for a private audience. Now called the Turin Erotic Papyrus, it reposes in the

*Writing porn began almost as early as writing itself. Archaeologists have found examples in Egypt, Rome, and Greece—more than a few penned by women.*

Egyptian Museum of Turin, Italy. Other explicit works, including a painted leather scroll, have turned up at Hatshepsut's Deir el-Bahari temple and elsewhere.

Again, amid the masses of papyri hidden in the ancient ruins of Oxyrhynchus, Egypt, archaeologists and researchers discovered a tantalizing fragment of a sex manual, a work of art by a Greek woman called Philaenis. This find proved even more shocking because it revealed that women of Greco-Roman times not only behaved as lasciviously as men, but they also wrote about the imaginative sex they'd had (and/or had fantasized).

Philaenis lived during Hellenistic times, on the Greek island of Samos or perhaps Leucadia (accounts disagree). She may have been the courtesan that inspired the coining of the word *pornography*. Whatever her day job, she began her literary odyssey by coming up with a killer title for her book. She called it *On Indecent Kisses*. Her erotic manual was clearly popular (judging by its mention by other writers, plus the number of papyrus fragments found at multiple sites), and centuries later would provide inspiration for Ovid's bestselling *Ars Amatoria (The Art of Love)*.

The introduction to her book begins: "Philaenis of Samos, daughter of Ocymenes, wrote the following things for those wanting . . . life." (The rest of the line is missing.) The author methodically organized her book into chapters, such as "How to Make a Pass," and "Seduction through Flattery" (a small fragment reads: "say that he or she is 'godlike'"). Other surviving chapter names include: "Cosmetics for Seduction Success"; "The Use of Aphrodisiacs"; "Abortion Methods"; and "Sexual Positions."

*On Indecent Kisses* evidently contained some suggestions for female-to-female intimacy that terrified males in ancient Greece and Rome, where the thought of women engaging in mutually satisfying behavior turned male stomachs. The brilliant seventh-century B.C. poetry and lyrics of Sappho of Lesbos had done much to bring attention to X-rated activity among gals out into the open, but the thought of lesbians (or *tribades*, as they were more commonly referred to then) had the average Athenian or Roman breaking out in hives. (See the entries on tribades and outercourse elsewhere in this book for more details.)

Philaenis's handbook for the voluptuary really pushed the outrage envelope, because it apparently included illustrations of sexual positions. Yes indeed: a *Joy of Sex* B.C., with how-tos for couples gay and straight. In the reign of Emperor Trajan the Roman poet Martial, who preened himself on hip vulgarity and flippant, ad hominem porn, found Philaenis's matter-of-fact nonfiction and art so horrifying that he scurried home to write scurrilous epigrams about her.

Another writer from Samos, a poet called Aeschrion, was even more dismayed to have "his" home island named as Philaenis's turf as well. In response, he wrote an epigram denying that she ever wrote lewd books or "did research" by consorting with men in that way.

For all the stir she caused, Philaenis was by no means the only gal to carry out such work. A talented female poet called Elephantis also did illustrated editions that focused on how to organize group sex. Wow. It got a mention from Roman historian Suetonius, author of the still-famous *Lives of the Twelve Caesars*. In his biography of Emperor Tiberius, he said that the nasty old voyeur owned a copy of her "learn through pictures" book. It got heavy use on the isle of Capri at his sexual pleasure park, where youngsters were forced to engage in group sex. According to Suetonius, it was used as a reference, "so that no one should lack a model for the execution of any lustful act he was ordered to perform."

Other feminine porn artists included Nico of Samos, called a writer of lewd books by Xenophon; and Astynassa, who took on the literary persona of Helen of Troy's personal maid to pen her book on sexual positions.

Although only a smidgen of biographical data has surfaced about male pornographers, nevertheless they did crank out a disreputable number of raunchy little books. Their numbers included authors Sabellus, Musaeus, Mummius, Sotades of Mantinea, Timon of Phlius, Botrys, and a fellow from fabled Sybaris called Hemitheon. The latter wrote a homoerotic novel called *Sybaritica*, cited for its "lubricity" by writers Martial and Lucian.

Purveyors of pornography back then evidently felt compelled to describe the postures of venery, as sex positions were called, and brag about the number they'd included in their book. Author Paxamus, for example, boasted of twelve positions in his tome called *Dodecatechnon* (Twelve Techniques). The poet Martial also commented on "the debauched books of Elephantis, with nine postures."

So what were the favorite Greco-Roman positions, anyway? Judging by the extant paintings and illustrations, one called the Rider was extremely popular. The woman sat proudly above the man, who was supine on his back. If she faced him, the pose was called *Venus pendula conversa*; if away, it was *Venus pendula aversa*. (See the amount of Latin you can learn if the topic is gripping enough?)

Another subset of titillating tales also became popular in the second century B.C. The first may have been written by Aristides of Miletus, a luxurious Greek city-state in Asia Minor. Called *Milesiaka (Milesian Tales)*, they were collections of short stories, told in the first person, using ribald language and salacious anecdotes of love and adventure. They appealed to male readers, these trashy novels; some were even found in the gear carried by legionaries.

As mentioned in the entry on masturbation, early porn books often enhanced private moments for many a lustful Roman or Greek, engaging in what the Victorians liked to call "self-pollution."

## THE PRIAPEIA:

### Before e-books there were tree-books

One of the ripest, raunchiest collections of printed matter ever made in ancient times was the *Priapeia*, a garland or collection of short Latin poems or epigrams. "Printed" isn't the adequate word to describe the *Priapeia*, which had a very unusual genesis.

*A Roman garden wasn't complete unless it boasted a statue of the god Priapus, whose fierce supersized member would guard the premises.*

Initially written on leather, papyrus, parchment, and possibly tree bark, these poems ran from two lines long to twenty or more. They were nailed or fastened onto the carved wooden figure of the god Priapus—and not just one Priapus, either. Most of the statues of this god adorned the lush walled gardens of the well-to-do, or sat inside temples throughout Rome. (Others appeared on board merchant ships, since Priapus was also the protector of sailors and patron god of navigation.)

Some statues were sophisticated images, beautifully carved and painted bright red. But many were deliberately crude, simply a tree trunk roughly shaped into human form. In both instances, the attention-getting body part of the Priapus god was his massive, at-attention virile member. In everyday language it was called a *mentula*, the street slang for phallus.

Priapus worship was said to have come from Greece, the cult later spreading to Italy. Other accounts insisted it was derived from the Egyptians and their adoration of Apis, the sacred bull. Like the older god Pan, Priapus's backstory included being raised by shepherds and being a minor deity of wilderness and woodlands.

In any event, these fierce scarlet images were very ancient fertility symbols, apropos for gardens filled with fruit trees, herbs, and edible plants. Priapus also protected livestock as well as wild animals. For property owners, the Priapus figure acted as a garden vigilante and an evil-eye deterrent. His oversize phallic aggression visually threatened fruit robbers, cattle rustlers, vegetable thieves, and any other no-good varmints with a terrible punishment: rape.

Thus the *Priapeia* poems attached to the Priapus figure—which poetically threatened the reader—added more emphasis.

How did the Priapus poetry come into being, anyway? It seems to have developed at a reunion of Roman literati, who were spending a relaxing day in the ultra-fancy gardens of Maecenas, swimming in Rome's first warm-water pool and swilling good wine. Maecenas, a tight friend of Rome's first emperor, was also the literary patron of Horace the poet and other well-known writers. His gardens were the first ones in Italy to be lush, Persian-style walled paradises.

Over the course of that jovial, competitive afternoon (or perhaps a series of afternoons) the group wrote poems and epigrams, then affixed them to the massive Priapus that stood guard on the grounds of the temple in the Maecenas gardens. Later, some ninety-five of these poems to Priapus were collected into a printed volume that saw publication in Rome. The "hard copies," as we'll call the ones not attached to the statues, became so popular with a wider audience that well-known writers of erotic or scatological themes, from Catullus and Petronius to Tibullus, were eager to add to the collection. And did so, with brio. Because of its ripely obscene content and often disturbing rape imagery, the *Priapeia* was for many centuries not translated into English.

## PHERENIKE OF RHODES:
### Cloaked in Olympic victory

Born into an athletic dynasty on the Greek island of Rhodes, Pherenike—whose name means "carrying victory"—grew up surrounded by testosterone and superstars, starting with her dad, Diagoras, a towering figure who won first prize in the men's boxing event at the 464 B.C. Olympic Games. (Back then, winners were awarded simple olive wreath crowns, but later got showered with golden perks as well.)

Her big, burly brothers continued the winning streak. In boxing and the ferocious boxing-wrestling event called the pancratium, Pherenike's brothers swept six different Olympic Games. Doreius, her youngest sibling, was the family standout. He took crowns in three successive Olympiads, plus eight victories at the Isthmian Games, seven at the Nemean, and more on the Great Games circuit besides.

As their sister, Pherenike probably cheered them on in person. As a youngster, and as an unmarried women, she would have made the long trek from Rhodes to Olympia with her family to see one or more of her brothers' triumphs. At the ancient Olympics, only unmarried women and girls (a euphemism for virgins) could attend; matrons were barred. No one could recall the reason or the start date for the ancient ban—or for its awful penalty: any Mrs. with the temerity to gate-crash would be hurled to her death off the Typaeum cliffs nearby.

While at Olympia, Pherenike may well have seen the Heraean Games, too. Every four years, just prior to the Olympics, footraces for girls and women were held on the same grounds. These competitions to honor the goddess Hera were more ancient than the Olympics themselves and three-time winners were honored with statues that stood alongside those of the Olympic winners in the sacred precinct.

In time, Pherenike married a sports-mad athlete named Callianax. They had two sons, who grew into husky lads—and likely contenders. In 404 B.C. her older son, Eucles, won his boxing event and brought the olive crown of Olympia home to his mother. Because she was now a married woman, Pherenike didn't get to witness his win.

*Even though Nike,
the deity of Olympic
victory, was a god-
dess, the ancient
Olympics barred
married women even
as spectators.*

In a few years, her younger son Pisodorus seemed primed for the boxing competition, and they entered his name into the boys' boxing event at
Olympia. But during the mandatory ten-month training period prior to
the Olympics, tragedy struck. Pherenike's husband, her son's trainer, died
suddenly. Pisodorus was staggered. So was his mother. But the new widow,
remembering she was part of the mighty Diagoras dynasty, didn't hesitate.

"I'll finish training you, son," she said.

And so began their well-kept secret, a clandestine training regimen.
Pherenike, who'd watched her brothers and husband box and train for
years, knew what skill sets her son needed to master. As muscular and
coordinated as the other males in the family, young Pisodorus had the tools
to be a winner. Speed, power, and elusiveness being key elements to success
in boxing, Pherenike soon had her son running laps and later, spending
hours pounding the millet-filled punchball. During sparring practice, wearing his ear guards and soft padded gloves, he bobbed and wove like an early
Muhammad Ali.

In June of 388 B.C., Pisodorus reported to the training area at Elis, the
place where all athletes spent the last month before the games.

In the July heat the ninety-eighth Olympic Games began, with religious
ceremonies and sacrifices to Zeus, Hera, and the other Greek gods. As a
first-timer, Pisodorus was probably nervous; he might have been even more
shaky had he known what his mother was up to. She wasn't a demure, hid-
den-away matron like those of Athens. A Rhodian from a family of athletes,
Pherenike was fit and moved boldly. She couldn't stand the thought of not
being there to support her son. Since she'd been to earlier Olympic events,
she knew what the official trainers wore, what they did, and where they
stood during the matches.

Pherenike dressed herself in the special full-length robe of a trainer, and carried the wooden staff they used. (She may have donned a fake beard and cut her hair as well, for all we know.) At any rate, her disguise passed muster, and Pherenike gained entry into the trainers' enclosure, which was surrounded by a low fence.

The herald's trumpet blared, and Pisodorus began his match. She'd done her job well, she saw. The teen moved quickly, overwhelming his opponent with left jabs, hooks, right crosses, and blows to the body. His speed and power awed her. The crowd roared their approval. At length, her son's opponent raised his index finger—the signal of defeat.

Pherenike couldn't contain herself. Letting out a war whoop of delight, she jumped the fence and ran to kiss her son. Either the high-pitched sound of her voice, or perhaps what her jump over the fence revealed, blew her disguise. The spectators, thousands of them, murmured in astonishment, which grew into a roar of outrage.

The ten Olympic judges were in a terrible quandary. No trainer had ever been revealed as a woman before! And a married woman—that was the real horror. Anxiously they conferred. Before long, they came to an ingeniously Greek solution. Pherenike would go unpunished—no fatal fling off the sheer Typaeum cliffs for her. With solemn faces, they announced that in light of her family's contributions to the glory of the Olympic Games, she would not undergo the penalty for breaking the taboo.

However, they quickly added, "From this day forward, trainers as well as athletes will participate in the nude at the Olympic Games."

Exultant, Pherenike and her son got to walk away from the Olympic Games together. From then on, however, she possessed lasting fame of her own, and a new nickname among the Greeks. They fondly called her Kallipatira, "good father."

## KOAN SILK:

### See-through is sexy

Although thousands of Greek vases and statues depicting naked gods, god-desses, men, women, and satyrs in varying states of excitement would seem to indicate otherwise, the Greeks were also fond of clothed ambiguity.

Ambiguity—as in first you see it, now you don't—could be highly erotic.

For over a thousand years, however, every stitch worn by the Greeks and Romans was made at home on looms that produced rectangular pieces of wool or linen. A shorter chunk became a Greek chiton or a Roman tunic. A longer piece of cloth, pinned or stitched at the shoulders and cinched with one or more belts, became a nice drapey gown, usually more demure than daring.

Another large piece of fabric, called a peplum or palla, served as a shawl or head covering when women went outdoors. The whole ensemble looked great on statues of shapely goddesses. On the average Greek or Roman gal, we'd call it the muffled look.

For ceremonial activities, however, such as religious processions, girls and unmarried women sometimes got to wear shorter chitons or tunics. During athletic competitions from the first century A.D. on, in which Greek and Roman girls and women around the Mediterranean took part, a female participant wore a short tunic with one shoulder strap, leaving one breast bare. Several statues still survive of female athletes in such garb, including a Roman copy in the Vatican Museum.

Only among Spartans young and old did women get to let it all hang out. Skimpy tunics were the norm. So was nudity during sports events.

So did any other Greek or Roman gals ever get to emulate Spartan sartorial freedom? Yes, indeed.

The Greeks called it the "Amorgian chiton"; the Romans, the "Koan vest." We'd call it "very sexy." It was a clingy, flattering gossamer gown that covered everything from neck to ankles yet revealed it at the same time. Its fabric: a feather-light, see-through silk.

Why do we know so little about it? Until recently, silk was thought to be a jealously guarded secret, exclusive to ancient China. And indeed it was—until clever traders from Persia and the Middle East hijacked a few silkworm eggs and the contraband eventually got to ancient Greece.

Another reason for our lack of knowledge: it was very tough to depict transparent cloth on a painting or carved in stone. So there are few traces of this garment in Greco-Roman art. One superb example does exist—the stone artwork called the Ludovisi Throne, which depicts the love goddess being lifted from the sea. On it, the sculptor has managed to show her body through this breathtaking fabric that clings to her.

By Aristotle's time or possibly earlier, wild silkworms were stealthily brought to the small Greek islands of Amorgos and Kos (not far from present-day Turkey), where their output was made into cloth. The insects were housed in mulberry trees. To make silk, the Chinese preferred to kill the butterfly inside the cocoon, whereas the Greeks allowed it to work its way out, breaking the threads as it went. Greek women on Amorgos, accustomed to making linen from flax, used the same technique, called hackling, to make their silk. The fabric soon got dubbed *amorgina* after the island, as well as *metaxa* and a confusion of other names.

*Spartan women bared more flesh than other Greeks. Their athletic females wore mini-tunics that covered just one breast.*

Naturally the stuff cost a fortune, but Greek women from housewives to *heterae* soon got their husbands, families, and lovers to cough up. By 411 B.C., when playwright Aristophanes first put on *Lysistrata*, the satirical play where women carry out a sex strike to keep their men from going to war, the fashion was red-hot among the Athenians. In the play, Aristophanes included lines about the women sexually teasing the men by coming forward "naked in their Amorgian chitons." These lines were understood, and roared at, by everyone in the audience.

When wealthy philosopher Plato wanted to send a thank-you gift to the daughters of the household where he'd enjoyed hospitality on Sicily, he specified in a letter: "Give the daughters of Kebes three tunics seven cubits long, not those expensive Amorgian ones, but the more ordinary kind made of Sicilian linen." Was that familial diplomacy? Or was Plato an aristocratic cheapskate?

After the Greek city-states fell into decline and were swallowed up by the Romans in 146 B.C., the victors saw the silky spoils as great gifts to bring home to their wives and lovers. In no time, Roman women were sashaying about in diaphanous splendor. (By this era, Rome already imported Chinese silk and highly prized it, although it lacked the sheer quality.)

Male writers, however, while busy ogling its female wearers, fumed over the alluring new trend. Pliny called Koan silks "the vestments that cover a woman while at the same time revealing her naked charms." He and others obsessed even more over the fact that men began dressing in Koan. Guys pointed to its lightweight fabric, claiming it was ideal to beat Rome's summer heat. But conventional Roman males stoutly, sweatily stuck to the well-swathed, head-to-foot woolen toga. Anything lighter or looser spelled decadence. Or the E word: effeminate.

## THARGELIA OF MILETUS:
### Mistress of the marriage-go-round

As the top-tier professionals of Aphrodite, the Greek sex goddess, *heterae* had their own stringent rules for business success: don't fall in love with the johns, and (Hera forbid!) don't marry the customers!

For years during the era of Persian king Cyrus the Great (576 to 530 B.C.), a spectacular courtesan named Thargelia topped the *hetera* popularity charts. Hailing from the Ionian Greek city-state of Miletus on the eastern shores of the Mediterranean, Thargelia was gorgeous and then some. She also had a solid reputation for charisma, shrewdness, and brains; nevertheless, she kept ignoring her coworkers' advice about marriage. According to the Greek sophist Hippias in his book *A Collection*, Thargelia tied the knot fourteen times!

Ms. T. wed a variety of well-known men and rulers, including Antiochus, the king of Thessaly. But all that pillow talk garnered her quite a bit more than wedding rings. The Mata Hari of her time and place, the spice in Thargelia's life largely came from double-agenting, not sex or marriage proposals. Among her male allies (if not her spouses), she was said to have included Cyrus the Great, for whom she did spying and intrigue.

Greek historian Plutarch, in his *Parallel Lives* biography, noted that "Thargelia, a great beauty, extremely charming and at the same time sagacious, had numerous suitors among the Greeks. She brought all who had to do with her over to the Persian interest, and by their means, being men of the greatest power and station, she sowed the seeds of the Median [that is, Persian] faction up and down in several cities."

Since the Greeks and the Persians were at each other's throats for centuries, notably the fifty-year (with time-outs) Persian War, from 498 B.C. to a peace treaty in 449, small wonder that the Athenians and other citizens of Greek city-states came to regard Thargelia's name as synonymous with "traitor."

The Athenians had extra-long memories. Nearly two hundred years after Thargelia, another beauteous and clever woman from Miletus came under deep suspicion for her role in politics—and her influence on men of power.

Her name was Aspasia; although a well-educated woman and the long-time live-in lover of Pericles, Athens' top politician and general, she was a non-Athenian and therefore a *metic*, or resident alien. As such, she was accused of persuading her man to wage war against the Greek island of Samos. Her alleged motive? The Samians had refused to call off *their* war against Miletus.

It helps to know that the city-states of the ever-belligerent Greeks fought nonstop with one another. Their quarrels often flamed into actual warfare, with resultant loss of life, atrocities, enslavements, and other gruesome outcomes. They hardly needed women such as Thargelia and Aspasia to incite them—but outspoken, sexually independent gals did make very convenient scapegoats. (And doubtless excellent spies, if they chose to be.)

Thargelia doesn't seem to have incurred official wrath. But Aspasia, invariably compared to her countrywoman Thargelia, certainly did. During her twenty years with Pericles, she got slandered onstage and off by poets, playwrights, and politicians galore.

When Athens went to war with Sparta in 431 B.C., the political climate got even nastier. Accusers lobbed a trumped-up charge of impiety against Aspasia. This delightfully vague accusation about ticking off the gods could legally be made by any citizen. Someone found guilty of impiety

*Like Thargelia, her fellow citizen of Miletus, Aspasia was an independent female who lived for philosophy and politics. Athenians loved to slander this intimate companion of Pericles.*

could receive the death penalty. As a non-Athenian, Aspasia couldn't even testify on her own behalf. Instead, her lover Pericles made an emotional plea regarding her innocence, and the case was dismissed.

Contempt for *metics* (and women who did not keep their lips buttoned) ran deep among the Athenians. Sadly, most of what little we "know" about Aspasia is malicious gossip, invention, and mud-slinging largely aimed at her dedicated love partner, Pericles. (More details about Aspasia in the entries on kissing and on Pericles and Aspasia as a couple.)

## MYSTERY CULTS:
### The origin of the orgy

Ancient orgies were not merely banal gatherings of horny civilians, eager to engage in group sex. Long-ago orgies involved initiation rites, strong intoxicants, wild dancing, spiritual secrets, religious ecstacy, and at times earthy debauchery, all of it focused around a deity or two.

The rites of these orgiastic cults, often called "the mysteries," were not free-for-alls or open to the public, either. Groups tended to be membership only. Members, called *orgeone*, were overseen by an adept called the *orgiophant*, who revealed the secrets and attempted to direct the activities.

Mention "orgy deity," and the name that immediately comes to mind is the wine god Dionysus and his Roman counterpart, Bacchus, but there were many other orgiastic cults and mysteries in ancient times. (Bacchus and the Bacchanalians also romp through another entry in this book.)

The great mystery religion at Eleusis, for instance. From time immemorial, this pilgrimage was made by thousands of Greeks to Eleusis, a hilltop village about fourteen miles from Athens. There, amid the strictest secrecy, rites were held, new members were initiated, and the ancient story of the vegetation goddess Demeter and her search for her lost daughter Persephone was reenacted.

The mysteries at Eleusis flourished for over 1,700 years, during which time hundreds of thousands of individuals from every corner of the Greek-speaking world were initiated into its secrets. The membership included emperors and slaves, women and men. To this day, most of what went on

*This was the temple complex of Eleusis, most famous and mysterious of the Greek mystery cults. The rites, still largely unknown to us, were carried out for 1,700 years.*

remains unknown. What few clues we have come from modern archaeology rather than the ancient literature.

To belong, individuals lodged in Athens for six months to attend the spring rites, called the Lesser Mysteries. In September, for the Greater Mysteries, initiates walked the Sacred Way from Athens to Eleusis. As they walked, they called out to bring Persephone back from the Underworld into the realm of the living. After they arrived outside the sanctuary, they danced all night without sleeping, then entered the Telesterion, the initiation hall, which held as many as three thousand people. There, initiates saw visions. Anthropologists have researched extensively and spun numerous theories as to the cause of these visions. One plausible scenario builds on the known fact that celebrants drank *kykeon*, a special potion that contained barley grain, symbol of Demeter, and ergot, a well-known fungus. Consuming ergot-laden grain produces symptoms of vertigo, visual distortions, and intense hallucinations.

Other psychotropic plants, including opium poppies, have also been suggested as the active ingredients of *kykeon*. Unlike other orgiastic mysteries, the one at Eleusis produced exaltation more spiritual than carnal. Members experienced ecstasy, Greek for "the flight of the soul from the body."

In his day, Plato wrote about another orgiastic group devoted to the moon cult of the Thracian goddess Bendi. It gained traction in Athens; originally as wild as the Bacchic rites, it became a watered-down festival for Athenians, featuring naked lads in a horserace by torchlight.

Not all orgies involved sexual congress. In fact, one of them removed sexual temptation in the most literal way. The cult of Cybele—later called Magna Mater by the Romans—had a huge following for six centuries. Its hardcore male adherents, called *galli*, paraded while high on mystical love for their goddess. In the throes of ecstasy (and possibly with a buzz on as well), the brand-new members of the *galli* chopped off their genitals and threw them into the crowds of parade watchers. (Veterans in the cult would have had no equipment to sacrifice but took part anyway.) Their three-day festival included one flagellation-filled day of blood, followed by Hilaria, the day of hilarity, where everyone shared a good laugh about the preceding day's mutilations. Scarcely anyone died during these do-it-yourself activities, or so the stoic *galli* claimed.

Other orgiastic cults centered around the worship of Orpheus, Adonis, Eumolpus, and the Cabeiri. Certain cults, such as the mysteries held on Samothrace, made snake handling part of the festivities; so did the snake-worshipping cult of Dionysus and earlier still, the Minoan goddesses on Crete.

By the time decadence-loving imperials such as the emperors Caligula, Nero, Domitian, and Commodus came and went, orgies were often secular vulgarizations, madcap parties of sexual frenzy for participants and voyeurs. Nevertheless, the mysteries great and small continued to exert a powerful attraction—one in which countless initiates found solace and spiritual ecstasy.

# PROSTITUTION:
## Love for sale, O.B.O.

As that venerable maxim of movie producers proclaims, sex sells. And it has sold since the misty beginnings of recorded history, with demand always outstripping supply. And sometimes stripping the supply as well.

Long-ago bawdy bodies of all genders were in the business of buying, selling, renting, loaning, and time-sharing sex. In fact, sex workers of one sort or another have been on the job even before the medium of exchange called money existed. The oldest profession indeed. Think about it: How do you suppose that hookers in Sodom and Gomorrah got paid?

The ancient world was also crawling with hierodules, temple slaves affiliated with hundreds of different temples, often called "sacred prostitutes" in service to that deity. Egypt had scads of religious harlots but few secular sex workers; music, however, was thought to be very erotic, so female musicians and dancers often had a sexual sideline.

In the Mesopotamian lands, ancient Sumer had ritual prostitutes from 2400 B.C.—and job offerings for secular entertainer-hookers both male and female. In addition, at the main ziggurat in the city of Ur, the head priestess and reigning male ruler performed a "sacred marriage" each year. A thousand years later in the same part of the world, Assyrian hookers had to abide by stringent dress codes, meaning they could not wear veils in the street like other women. If a prostitute defied the ordinance and got caught sashaying around in a veil, her punishment was a stinging fifty blows. Nearly as dismaying, she also had bitumen (a tarlike substance) poured on her head.

About 600 B.C. or so, sex worker slaves received official status in Athens under lawmaker Solon, who set up the first state brothels. He also began a gladsome revenue stream for the city by taxing other prostitutes (called *pornai*) on their earnings. *Pornai* wore special clothing, follow-me shoes, and wigs or other distinctive hair signals.

*Sex workers paid taxes and came in all price ranges, from eye-candy courtesans to brothel slaves and streetwalkers.*

Hooking, called "browsing" in ancient Greek street slang, had a gamut of options and pricing levels. Among them: the plain vanilla brothel slave at one obol, the smallest coin; the street freelancers; the intermediate "sex optional" flute players, dancers, and musicians hired as entertainment at the all-male drinking parties. And on up the scale to sleek courtesans and, at the top, the educated and witty *heterae* or "companions." The latter, mostly resident aliens from other parts of Greece, were educated freeborn women. Ideally, a *hetera* strove to have a circle of well-heeled men friends, each of whom picked up the tab for the different cost centers of her life: rent, clothes, jewelry, and so forth.

Some *heterae*, such as one of the two famed seductresses named Lais, chose to time-share. In her case, she charged top drachma to a wealthy philosopher named Aristippus for her time and services two months of the year, then spent an equal number of sleepovers with the raggedy, outrageous Diogenes of Sinope. She must have had a real passion for Cynic philosophy, since Diogenes' "home" in the Athens marketplace was a *pithos*, a large clay jar that once held wine or olive oil. Lais may have shared quarters with Diogenes' pack of stray dogs as well!

Athens' nightlife was dull compared to that in the lively Greek metropolis of Corinth, located on the skinny isthmus joining the two parts of the Greek mainland. A mecca for prostitution, it boasted crowds of hierodules and equal numbers of secular call girls called the "colts of Aphrodite," the sassy, stratospherically high-priced courtesans of that city.

Athens and many other Greek city-states in Greece, Italy, Sicily, and Asia Minor also had a significant number of young male sex workers. Like their female competition, in Athens the boys tended to congregate on the Lycabettos hill, around the Ceramicus district, and in the port of Piraeus.

*Athens' most outrageous citizen, Diogenes, often shared his earthenware
digs with stray dogs and famous floozies.*

They also favored cemeteries, which provided nice flat surfaces for al fresco
bedding down and lots of "facebook" space for advertising one's services.

Rome, and later the entire Roman Empire, provided the same staggering variety of paid sexual services as the Greek-speaking world, just a tad
more bureaucratic. From 180 B.C. on, taxes were assessed on prostitution and
brothels. Freelance entrepreneurs had to register, giving their given name,
place of birth, and hooker handle, plus declaring the amount they intended
to charge. Failure to officially register carried a fine, plus a good whipping.
Despite that possibility, venturesome freelancers might have outnumbered
the street-legal hookers. (Check out the entry on adultery for other details.)

Throughout Italy, brothels and X-rated businesses abounded, from tavern-cathouses to other joint ventures where sex on demand was readily available. There were also streetwalkers of both genders who specialized in stand-up business, shall we say, beneath many of the smaller triumphal arches in Rome's central district. Since the arches were called *fornices*, the activity generation in their vicinity became known as fornication.

Then as now, middle management often muscled its way into the flesh for cash trade. Roman whores both male and female were often managed by a *leno*, or pimp; in Greece, it was the hated *pornoboskos*, or "whore-shepherd."

Although long-ago ladies (and a few gents) for play and pay were often celebrated in song, verse, art, and literature, you will look in vain for their own words about happiness (or lack of it) in their own lives.

## MALE GARB:
### Clothes made the man—& the hooker

One of history's intriguing puzzles: the world-famous Roman toga, a prestige garment, could only be worn by freeborn males who had reached the age of fifteen, when manhood officially began for Romans. The sole exception to that rule? The fashion-forward female prostitutes of Rome, who proudly wore the toga as well. How this contradiction came to be is lost to us, but one can easily see why the hookers took to it. Like the garb of a nurse, the toga made services on offer instantly recognizable.

The typical toga, an off-white hemisphere of wool, contained yards of material. Its thickness and weight would have done a good job of keeping streetwalkers warm on windy street corners, and could also have served as a comfy ad hoc trysting spot.

Even in later imperial centuries, the most sophisticated era of Roman times, togas would have been difficult to clean, post-tryst. Since no effective soap existed (and Romans disdained the early "soap" used by the barbaric German tribes), woolen garments were "washed" in stale urine and potash, then given a sulfur treatment to whiten them.

Another minor mystery: American universities have long maintained fraternities and sororities galore, all of them using Greek letters and names. Traditionally, frats have long been fond of throwing what they call "toga parties," named after a garment that was distinctively Roman. The Greek, elite or not, wouldn't be caught dead in a toga. Instead, males wore the *himation*, a billowy, bedsheet-shaped piece of wool, casually tied or wrapped around the waist and over one shoulder, allowing air to circulate and room to dangle, if you know I mean. Since the Greeks tended to scoff at the notion of briefs, unpremeditated frontal nudity was commonplace. In sharp contrast, Greek slaves and working-class men doing hard physical labor wore loincloths, separating them from men of leisure.

Our humble but ubiquitous T-shirt also had its beginnings in ancient Greece. Men, especially the manual laborers, often wore a sleeveless muscle tee that varied in length. Their tee was called a tunic; at times, it was referred to as a *gymnos*.

The word *gymnos*, however, had dual meanings. The Greek *gymnasium* took its name from *gymnos*, which could mean "dressed only in the *gymnos*," since it sometimes served as workout gear back then. But most of the time and in most contexts, *gymnos* meant "naked."

The root also shows up in *gymnosophists*, the name that Alexander the

*The classic woolen toga exemplified a man of leisure but it also served as an identity badge for Roman prostitutes.*

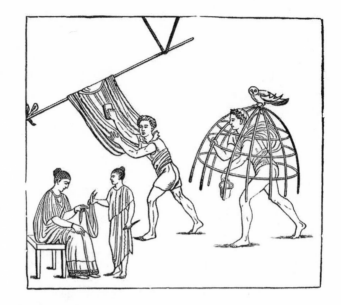

*The trouble with togas? Keeping that white wool clean. Lacking soap,
ancient dry cleaners used human urine to do the job.*

Great and the Macedonians gave to the naked philosophers they bumped
into during their lengthy stay in India. Although the Greeks used the terms
*brahman* and *gymnosophist* interchangeably, the former was an orthodox
priestly caste. The latter men were equally skeptical of Brahman beliefs
and of the Jain philosophy of nonviolence. They were rebels who lived "sky
clad," out in nature rather than in towns. Like the Spartans, these naked
sages praised the simple life, calling nudity healthy, efficient, and a great
method of building endurance. Even today, those beliefs remain embedded
in the male psyche, as most women would affirm.

## PULCHERIA OF BYZANTIUM:
### Power chastity rocked

Hardly anyone thinks of Byzantine women, power politics, and lifelong chastity in the same breath, although at least one chose this route to reign in a big way during the last centuries of the bifurcated Roman Empire.

Pulcheria was the precocious powerhouse example. At fifteen, she stepped up as regent empress for her weak young brother Theo, thereby running the eastern half of the Roman Empire from Constantinople. Her era, the centuries when Christianity really took hold, opened a new avenue of independence for women: career chastity. Not just as nuns or mother superiors, either. Pulcheria was astute enough to see that the best way to keep her autonomy was to give herself, body and soul, only to the church. Her "virgin for life" ceremony, being Byzantine, was gloriously pompous and dazzling. She was much applauded. As a mark of approval, the Roman senate also gave her more political power by declaring her Augusta in 414. That title got her treated equally among other rulers and men of power. Her face appeared on a variety of classy gold coins, too, showing her being crowned by the right hand of God, no less.

As regent empress, Pulcheria immediately fired the eunuch tutor in charge of her little brother's education. Now her first order of business was to make him into a figurehead emperor; she personally tutored him on his studies, his duties, and even his choice of a mate. When

*Being a Byzantine empress was swell. Even better was Pulcheria's approach to it: career virgin.*

she wasn't reciting passages from Scripture or fasting twice a week, big sister put young Theo through his paces. A sampling of her lesson plans: how to speak with dignity; how to walk; how to restrain loud laughter; and how to ride a horse in an imperial fashion.

A kind boy, Theo was careless and easily swayed. This being Byzantium, palace intrigue and outsider coup attempts were omnipresent. As Theo went through puberty, aristocrats fielded their own marital candidate from Antioch, a sleek Greek named Eudocia. Although she was still Theo's puppet master, Pulcheria could do little to thwart him when her opponents managed to dangle their bride material in front of the teen, who snapped at Eudocia like a hungry trout.

Pulcheria still had supreme control; her brother was a trusting soul, too trusting. To show him the error of his ways, she placed a document on the table before him. He duly signed without reading it, as he'd always done. With a sigh, his big sister then made a point of reading aloud what he had just signed. It was a contract giving Pulcheria a new slave: Theo's new wife! They all had a hearty fake laugh, as she finally tore it up.

Her credentials as the true CEO of Byzantium fully established, Pulcheria forged ahead with her organizational plans while not neglecting her piety projects, including a massive amount of church building.

Truth be told, Theo enjoyed having his older sister micro-manage; in fact, when a small war with Persia bubbled up in 420, he told everyone that her extreme piety—and her strict chastity—was directly responsible for the success of the Byzantine armies in the field.

As the years rolled on, a rift developed between Theo and his wife Eudocia; at length she slunk off to the Holy Land, ostensibly to make a pilgrimage. Pulcheria couldn't help but gloat a bit; she gloated even more whenever Pope Leo wrote or came calling, asking for her help in the latest theological quarrels.

In the summer of A.D. 450, her beloved brother Theo—evidently forgetting momentarily how to ride a horse in true imperial fashion—fell from his mount and injured his spine. Two days later, he died. Before he did so, he had a heart-to-heart with his sister and an obscure military officer named Marcian about a premonition he'd had. In it, he saw Marcian ruling Byzantium. Dream premonitions being one of those omens you didn't ignore in old Byzantium, he urged Pulcheria to wed Marcian.

Pulcheria was already worried, pondering her future, since legally the Roman senate would not make her (being female) sole ruler, even though they respected and feared her. After Theo died, she was shattered, spending the next month arranging for her brother's huge public funeral. At the same time, she entered into negotiations with the mild-mannered Marcian. And they came to terms—her terms, naturally. The first being, absolutely no sex. She was a career virgin, by God, and intended to stay that way.

Pulcheria had three glorious years to run things her way before she left the material world in A.D. 453. Because she loved Constantinople and its people, she left all her worldly goods to local charities and to the poor—a staggering amount of real estate and other property. As befits a martinet to the last, she bossily instructed her husband Marcian to do the same. Or else!

Possibly garnering the most Obscure Roman Emperor award, Marcian peacefully ruled for three years before dying of gangrene. We still don't know if he followed Pulcheria's postmortem orders.

# Legendary Loves &
# Sometimes-Real Romances

# THE SACRED BAND:

## They were called "an army of lovers"

Hardly anyone ever mentions Thebes, thirty-three miles northwest of Athens in the region of Boeotia, once a powerful urban center that dominated the rest of Greece. (If mentioned at all, it is invariably confused with the Egyptian Thebes, a city straddling the Nile River that was Egypt's capital for centuries.)

Grecian Thebes was home to the Sacred Band, a powerhouse special military force comprised of 150 pairs of older male/younger male lovers. Today it's often confused with the Three Hundred, the band of Spartan warriors who in 480 B.C. held off the gigantic Persian army of Xerxes at the pass of Thermopylae long enough to give Greek allies time to meet the foe at Marathon. Recently popularized in films and comics, the Three Hundred had many parallels with the Sacred Band, as you'll see.

How and why did the Sacred Band come into being? According to Greek historian Plutarch (himself a native Boeotian), this elite force took its inspiration from a quote in *The Symposium* by Plato, written seven years before the group's formation, which said in part, "If only there were a way of contriving that a state or an army should be made up of lovers and their beloveds, they would be the very best governors of their own city, abstaining from all dishonor, and emulating one another in honor."

Democratic Thebes was known for its serene acceptance of same-sex male relationships. There, lovers pledged their devotion at a tomb sacred to the cult of Hercules and his young lover Iolaus. After pledging, male couples often lived together in a marriage recognized by all citizens.

Soon after the year 404 B.C., all of Greece began to suffer under the harsh regime of the Spartans, newly victorious over the Athenians and its allies during the Peloponnesian War. In reaction, the Thebans handpicked three hundred men who were committed couples from the ranks of their existing citizen army. They trained together, coming up with inventive maneuvers—such as deeper phalanx formations and the use of shields as offensive weapons—which eventually became part of their "shock troops" strategy. By degrees, they made their city preeminent, recognized by other Greeks as a top military power.

In 375 B.C. they beat the Spartans by defeating an army three times their size. Four years later, under the leadership of generals Epaminondas and Pelopidas, they decisively kicked Spartan hiney again at Leuctra—called by many historians the most important battle ever waged, Greek against Greek.

The victories of the Sacred Band let the Thebans and other Greeks dare to hope that the Spartans were not, in fact, invincible. Thebes' extraordinary general Epaminondas (a philosopher and orator when not on the battlefield) then carried the ball forward, freeing the large provinces of Arcadia and Messenia from Spartan rule, and laying successful siege to Sparta's capital as well.

But a new power emerged that even the Sacred Band could not quell. As a teen, king-to-be Philip II of Macedon had spent three years (368 to 365 B.C.) as a hostage in then-triumphant Thebes, where he studied (and later copied) their fighting methods and strategies. Once he became king, Philip set off to conquer all of Greece, eventually confronting the Athenians and Thebans at Chaeronea in 358 B.C., with his eighteen-year-old son Alexander (later dubbed "the Great") as second in command.

*Philip of Macedon*

*King Philip, a busy bisexual, admired the Sacred Band of Thebes, whose all-gay warrior couples he nevertheless slew.*

There he confronted the Sacred Band—which he attacked with his army of cavalry and troops using long spears, the Macedonian way of warfare. The members of the Sacred Band stood their ground, fighting fiercely, until all three hundred men perished.

Greek historian Plutarch wrote about the moment after the battle, when King Philip found their bodies and learned that this was the band of lovers and beloveds: "He burst into tears and said: 'If anyone who thinks that these men did anything disgraceful, may they perish miserably.' " (Plutarch, who wrote these words four hundred years after Philip, also noted that public pledges by male lovers were still part of Theban daily life.)

On that battlesite, the common grave of the Sacred Band was topped with a memorial of a huge marble lion that stands there still, having been restored in 1902 by the Order of Chaeronea, a secret society of English homosexuals.

History often piles irony upon irony; such was the fate of King Philip II of Macedon. After destroying the Sacred Band, Phillip would meet his own death at the hands of a man called Pausanias the Elder. The assassin was one of Philip's former male lovers.

## ALEX & HEPHAESTION:

### Love conquers all—even Alex the Great

Theirs was a love often compared to that of Achilles and Patroclus, the great heroes of the Trojan War; the comparison is apt. Homer's *Iliad* revolves around the relationship—by turns friends, lovers, and male bonding in a war setting. As Alexander and Hephaestion would do, Achilles and Patroclus face injury, treachery, and tragic loss.

Before he was even Great, Alex knew and loved Hephaestion, who was probably one year his senior. Sons of Macedonian nobles, they were boyhood chums who studied in tandem with philosopher-teacher Aristotle in a green and lovely part of Macedonia called Mieza. Aristotle, invariably thought of as "Athenian Greek," was actually from Macedonia; Philip II hired him to give his son and a select few of his peers the best possible education.

Besides Aristotle's lectures and classes, the two boys learned to ride, sail, and fight on foot and horseback, skills that they'd need as warriors. Did the teens become intimate at that time? We cannot know, but it seems likely.

At age eighteen, Prince Alex got his first taste of warfare at the battle of Chaeronea in Greece. He led the successful charge against the enemy—and his performance stunned his father.

By the time that steadfast friends Alex and Hephaestion were twenty and twenty-one, King Philip II had been assassinated and his son took on the mantle of leadership. With alacrity and skill, Alex and the Macedonian fighting force began what would become his decade-long world conquest, moving south through Greece and then into Asia Minor.

In May of 334 B.C., the Macedonian juggernaut reached the ancient city of Troy. Alex and his best bud immediately went to the resting place of Achilles and Patroclus to lay wreaths on their tombs. Afterward, they ran a footrace in the nude to honor their dead heroes. This much-told story cemented the general belief that the two were lovers.

Their army continued to record victory after victory as they worked their way south and east. At the battle of Issus, the Macedonians defeated the Persians for the first time. Persian king Darius was killed and his queen Statira captured. In her first meeting with Alexander, the queen immediately kneeled in front of the taller young man—Hephaestion. Terrified at her blunder, she began to apologize to Alex, who said, "Don't worry, Mother. Everywhere, he is Alexander, too."

In that long-ago egocentric and boastful world, his graceful and great-hearted tribute remains one of the most moving endorsements of love and friendship.

In our world, where sexual identity is often parsed into neat categories, Alexander and Hephaestion would both be called bisexuals, since they subsequently married a variety of women and also carried on love affairs with ones they did not wed. Despite both men's affection for their women and Alex's probable liaison with the Persian eunuch known as Bagoas, the tight bond between them continued.

Alexander the Great

*Like his father, Alexander the Great was bisexual. He, however, maintained a steadfast love for his partner Hephaestion until death parted them.*

Hephaestion was not a great warrior, but he did a good job, commanding under the most trying of circumstances. He was an excellent organizer and a skilled diplomat by all accounts; Alex trusted him implicitly. Unlike others in the inner circle, Hephaestion never betrayed his commander or let him down. That says much about his character—and likewise the character of Alex, who wasn't always a benign and loving leader, either.

In 330 B.C., Hephaestion uncovered and revealed a plot against his friend's life. Inevitably that made others more jealous of his special relationship with Alex, given the power struggles between ambitious men in the inner circle.

After years of harsh battles, difficult weather, struggles through awful terrain and unknown territories as far as India, Alex's four armies, including one under Hephaestion's command, rejoined Alexander at a place called Carmania in southwest Asia (today's Iran). In December of 325 B.C., they celebrated wildly, Alex decorating his key officers and giving some of them, Hephaestion included, golden diadems. A few years earlier, these macho Macedonians would have considered these crowns effeminately Persian, but in their travels they'd all become more accepting of others' customs.

Next, since Alexander never did anything in a small or conventional way, he organized a mass wedding ceremony between eighty of his top Macedonian officers and eighty Persian princesses who'd gotten a Greek education in the five years since Alex had conquered their nation. Days of lavish ceremonies followed, with Hephaestion marrying a daughter of Persian king Darius, and Alex tying the knot as well. All seemed smooth sailing now; Alex was happy and busy with plans for sending a naval expedition to Arabia.

Then it all came crashing down. In the fall of 324 B.C., Alex came to Ecbatana, one of his new capital cities. Naturally the Macedonian boys threw a drinking party. The next day, Hephaestion fell sick. A hangover, everyone assumed. Seven days later, he died of a fever.

Alex was beyond stunned. He had lost what he called "the friend I valued as my own life." As historian Arrian wrote, "Alex flung himself on the body of his friend and lay there in tears, refusing to be parted until he was dragged away forcefully by the men in his inner circle." Plutarch noted that "Alex ordered mourning throughout the empire, and asked the oracle at Egyptian Siwa if the god Amon would permit Hephaestion to be worshipped as a god." Amon refused but did permit Alex's lover to be worshipped as a divine hero.

Hephaestion's funeral was spectacular and costly, the equivalent of millions of dollars in today's currency. The funeral pyre resembled a Babylonian ziggurat, seven stories high, loaded with 240 ships and scenes rendered in gold of centaur battles, lions, and bulls. Part of Babylon's city walls were demolished to build the platform for the pyre, and according to Greek historian Strabo, it took ten thousand workmen two months to clear the site afterward.

The permanent memorial to Hephaestion that Alex planned may never have been completed. In a strange echo of his lover, Alexander himself was to die, unexpectedly, of a mysterious fever the following June of the year 323 B.C.

## SERVILIA & JULIUS CAESAR:
### History's first cougar

Ashton Kutcher wasn't the first famous man to fall in love with an older woman. Some 2,100 years ago, a man universally famous in his time (and ours) fell hard for a Roman patrician pushing fifty, with four kids and two marriages under her belt.

Her name? Servilia Caepionis. She came from one of Rome's most distinguished families. A shrewd, well-connected political dynamo, she remains unsung even after being brought to vivid life in several films and television series in recent years.

Her thirty six-year-old lover? None other than Gaius Julius Caesar.

The two met while Servilia was raising her children from her first and second marriages. After an immediate and mutual attraction, she became

Caesar's mistress around 64 B.C. Julius soon gave his lover a gorgeous black pearl rumored to have cost around six million sesterces—a huge sum in any language. She stayed married to her second husband, Decimus Silanus, who seems to have been a go-along guy. It paid off, too. A couple of years later, Caesar supported Silanus in his successful political bid for Roman consul.

Likewise, Caesar's string of three wives seemed to have put up with the long-term arrangement.

Like her lover Caesar, Servilia was outrageous—even reckless at times. In 63 B.C., her half brother Cato, also a senator, and Caesar opposed each other during a fierce debate over the Cataline conspiracy. At one point, someone handed Julius a letter—which Cato took to be from the Cataline conspirators.

"Read it aloud!" Cato demanded. Oh, boy. As the smokin' hot note from Servilia was read to the titillated Roman senators, Cato learned that his half sister had been doing the wild thing with his senatorial opponent. Awkward moment. And small wonder that Cato and his conservative clique became even more rabid foes of Julius Caesar.

Caesar spent years away from Rome, fighting wars, conquering Gauls, raising money, and building his power base. Despite his long absences—or perhaps because of them—his relationship with Servilia remained feverishly hot, lasting for two decades until his shocking assassination in March of 44 B.C.

Roman high society was a complex one and relatively small, meaning that most people became intimately connected (and thus obligated) by multiple marriages, divorces, adoptions, and melded families.

JVLIVS CÆSAR
(from the Naples bust)

*The passion of Julius Caesar's life? Servilia, his lover for decades. Tragically her own son Brutus spearheaded Caesar's murder.*

Thus when Julius Caesar was murdered on the Senate floor, Servilia not only lost the love of her life—she also became the horrified mother of an assassin: her son Marcus Brutus. She also found herself the mother-in-law of another key man in the assassination, since Cassius was married to her daughter Junia Tertia.

In the aftermath, a grieving Servilia sought to protect her murderous kin from the dire consequences of their actions, but failed. Her astute political advice, which she freely offered to friends in her political circle, including Cicero, was also rejected for the most part. She, however, survived the years of chaos and bloody civil war that tore Italy apart following the assassination—about the only one in her elite circle who did. Servilia ended her days at the country home of Titus Atticus, the great-hearted friend of Cicero, who had also mentored her son Brutus.

Servilia may not be recognized as a trailblazing "cougar" like modern-day icons from Mae West to Madonna. Nevertheless, her fascinating love story cries out to be told, doesn't it?

## ORPHEUS AND EURYDICE:
### Into the mouth of hell for his mate

Orpheus was a musican, and a good one. He wrote music, too. He not only had rhythm, he could also charm wild beasts, sway the trees, and even change the course of rivers with his songs. No wonder Eurydice fell for him.

He was a kind and gentle guy, not one of those rowdy troubadours on the make. His mother was a Muse—the source of his musical roots; his dad, a prince from Thrace. Or maybe a king. He'd also mumbled something about being the son of the god Apollo.

She couldn't even remember how and where they met, but it was love at first glance. Orpheus wooed her with stories of his adventures with the Argonauts, and how he'd played his lyre when their ship passed the islands of the Sirens. His wild and beautiful music had kept the men from hearing the bewitching siren songs and crashing upon the evil rocks around their shores. A hero, that's what he was.

She learned he was a prophet, and had practiced the magical arts. He'd been around; he'd even been to the Underworld and back, he said.

Finally, after he'd told her all his stories, he said, "Eurydice, will you marry me?"

Of course she would, and did. Their wedding took place among her people, the Cicones. An outdoor affair. Afterward, she went for a stroll among the tall grasses in the glow of the sunshine. She was so happy. And then it happened: one of those damned satyrs showed up—they were always crashing weddings, the horny little creeps—and started chasing her. She ran fast, and was pulling away from him, looking for Orpheus, when suddenly she stumbled and fell, right into a nest of writhing vipers! Terrified, she scrambled out, but one snake bit her on the heel as she made her escape.

Oh, Orpheus . . .

He'd only been gone from her for a few minutes, half an hour tops; he'd just gone to have a congratulatory bump with the boys. Where could she be? When he found Eurydice, she was lying in the grasses, a calm smile on her beautiful face. She looked as though she was taking a nap, awaiting his return. Her bloody heel, the hiss of the nearby snakes, told the rest of the story.

His new bride, dead. Orpheus thought his heart would split in two with sorrow. Numbly, he picked up his lyre and began to play. His song, heavy with grief, wafted out into the world. Hearing the notes of his music, all of the gods and goddesses began to weep.

He played for hours, grieving in his own way. Finally, one of the gods whispered to him, "Go down to the Underworld, boy, and fetch her back. You alone can persuade Hades and Persephone to release your new bride."

Drying his tears, Orpheus once again took the fearsome journey into the Underworld. Although fear made him icy cold, he struck the strings of his lyre and began to sing. "In the end, every lovely thing goes down to you, O Hades, you are the debtor who is always paid. But I seek one who came to you too soon. I only ask one small thing, that you lend her back to me, for my love is too strong a god."

His pleading song was so eloquent it made tears of iron run down Hades' cheeks. "Your wish is granted, just stop that dreadful wailing," Hades said. "You may take Eurydice back into the light of day, under one condition."

Orpheus, trembling with happiness and fear, asked, "What must I do, O King of Tartarus?"

"Have her follow you—but do not look back at her until you reach the upper world."

Orpheus exploded with joy at these words, and at the sight of his beloved's ghostly form. The two lovers went through the great doors of Hades' kingdom and began the trek to the earthly world. It was a long journey, uphill of course, dark and torturous; by the time Orpheus reached the sunlight, he'd grown anxious. Was Eurydice still behind him? He needed to see her! He turned, holding out his arms for her; and there she was, smiling—but still in the shadows of the Underworld.

In desperation he lunged after her, but it was too late. He thought he heard her whisper, "Farewell," and she was gone. Orpheus cried out to Hades for another chance, but he was only met with silence.

Stunned, disconsolate, Orpheus began to wander through the wilderness of Thrace, playing his music, his only comfort. At length some Ciconian women of Eurydice's people happened upon him. They were already unhappy about the whole Eurydice affair, and started throwing sticks and stones at him to shut him up. But the music of Orpheus was so haunting that even the inanimate objects refused to hit him.

Well, that did it. The women, who were already wearing their maenad gear for an upcoming Dionysian orgy, tore Orpheus to shreds and decapitated him.

They threw him into the river—his body, head, and lyre—but even as they floated out into the great sea of the Mediterranean, Orpheus's head and his lyre kept on singing and playing. All of his parts floated to the island of Lesbos, where locals reverently gathered them up and built a shrine in his honor. The Orpheus head became an oracle that gave prophesies until the god Apollo got into a jealous snit and silenced it.

There were as many variations on the Orpheus and Eurydice story as there were Greeks, making the Orphic literature rich as well as contradictory.

Centuries later, in Plato's time, certain men became wandering beggar-priests of what was called the "Orphic life," practicing vegetarians who abstained from eggs, beans, and sex in order to pass along the ancient teachings and exquisite musical poems of Orpheus.

*A maenad might look harmless but a band of them in full riot gear tore Orpheus the musician to shreds.*

## SELEUCUS & FAMILY:
### Father-son solution to forbidden love

Besides conquering the world, Alexander the Great had another ambitious goal: to meld the cultures he conquered into one Greek-speaking entity. One of his bright ideas? After defeating the Persians, he selected eighty of his best and brightest Macedonian officers—including a shrewd young commander named Seleucus—to marry an equal number of dazzling Persian noblewomen. With cross-cultural procreation in mind, Alex splashed out lavishly for the spectacle. One of his less subtle party favors? Gold and silver nuptial couches for each couple.

Over the long term, Alex's efforts fell flat—except for Seleucus, who adored his Persian bride Apama. Of the eighty, they were about the only pair to remain married. (Full disclosure: an adventurous princess, Apama had already hit the mattress with Seleucus. Several years earlier, she'd traveled to faraway India with her lover, where she'd given birth to their first child, Antiochus.)

Apama and Seleucus went on to have three more children. It's rash to speculate about personality traits of long-ago people, but Seleucus, despite his job description, appeared to adore his wife and treat her well. On the other hand, he was one of those aristocratic Macedonian males, a group notorious for collecting wives, especially those who came with additional real estate.

Some twenty years after Alexander the Great's death in 323 B.C., King Seleucus controlled mammoth chunks of the regions we now call Turkey, Syria, Arabia, Iraq, Iran, and even a piece of India that went beyond what Alexander had won.

When Seleucus turned sixty, he lusted for just a little more territory—and thus married a superb young specimen named Stratonice, kin to several other Macedonian generals who'd been part of the Alexander inner circle. Taking his new bride to his capital of Antioch, Syria, the king named another city after Stratonice to make her feel at home. In addition, he gave his young wife "honorary goddess" status by setting up a local temple to worship Stratonice as Aphrodite.

These attentions may have given heartburn to Seleucus's longtime wife Apama, who'd already had various cities named after her. Being older and

*This celebrity case of love sickness had a happy ending: son wins dad's new wife, first wife retrieves original husband.*

wiser, she resigned herself to the newcomer. By now her son Antiochus was a strapping young man, training to succeed his father.

Suddenly, however, he fell ill with a mysterious disease and stopped eating. In despair, Seleucus paid outrageous sums to bring in Erasistratos, the most famous physician in the Greek world, to take the case. The doc was initially stymied because he couldn't find physical symptoms of the malady. Being, however, a believer in psychosomatic disease, he hung out in the sickroom, observing family and friends as they came and went. All the visitors seemed to drain Antiochus's vitality, with one exception: Stratonice, the young queen in blooming health.

Erasistratos was a learned man. He also adored the love poetry of Sappho, who'd lived several centuries earlier. He was familiar with her apt descriptions of passionate love—flushed face, sweaty body, faltering voice, irregular heartbeats—and he saw all these symptoms in Antiochus. Clearly the young man was lovesick; and at the same time, he recognized and felt guilty about the inappropriate nature of his passion for his stepmother.

So the doctor took King Seleucus aside, saying to him, "Your son has the disease of love for a woman, but a hopeless love." Being a ruler and used to getting his way, Seleucus was astonished, demanding to know how to rectify the situation. Since he knew that the king loved his son dearly, Erasistratos delicately told him that Antiochus was in love with Stratonice.

After the initial shock, Seleucus clearly saw that he should step aside and let his son follow his desire. (Never mind what Stratonice thought; it was 293 B.C., after all.)

When the whole matter was resolved, King Seleucus then announced to his people that he was handing over the reins of his Upper Asia empire to the next generation, his son and Stratonice.

He actually offered to marry the young couple.

In this heartwarming story (written about by Greek historian Plutarch and others), everyone achieved happiness in this odd situation, even and especially Apama, the faithful first wife of Seleucus, who got him all to herself until his death at age seventy-seven. Young Antiochus the First won his true love and joyously went about founding nearly as many cities as Alexander the Great. The Seleucid dynasty and empire remained a vigorous force in the world and stayed independent of Roman rule until 190 B.C.

## HELEN OF TROY:
### Homer launches a durable hit

The face that launched a thousand ships? Oh yeah, the ravishing Helen of Sparta. (She was born a Spartan; the Troy add-on came later.) Didn't she elope with a guy named Paris? And cause the Trojan War somehow?

Well, yes and no.

Before reading further, keep in mind that her entire story with all its contradictions and implausibilities is the equivalent of an early reality show. Yes, there were Mycenaean princesses in the twelfth century B.C. And yes, there were places called Sparta, Troy, and Athens, and indeed, they often fought wars.

Helen's dad was King Tyndareus of Sparta, although the god Zeus also claimed paternity. When she was twelve, King Theseus of Athens abducted and raped her. In some accounts, she gave birth to his child. Eventually, Helen's brothers engineered a revenge kidnapping to return Helen to Sparta.

Although a little shopworn, Helen was put on the eligible bride list. Masses of suitors responded. Frankly terrified at the mob of aroused males around the palace door, Tyndareus stressed over his decision. Odysseus, one of the suitors, sensing an opportunity, offered to help Tyndareus if the king would support his courtship of the babe he *really* had his eye on: Penelope of Ithaca. Odysseus then devised an oath that all the suitor dudes had to take. He made them agree to defend whoever won the bride, swearing the oath on the innards of a freshly killed horse, so everybody knew the king was dead serious.

The contest for Helen's hand in marriage was on.

The suitor competition was won by Menelaus, partly because he had pricey guy-toys—sixty ships. He and Helen settled in, starting having babies. He was tickled at daddyhood—plus Tyndareus had stepped down, and they were now rulers of Sparta.

On the other side of the Mediterranean lived a young prince of Troy named Paris. For some inexplicable reason, Olympia's head deity Zeus tapped Paris to judge his upcoming "most beautiful goddess" contest—there were three contestants, and boy, did Aphrodite want to win. She offered Paris a bribe: name her as hottest goddess, and she would make sure that he would win the world's most beautiful mortal woman. Paris readily obliged, and the love goddess got the crown, enraging rival deities Athena and Hera.

Now it was Aphrodite's turn to hold up her end of the bargain. So she helped Paris get himself invited to Sparta, where King Menelaus threw a nine-day welcoming feast for him. During the partying, Paris started wooing Menelaus's wife, even writing "I love you, Helen!" on the wine-spattered tablecloth one night. Fortunately, Menelaus noticed nothing. Soon thereafter, he was called to faraway Crete to bury his grandfather; naturally he asked Helen to run the kingdom and entertain their guests.

He had barely sailed out of sight when Paris and Helen made plans to run away. She'd already been abducted once, so she knew the ropes. Thinking ahead, she left all but one of her kids behind but had the foresight to pack gold, some palace treasures, and five serving women.

After various adventures at sea, the couple arrived in Troy to great acclaim. To a man, the Trojans thought Helen was totally hot. Soon after their arrival, Helen found a stone dripping blood near the castle and immediately recognized it as a powerful aphrodisiac. From that moment on, she dribbled it on Paris's cereal every morning to keep that testosterone percolating. Soon fertile Helen began popping out more babies.

*Helen of Troy, the most popular reality show of the twelfth century B.C., was all about making love and war.*

Meanwhile King Menelaus had returned from Crete and was quite disgruntled at the abduction of Helen. He immediately went to Mycenae to lobby his brother-in-law Agamemnon. "Dang it, I'm the injured party here! Paris really abused my hospitality."

Agamemnon sympathized. "If our demand for Helen's return, and a decent compensation offer, aren't forthcoming from King Priam, Paris's father, we'll go to war!"

King Priam stonewalled them; so Menelaus immediately rounded up all the suitors who'd stood on the bloody horse entrails and sworn that they'd defend whoever won Helen's hand, insisting that the crime needed swift punishment. Or, as he put it, "Nobody's wife is safe!"

In that shaky fashion, the Trojan War began, with most of the Greek kings and leaders siding with Menelaus against the Trojans.

Helen may not have launched a thousand ships (a few hundred is more like it), but she was an amazing catalyst.

During the war's ten-year duration, Helen would come to regret her part in it—and the Trojans would come to hate her for the deaths she caused. But not Paris's family. In fact, when Paris got killed, Helen coolly moved on to his brother Hector—and then to his youngest brother.

When Troy surrendered, the city afire, Helen once again confronted her husband Menelaus, who'd sworn to kill his faithless wife with his own sword. As the enraged king lifted it to strike, Helen let her robe slip from her shoulders. At the sight of her still-magical breasts, he dropped his weapon. Pretty awesome, given the number of children she'd birthed and nursed.

We don't know much more, other than that cults devoted to Helen of Troy sprang up around Greece, from Sparta to the Greek islands and

Athens. Even more extraordinary is the worshipful durability of her legend to the present day.

## PERICLES & ASPASIA:
### Married to love, not to marriage

You think it's tough being a single woman and a foreigner in our country today? Try being an unattached non-Athenian during that Greek city-state's Golden Age, roughly 480 to 399 B.C. Aspasia, for example, a delightful and charismatic Greek who emigrated from Miletus in Asia Minor, continuously bumped up against Athenian sneers toward nonlocals.

Having a superb education and a gift for eloquence didn't do much to improve Aspasia's reputation, either. She may or may not have been a courtesan or *hetera*—the latter being a Greek term for the classiest female companions. She was certainly labeled those things, and epithets even coarser, such as harlot and brothel keeper.

Although we have very little in the way of reliable testimony about her, one fact does seem clear: she entered into a long and loving relationship with the most brilliant political and military leader that Athens ever had. She and Pericles had what may have been the most rewarding long-term affair between consenting heterosexuals. In Athens, that was saying something.

Because she was a non-Athenian, she and Pericles could never marry. Thus they were in a no-man's land in terms of legal standing—unable to be a wife, she had a shadow existence as his mistress. In Rome, there existed a legal cohabitation called concubinage between

*Athens had a Hall of Famer in Pericles: canny general, brilliant politician, and truly great husband material.*

a free man and a free woman who for some specific reason could not marry. Athens, however, did not recognize that sort of arrangement; Greek concubines were slaves, not free women.

On the other hand, the idea of marriage Athens-style would not have been very appealing from Aspasia's point of view. She was a dame who could participate deeply in the political, intellectual, and creative life of her home city of Miletus, a place where women had more independence of movement, more options, more say-so.

In Athens, marriage was something that male citizens aged thirty and up dutifully did in order to beget legitimate offspring. Everyone wanted children, despite the risks. But in marriage, the typical Athenian lass went from childhood to bride to life as a secluded matron somewhere between the ages of thirteen and fifteen. Marriage partners were arranged by the families, based on connections, wealth, who had the most sublime ancestors, and how much dowry the girl's family was able to offer. Love and affection were very low priorities, if considered at all.

After marriage, Athenian husbands could continue to patronize prostitutes and dally with slaves of either gender. Athens nightlife consisted of a round of dinner and drinking parties, where the guests were all males and various female sex workers were on offer, from flute girls and other entertainers to *heterae*. The latter were independent women, most of them non-Athenians like Aspasia, who could pick and choose their lovers. And often choose their male clients, who paid for the evening's privilege of their lively conversation, sexy flirting, eye-candy appearance, and optional sexual services.

After marriage, Athenian wives stayed home. Whether newlywed or nearly dead, married women never ever got taken out to dinner. (The only exceptions? Women from poorer families who had to work to keep bread and feta on the table.) From time to time, husbands would spend evenings at home, usually with the goal of impregnating the little woman.

Given these polarized circumstances, love, affection, and even communication between married couples was probably in short supply.

Unlike today's couples, Aspasia couldn't effectively argue that she and Pericles should go live in her home city, where they could be married. He was Athenian and an important man in his city. Greeks were rooted to their homes, their birthplaces. (They still are, for that matter.)

Aspasia and Pericles went on to have a son together and probably did long to wed. Ironically, however, because of a law Pericles himself had passed, stipulating that Athenians could only wed other Athenians, he had legislated away that possibility! Aspasia never complained (that we know of) about the hardships of a relationship without formal recognition or rights, or those of Pericles Junior, who was born as his dad neared fifty years of age.

Pericles had two boys from a former marriage, both of whom he saw die in the Great Plague of 430 B.C. After he was no longer leader of Athens, an anguished Pericles did some hard groveling to persuade Athenians to amend the citizenship law so that his son with Aspasia could become a citizen and legitimate heir.

Tragically, in the autumn of 429 B.C. Pericles too was stricken—the victim of the second wave of the Great Plague. (Today's scientists now think it was an epidemic of typhoid fever or, alternatively, of the ebola virus.) Aspasia survived him but did not witness two final tragedies: the death of her son Pericles, who'd become an Athenian general; and the suicide of Socrates, Aspasia's firm friend and supporter.

## BERENICE & TITUS:
### Jewish princess almost makes empress

A romantic at heart, gorgeous and zaftig Berenice didn't plan on being married thrice and widowed twice. She didn't plan on committing incest, either. Things just worked out that way.

Berenice belonged to the elite Herodian clan, a dynasty that had ruled the Jews for over a century. Over time, many of the Herodians had lived in the imperial household in Rome and had gotten educated with the emperor's kids, but Berenice did not get that luxury. Chased by creditors, her hapless dad, Agrippa, shuttled the family between Palestine, Syria, and Judaea province until A.D. 37, when their luck suddenly changed.

A new Roman emperor, Caligula, occupied the imperial chair. Being a longtime pal of her dad's, he appointed Agrippa to govern chunks of the province of Judaea. On the heels of that announcement, she had a marriage offer from the richest Jewish family in Alexandria, Egypt. Since Berenice hadn't hit puberty yet, the wedding was scheduled for A.D. 41, when she would turn thirteen.

That same year, Caligula was assassinated and Claudius became the Roman emperor. This continued Berenice's streak of luck, since Claudius was another one of Dad's friends, made during his Roman childhood. Berenice was only halfway through her teens when her first spouse died. The family wasted no time in arranging another marriage, this go-round with her own uncle Herod. No spring chicken, Herod, but he did his best, giving Berenice two sons. Unfortunately, the strain of having toddlers and a teenage wife-niece put him in the grave four years later.

Now a woman, Berenice eagerly moved in with her brother Agrippa

II, a year older than she. Before long, ugly rumors of incest surfaced, but Berenice took it in stride, having already committed incest with husband number two. Eventually Berenice asked her brother to find her a decent new mate. Somebody with a little spark and longevity would be grand, she thought.

He came up with Polemo, the king of Cilicia (in modern-day Turkey), who seemed to enjoy her sexy dowry more than he did her. Into divorce court she went, and back to cohabit with her brother, gossipers be damned.

With her wealth, intelligence, and gift for diplomacy, Berenice gradually found herself doing meaningful work as an active philanthropist and an ad hoc arbitrator between Jewish and Roman factions. Eventually she was looked at as an equal partner in co-rule with her brother Agrippa. From time to time, she fretted about her personal life; she wasn't getting any younger. But she, like all Jews, had bigger issues to worry about. For some time, the Romans had discriminated against the Jews, favoring Greek populations in the Holy Land.

Things got uglier when a Roman-appointed governor stole from the temple in Jerusalem. The Romans crucified the leaders of the ensuing riot. Although Berenice and her brother pleaded with the Roman authorities on behalf of the Jewish population, their efforts went unheeded. As the situation grew more intense, the Jewish insurgents turned against the Herodian families and burned down their palaces, citing their close ties with the Roman imperial families. Berenice kept trying to negotiate on behalf of the Jews but was nearly killed in one of the skirmishes roiling throughout the city.

By A.D. 66, a rebellion was in full swing; the Romans responded harshly, sending General Vespasian and later his son Titus, along with 60,000 seasoned soldiers, to crush it. After three years of merciless siege, the Romans retook Jerusalem. And Rome (along with the Jews) had a new emperor: Vespasian himself.

Bernenice's entire family had fled north to the Galilee. The war came to an end at a heinous cost: the holy city of Jerusalem sacked, countless dead, and nearly 100,000 Jews taken as prisoners of war.

Amid the carnage, somehow Berenice met the man she'd been longing for. It was the emperor's son Titus, eleven years her junior, who would later be called "the delight and darling of the human race," a genial man gifted with extraordinary personal empathy. Two nations at odds and different religions separated them, but it did not seem to matter. They fell deeply in love. As deft with languages as he was keen in military matters, Titus wrote poetic verse, played the harp, and sang to her.

They had a mere year or two together in Judaea before he was called back to Rome to assist his father Vespasian in the monumental task of governing the empire.

Berenice and Titus did not see each other for four years. In A.D. 75, she and her brother Agrippa II came to Rome. Very soon she was living openly and lavishly with Titus in the palace. Their love was still ardent, but their lives were not without unpleasantness.

People had long memories. Romans saw her as "Little Cleopatra," an echo of the foreign queen who'd tried to co-opt the empire and its ruler. The public gossiped and fumed over her "barbaric" jewels, particularly a huge diamond she often wore. Titus and Berenice were publicly denounced by outspoken philosophers, and when Titus punished those who trash-talked his love, it made the situation worse. Finally, Emperor Vespasian, who'd always liked Berenice, regretfully ordered Titus to dump her.

In terms of influence and political pull, Berenice of the Herodians was at her most powerful but Roman public opinion trumped true love. As the historian Suetonius said in his biography of Titus, "He sent her away though he was unwilling and so was she."

She'd had just two more years with her lovely prince. But leave she did, with dignity. When Vespasian died in June of A.D. 79, however, she hurried back to Rome. A fresh start! Now her lover would put things right, convince the world that they belonged together. He didn't. He sent her away again, mumbling platitudes about "timing" and "public perceptions."

Time, fate, and circumstance were no longer their allies. Two months after her arrival in Rome, Mount Vesuvius erupted, creating a national disaster that Titus had to handle immediately. On the heels of it, a massive fire

*Rome's Colosseum, originally known as the Flavian Amphitheatre, played a part in the ill-fated romance between Titus and Berenice.*

hit Rome, followed by a deadly wave of plague. Titus had his hands full. He did all he could to comfort and console his people.

It wasn't enough—so he gave them entertainment. The Flavian Amphitheatre (known to us as the Colosseum), begun by Titus's dad and dedicated to him, had finally reached completion in A.D. 80. To cheer the battered spirits of the Romans, Emperor Titus immediately held one hundred days of games in the arena, the most elaborate and costly bloodfest ever witnessed.

Berenice tried to comfort herself about the realities of rule that her lover faced. He would send for her later, when things got back to normal. Normal never arrived, however. On a September day in the year 81, Titus died suddenly of a fever. He was forty-two. His grieving lover Berenice, now fifty-three, disappeared from public notice, the rest of her life unremarked to this day.

## HADRIAN & ANTINOOS:
### Turned his lover into a god

No one really expected a Roman emperor to behave himself when it came to his relationships; marriage was often a dynastic affair, political and calculated. Still, the most egregious example of a one-sided commitment may have been the loveless yet highly public marathon marriage between Emperor Hadrian and his empress, Sabina.

Starting with the wedding night, relations between Sabina and Hadrian went from tepid to ice-cold. All of thirteen or fourteen at the altar, Sabina may have been a sweet kid; over time, loneliness and lovelessness turned her arid and sour.

The couple never had children. Sabina was rumored to have outwitted pregnancy through abstinence and/or anal intercourse. In any event, she didn't face overwhelming male demands in the bedroom, since throughout their marriage Hadrian played the field, and on both teams. His affairs with married women were so plentiful that he was publicly accused of "addiction" to them.

Many Roman emperors collected boy-toys by the dozen, and Hadrian was no exception. Spiritually and culturally, he considered himself more Greek than Roman, so the classical Athenian relationsip of *erastes-eromenos*, mature men hooking up with teens, suited him beautifully.

But on a goodwill trip to Bithynia in Asia Minor, Hadrian's wife Sabina was confronted with the last straw. Hadrian met a curly-headed young teen with deepset eyes, his demeanor by turns shy and soulful. The emperor, now pushing fifty, was smitten. From that moment on, Antinoos never left Hadrian's side.

While Hadrian dutifully took care of state business, built splendid and lasting structures (Hadrian's Wall and the Pantheon makeover, for instance), carried out wars, and extricated Rome from other conflicts, he spent more than half of his twenty-one-year reign getting to know his subjects and his empire, making years-long trips from Germany to North Africa, from Greece to the British Isles. Empress Sabina was obliged to accompany him.

They weren't alone by any means. His retinue numbered over a thousand. Around A.D. 128, Hadrian and company, including his lover Antinoos, his wife, her attendants, plus a sea of aides and hangers-on, embarked on another grand circle tour, this time headed to Asia Minor, Greece, Palestine, and Egypt.

*The eloquent, intelligent face of Emperor Hadrian, one of Rome's better rulers.*

As they traveled, the emperor's couriers kept him apprised of political news, army movements, and disasters. Like other superstitious men in high places, Hadrian also got daily updates on portents, omens, scary dreams, and astrological news. An astrology adept, Hadrian obsessively checked his stars. He even forecast the date of his own death; and correctly.

In the year A.D. 130, while they were in Alexandria, Egypt, Hadrian felt a growing unease. Did some new catastrophe loom in his immediate future? In the fall, he looked up a magician named Pancrates, who demonstrated a spell involving mice, beetles, frankincense, myrrh, and dung that was guaranteed to kill a man in seven hours. After the spellbinding, a man showed up and promptly expired on the seventh hour. That was "proof" enough for Hadrian to pay a huge fee for Pancrates' services.

Intimations of tragedy continued to plague Hadrian's mind. One balmy October evening, as everyone excitedly discussed the field trip that Hadrian, Sabina, and their high-status guests were to take the next day, Antinoos disappeared. A frantic search ensued on land and in the Nile, but the boy was never seen again. The cruel mystery of his disappearance drove Hadrian wild with sorrow. Antinoos would have been eighteen years old.

Within weeks, Emperor Hadrian made Antinoos into a god. Earlier emperors and empresses had been deified, but they were imperials. Deifying a commoner, a non-Roman, a catamite? Appalling bad taste to honor a sexual companion. Sacrilegious, perhaps. Ignoring the disapproval and snide remarks of Romans high and low, Hadrian commissioned the building of temples around the Mediterranean Sea, and ordered that worship of Antinoos commence empirewide. Immediately.

To give people something concrete to worship, Hadrian set in motion the last new era of Greek sculpture, commissioning what was likely over a thousand statues and busts of his young lover. Hundreds still remain on display at museums worldwide; as Elizabeth Speller, author of *Following Hadrian*, describes them: "A new face appeared, and it was one of manly, though submissive beauty . . . a well-proportioned body, with downcast eyes and thick, curly hair nestling at the nape of the neck."

Hadrian's grief and grandiosity had no bounds. On the east banks of the Nile, at the spot where his lover had vanished, he founded a city called Antinoopolis. No expense was spared to make it splendid and luxurious. Before the city even rose on the site, the emperor honored Antinoos with a Great Games competition and festival.

A huge, hieroglyph-covered obelisk now reposing on the Pincian Hill in Rome may be a memento of those first games. On it, an inscription more lengthy than memorable, written by Hadrian, included these phrases: "The god Osiris-Antinoos, the justified—he grew into a youth with a beautiful countenance and magnificently adorned eyes . . . whose heart is in very great jubilation, since he had recognized his own form after being raised again to life and seen his father, God of the Rising Sun . . . The god whose place this is, he makes a sports arena in his place in Egypt, which is named after him, for the strong ones [athletes] that are in this land, and for the rowing teams and the runners of the whole land and for all men who belong to the place of the sacred writing where Thoth is present. They receive the prizes awarded and crowns, while they are repaid with all sorts of good things."

*Antinoos, the sultry young nobody that Hadrian desperately loved and lost. His unexplained vanishing act led to the final flowering of imperial art.*

Despite the initial scorn and shock at Antinoos's

deification, he came to be enthusiastically worshipped alone, or in conjunction with other gods from Dionysus to Osiris, for centuries around the empire but especially in the eastern provinces and the boy's native Bithynia, today the northwest coast of Turkey.

The lovelorn emperor never got over his loss; and no one ever discovered why or how the boy vanished. The body was never recovered, either.

Was his death foul play? An accident? Suicide? Murder by a jealous rival? Or, as some have theorized, was it Antinoos's gift, a deliberate and loving sacrifice of a life to preserve the safety of the one who ruled? That question remains unanswered, but it's one of history's most heart-rending, fascinating mysteries.

And Sabina? Marital longevity won her what love could not. When she died in A.D. 137, her husband Hadrian had her deified as well. The marvelous bas-relief of her apotheosis still holds pride of place in Rome's Palazzo dei Conservatori museum.

# Love Hurts. But Changing Gender Really Smarts

## EUNUCHS & CASTRATI:

### Sensitive men, the hard way

By and large, Greek and Roman males scoffed at men who exhibited feminine qualities such as—ugh—sensitivity. Greek philosophers, Aristotle among them, affirmed that physically and mentally, females were a defective sort of male. Thus to be a man meant macho, and lots of it.

The thought of being born a female was distressing enough to male minds—equally dire was the idea of male castration. Nevertheless, eunuchs, some of them castrated forcibly and others, wince, by choice, were much in evidence in ancient societies, beginning with the Egyptians, Assyrians, Persians, and other cultures and becoming fairly commonplace among the Greeks and Romans.

Although we sometimes use the words *eunuch* and *castrato* interchangeably, they were not. Roman law, for example, made a clear distinction between eunuchs, defined as men who were impotent due to accident or birth circumstances, and/or indifferent to the female gender by nature; and castrati, who were unable to procreate because of genital mutilation.

The castration procedure, whether carried out before puberty or after, was grisly. It was also fatal to a shocking percentage of victims. Archaeologists excavating in Roman Britain sites found one of the tools used: a heavy, serrated bronze implement that clamped around the scrotum and removed the offending parts from their owner. Simpler tools, such as razors, shards of pottery, or pieces of obsidian, were also utilized in this agonizing operation. Some victims lost the whole package, while others, called *spadones*, were divested only of their testicles.

What motivated this bloody business? One was the perennial sex slave market for handsome sweet-voiced young boys with smooth hairless skin. (Fifteen centuries later, this would again create a job market for castrati singers in Renaissance Italy.) Another driving force: to provide gelded workers for intimate settings, such as the harems and women's quarters of rulers in regions of Persia, Egypt, and the Middle East.

A third reason was the illogical but firm folk belief that castrati and eunuchs made the most loyal and discreet employees. Because these men could produce no heirs, it was thought they were less apt to usurp power or throne-grab. Government bureaucracies around the ancient world had great need of such workers in middle management, and a mountain of evidence exists about the careers of thousands. In addition, a significant percentage became top advisers for a roll-call of Roman emperors, from Claudius and Nero to Gordians I and II.

During later imperial centuries, the growing demand for eunuch slaves impelled Emperor Hadrian to try to curb the market by passing laws; he failed, as did later emperors Nerva and Diocletian.

A fourth motive existed for male castration: the goal of religious chastity, which Egyptian priests had long exemplified. Around 204 B.C., the religious cult of the goddess Cybele came into being. Its persistent popularity spread from Asia Minor to Rome, where the deity was renamed Magna Mater. The cult literally created its membership of male disciples who, to show their devotion, castrated themselves in public. (You can read more about them and other ecstatic mystery religions elsewhere in this book.)

*The goddess Cybele of Asia Minor demanded a lot from her male devotees. Worship wasn't enough; she also required the DIY donation of their private parts.*

Other sects around the Greco-Roman world had followers who emasculated themselves; in the second and third centuries A.D., the fast-growing Christian movement tried but also failed to keep its adherents from such extreme demonstrations of chastity.

The most notorious do-it-yourselfer? Theologian, teacher, and writer Origen of Alexandria. One account says that he was motivated to wield the knife upon reading the passage of Matthew 19:12 that says, "There are eunuchs who have made themselves eunuchs for the sake of the kingdom of heaven." Another reason: once castrated, he could teach female disciples without temptation. His castration around A.D. 200 led to a bizarre squabble among bishops as to whether such Christian activists could remain in the church. By 325, however, the Nicaean church council met to prohibit the practice of castrating oneself, so clearly Origen had imitators.

The abusive practice of making eunuchs and castrati out of men and boys flourished to an even greater extent after the Roman Empire lost traction to the Byzantines. During the thousand-year run of the Byzantine Empire, headquartered in Constantinople, eunuchs and castrati became even more visible as power players—and even more often, as tragic pawns in the sexual slave trade.

## EUNUCH PROFILES:
### Household names without heirs

Philaeterus became a eunuch in boyhood, the result of an accident. That did not stop him from becoming a shrewd and able officer who served in the armies of Antigonus and Lysimachus, two of the successor generals snarling over the conquests up for grabs after the death of Alexander the Great. In the succession wars, he was eventually promoted to commander of his hometown, the fortified city of Pergamum in Asia Minor (near Izmir in present-day Turkey). He took advantage of his plum assignment to switch sides—and declare his independence from the rest of the quarreling generals.

He ruled Pergamum for nearly forty years. Since it was a wealthy city, it had a fat treasury—and with these civic funds, Philaeterus made his hometown even more beautiful than it had been. He was also a generous benefactor to neighboring cities. Because he had no heirs, he adopted his nephew, Eumenes, to found the Attalid dynasty. After his death in 263 B.C., his successors continued to honor him on the city's handsome coins.

Halotus, whose name is inextricably linked with Roman emperors Claudius and Nero, was a political survivor. In his post as the official food foretaster to the imperial family, the youthful eunuch guarded the health and welfare of Claudius until that disastrous October of A.D. 54, when his employer turned up dead of poisoning. The conspiracy must have included Halotus. That said, the major player was definitely Agrippina, Claudius's niece and fourth wife, who'd likely become restive over her chronically ailing husband's inexplicably long lifespan.

Once Agrippina's evil cherub Nero reached his teens and got his official manhood toga, Emperor Claudius's goose was cooked. Common sense would dictate that the goose of Halotus would be done for as well, since every conspiracy needs a fall guy.

Apparently not in this instance: wily Halotus bounced back, even retaining his cushy foretaster job throughout the fourteen-year reign

*Eunuch Philaeterus of Pergamum, an unsung success story, was a terrific general and city administrator who founded a dynasty despite his lack of progeny.*

of Emperor Nero. As a further triumph, Halotus survived Nero's downfall! He went on to become the gastronomic confidant of short-lived Emperor Galba in A.D. 69, called "the year of the revolving emperors."

Bagoas, although not of the Persian nobility, became an excellent administrator and the number-two eunuch of Persia during the regimes of Artaxerxes III and IV. Thanks to his twin talents as poisoner and assassin, Bagoas did away with two generations of Persian despots, thus allowing the military forces of Philip II of Macedon (and later his son, Alexander the Great) to conquer the Persians and bring an end to the Achaemenid empire. According to some sources (and Mary Renault's superb novel *The Persian Boy*), Bagoas may have had a *petit* dalliance with Alexander the Great during his time in Babylon.

This eunuch's dazzling career finally came to a screeching halt when Persian king Darius III caught wind of Bagoas's murderous plans for him—and Darius forced him to drink a fatal cup himself.

In late imperial times, Eutropius came to the fore. Although eunuchs and castrati won favor with rulers because of their loyalty and lack of ambition, Eutropius didn't fit the mold. A mid-level official in the busy Byzantine bureaucracy, he came to the attention of Arcadius, the current emperor, by fielding the most attractive marriage candidate, Eudoxia by name. On the strength of that feat, he became the emperor's top adviser.

Eutropius had other useful skills. In A.D. 398, he was able to pull off a military triumph by thwarting the invasion of the Huns. The following year he was appointed consul—an achievement of such magnitude that the Roman senate, along with other patricians, went ballistic, demanding his removal. They probably admired his corporate ladder-climbing skills, but a eunuch consul? No way. Eudoxia, that ungrateful empress, gave him the thumbs-down. That was followed by a really bad omen: a major earthquake rocked Constantinople. Sent into exile on Cyprus, Eutropius was later beheaded on a specious charge.

## HERMAPHRODITES:
### Early warning signs from the gods

In Italy and surrounding lands, long-ago folks saw warning signs all around them, so many that they had to be organized into supernatural categories: portents, *ostents*, prodigies, and *monstra*. (These terms, used by soothsayers and augurs, meant tokens, acts, or events that offered clues to important or calamitous future happenings, acts so rare or extraordinary as to inspire wonder; *monstra* could be abnormal or simply wondrous. From *ostent*, we now have *ostentatious*; from *portent* we derive *portentous*; from *prodigy* we get *prodigious*; and from *monstra*, we get *monster*.)

These occurrences were interpreted as signals that something was amiss between heaven and earth, that something bad was about to happen. What kinds of omens seemed truly ominous two thousand years ago? The report of a shower of frogs, for instance. The sight of a statue of Jupiter sweating blood. Even the infrequent birth of triplets was an occasion for mass hysteria.

But the prodigy that really set teeth to chattering was the terrible news that a hermaphrodite had turned up somewhere. Ancient Greeks and Romans had a morbid fear of hermaphrodites, who today might be called transsexuals. They looked at sexuality as a spectrum of actions, but gender identity was different. A hermaphrodite, whose body mingled masculine and feminine equipment, or who self-identified as another gender, disturbed

*The symbol for hermaphrodite, a frightening phenomenon in ancient times. Although the Greeks had a demigod named Hermaphrodite, when one appeared in human form, panic broke out.*

the social fabric. Alternatively, the neither-nor aspect of a hermaphrodite might represent divine displeasure.

Once an individual had been reported to the authorities and declared an official prodigy, that prompted an emergency meeting of the Decemviri, a group of ten bigwigs from the Roman senate. These old boys consulted the Sybilline prophesies, a collection of ancient oracles. These readings told Romans exactly what to do when such an unlucky creature showed up.

How had this phobia arisen in the first place? Early in Greek history, a modest cult had arisen to honor a demi-god named Hermaphrodite. As the myth went, this fifteen-year-old son of Hermes and Aphrodite (Mercury and Venus, among the Romans) was being stalked by a comely nymph named Salmacis. Although the teenager rejected her advances, she managed to wrap herself around him while bathing and persuaded a more powerful deity to grant her wish—that they would become inseparable. As the poet Ovid later put it, "Their bodies became one, no longer two, nor could you say it was a boy or a girl. They seemed neither—or both."

The cult was not widely popular, but small images of the demi-god Hermaphrodite could be found in many households.

On a scientific level, a hermaphrodite of long ago, also called an androgyne or "man-woman" by the Greeks and Romans, could represent one of two possibilities: a woman who at some point, often explosively, turned into a man; or a person who visibly exhibited male and female sexual characteristics at the same time. (The next entry relates the fascinating case study of such a person.)

A person—even a small child—identified as a hermaphrodite often became a scapegoat. For instance, during a period in Italy that saw a stinging shower of stones occur, along with lightning bolts that scorched peoples' clothes and struck the temple of Jupiter in Rome, a twelve-year-old hermaphrodite was discovered in Umbria. At the urging of priests and soothsayers, he/she was put to death. At other times, the putative hermaphrodite might be banished, or cast adrift in the sea.

From the Roman point of view, it seemed important to document as well as punish hermaphrodites, who showed up regularly in ancient accounts. (Any survivors unhappy with their gender kept low profiles.).

By good fortune, two of the Sybilline oracular poems about hermaphrodite appeasement have survived to our day. Given wide distribution by the Decemviri senators, these poetic commands were directed at the general public. A couple of examples from the verses: (1) Give the goddess Persephone the most beautiful thing in the world; (2) Sacrifice a black ox to Hades; (3) Make prayers to Apollo and be sure that everyone wears a garland.

Dealing with the threat of a hermaphrodite two thousand years ago has parallels to our own planetary dilemmas, as the mournful last lines of the Sybilline poem make clear: "If you perform the prescribed rites, the calamity will still come, but it will not come in your lifetime." We would call that the "pass the problem along to your grandkids" solution.

No matter how the gods were placated, or to what degree, a number of fearsome hermaphrodite sightings did occur in Rome during the imperial centuries. Emperor Claudius—perhaps because he himself had a stammer, a limp, and other physical disabilities—displayed a more enlightened attitude toward human oddities. On one occasion, a thirteen-year-old from a distinguished family who turned from a maiden into a male on her wedding day was brought before him. Instead of banishment or worse, Claudius chose to look at the prodigy as a gift from the gods. Just to be on the safe side, however, he quickly built an altar on Capitoline Hill to a special cult dedicated to Jupiter, Averter of Evil.

## HERAIS, AKA DIOPHANTOS:
### Close-up of a gender change

These days, it's thought that many of those accused of being hermaphroditic in ancient times suffered from a medical condition called hypospadias or male pseudo-hermaphroditism. Initially identified as females, their true gender was male, often coming to light at puberty. Greco-Roman literature is littered with tabloid-style reports of newly married women who suddenly developed male organs, to the dismay of their bridegrooms.

Here is the real-life story of Herais, as told by Greek historian Diodoros of Sicily, whose invaluable account relied more on medical and social details than superstition.

She was born the daughter of an Arab woman and a Macedonian military man named Diophantos; after her dad retired, the family settled in a Greek-founded town called Abae on the Arabian peninsula.

At that time, a weak king called Alexander Balas ran their part of the world; he'd been handed Arabia and the throne of Syria, but his political strings were pulled by Egypt and Rome. Like everyone else, Balas liked to drop by his favorite oracle from time to time. At the one in Cilicia he was told, "Beware of the place that bore the two-formed one." Just like fortune cookies today, oracles specialized in enigmatic phraseology, so Balas simply stored the ominous message away for future reference.

Meanwhile, Herais grew into womanhood. Her father did the expected, giving her a dowry and her hand in marriage to a gent named Samiades. About a year after they wed, her husband took an extended journey, while Herais remained at home.

While her husband was away, Herais fell ill with a disease no one could diagnose. A painful tumor developed in her lower abdomen. The feverish young wife got sicker and sicker until the darn thing burst open—whereupon a fully formed set of male genitalia emerged from her body. Instantly Herais felt better, aside from being horrified at her gender transformation.

Her parents were equally dumbfounded. And frightened. After Herais recovered, she (or rather, he) began wearing her normal women's clothing again and went on being a housewife, for lack of a better idea.

Her anxious parents worried about their daughter; they knew that surprises like this were invariably unwelcome. Prior to this development, what kind of conjugal relations had she and her husband had? What on earth would they do now? Could this marriage be saved?

When Samiades returned, the situation grew even more tense. Herais refused to have intercourse and avoided him like the plague; so did Herais's father whenever Samiades tried to talk to him about the weird female troubles he was having with his wife.

The in-the-dark husband finally got so enraged that he sued his father-in-law, which meant that Herais had to appear in court as well. When the jury or judge convicted Herais of failing to meet her marital obligations, the dual-gender witness had had enough. Lifting her gown in full frontal nudity, Herais spoke directly to those present, demanding, "Which of you would compel a man to have sex with another man?"

This display brought down the house, and Herais and her father were acquitted. Samiades was staggered. (He would later find that he greatly missed her; eventually he killed himself, naming Herais as his heir.)

Meanwhile, due to the traumatic nature of her transformation, Herais's groin was frankly a mess. Surgery was undertaken, and as author Diodoros reported, "The male organ had been concealed in an egg-shaped portion of the female organ. Since a membrane had abnormally encased the organ, an aperture had formed, through which bodily secretions were discharged. In consequence, they [the doctors] found it necessary to scarify the perforated area and induce cicatrization [scarring]. Having thus brought the male organ into decent shape, they gained credit for applying such treatment as the case allowed."

Now that Herais was well and truly outed as a male, she began dressing as a man, officially changing her name to Diophantos, like her dad's. Not only that, she decided to pursue a more active career by joining the army of King Alexander Balas as a cavalry officer.

Remember the ominous "fortune cookie" message that Balas received at the oracle? While in his service, the newly male Diophantos may have even witnessed Balas's demise. He was assassinated by supposed friends in Abae, the town that had indeed seen the birth of a "two-formed one": Herais.

## INFIBULATION:
### Genital lockups, male & female

Greek and Roman slave owners tried various methods to prevent sexual activity between their slaves, or between slaves and members of the household. Substances, such as hemlock juice, for instance, would be applied to the male testes of slaves at puberty.

Far more often, though, they employed a sadistic means of genital control called infibulation. On the uncircumcised phalluses of boys approaching puberty they made a series of perforations in the foreskin, using a needle. After the holes healed, they inserted a fibula, a large bronze forerunner of the safety pin, through the foreskin. Sometimes the luckless wearer was fitted with larger bronze rings that were welded shut by applying red-hot charcoal.

This horrendous practice is on visual display at the Louvre Museum in Paris, where two larger-than-life, very nude statues of Roman slaves can be seen. They clearly show infibulation and what it did to phalluses—as well as what infibulated life must have been like.

Believe it or not, infibulation was thought to be the more "humane" approach. Masters ordered male slaves to be infibulated rather than subject them to castration, given the much higher likelihood of their death in surgery. It was also a common practice to infibulate gladiators—the rationale being to preserve their vigor. (Three-quarters of all gladiators were slaves and thus had no say in the matter.)

Flesh-crawling as it sounds, in Roman times a few free men actually infibulated by choice, to be hip and desirable. Comedy actors, dancers, and musicians did it, hoping to attract well-heeled sexual partners who would pay to play by unchaining them temporarily.

Members of religious sects, including the early Christian church and ascetics of various persuasions, also used infibulation to control their earthly desires.

From Greco-Roman times forward, the practice of infibulation has had staying power. Some statuary and art from the Renaissance, for example, depicts piercing of the male genitalia, often with oversize metal rings.

In the eighteenth century, population control advocates like Malthus and his followers lobbied for compulsory infibulation for anyone over fourteen years of age who was deemed unfit to procreate. His list included criminals, those with chronic diseases, beggars, unmarried servants (!!), apprentices, and rank-and-file soldiers.

During the Victorian era, prudish Western societies went hysterical over masturbation, again warming to the idea of locking up the sexual organs in a variety of ways.

The age-old desire to control or ruin the sexual capacity of others still exists today—now, however, mainly aimed at crippling women. From Greek times forward, there were reports of female slaves being infibulated with small metal rings but little in the way of evidence, other than some suspicious-looking metal remnants found in the graves of female slaves from Britain's Roman era.

In Europe during the Middle Ages, prior to departure the crusaders often installed chastity belts on their wives. The name sounds more humane than the object. "Chastity belts" had chain-mail metal parts and locking mechanisms.

In today's world, in parts of Africa, Asia, India, and the Middle East, a procedure even viler and more extensive than infibulation or chastity belts continues unabated. Operating under the guise of religion or tradition to protect chastity, this pharoanic or Sudanese circumcision, as it is known, produces dreadful mutilation in millions of young girls. Those who perform it completely remove the clitoris and labia minora, roughly sewing what's left of the sexual organs together. Alternatively, they bind the victim's knees and thighs together until the tissue heals into a scar. Often carried out under filthy conditions with unsterilized instruments, the operation has a high mortality rate. Females who do survive often suffer severe health problems, social shunning, agony during sexual activity, and high risk during child-bearing years.

Most of these women are not slaves, as the majority were among the infibulated victims of the ancient Greeks and Romans. Nevertheless, they are far from free to control what happens to their own bodies.

## MARRIAGE:

### No shotguns, but everyone from Sparta to Rome had to get married

Interesting, how ancient Athens is always viewed as the glorious, creative, democratic society, and its bête noir, Sparta, as the drear and repressive military society. If you were born back then, your opinion just might have depended on which gender you were.

Although the Spartans had a rep as glumly laconic folks, growing up in ancient Sparta was a far from gloomy affair. For girls, anyway. From toddlerhood, they got acquainted with little boys as playmates, engaged in competitive sports with them, went swimming (and dancing) in the nude. Girls even got to drive chariots in various annual festivals. Spartan girls didn't marry until age eighteen, and they ate a healthy diet—unlike their counterparts in Athens, who were kept indoors, fed poorly, and married off as soon as they menstruated.

It wasn't that the Spartans were progressive. They had eugenic reasons in mind: healthy young women produced healthy babies—and male babies were needed to feed the Spartan war machine. (Male babies were examined at birth; any with physical defects were immediately exposed or put to death outright.)

Although boys left their mothers at age seven to live in literally spartan barracks, eat meager rations of wretched food, and train insanely to become the toughest soldiers alive, they still had male urges. Unlike Athens and other Greek city-states, these urges could not be satisfied at the corner brothel, because Spartans did not allow prostitution inside their small city of 8,000 citizens. Growing boys had no access to slaves male or female, either, who in other locales would be obliged to submit to free men. The Spartans had Helots to do their grunt work; these unfree individuals were slaves of the state, not owned by individuals. Helot families lived in the country, and thus were less vulnerable to sexual abuse.

The Spartans devised a rather clever sexual escape clause; free males between the ages of twenty-one and thirty, and unmarried females over eighteen could engage in what books on Spartan history sometimes euphemistically call a "secret abduction" but was more like an elopement. Their first assignation took place after dark (flaunting the boy's curfew, since he lived in the barracks). After shaving her head boy-style, and dressing in a tunic like the ones preteen boys wore, the young woman would await her new lover. These "secret" meetings were not between strangers; these girls had known these boys all their lives, since they'd played together as youngsters.

*Few paintings of real-life couples have survived, making this portrait remarkable. These two are middle-class successes, not aristocrats, who likely perished in Pompeii during the A.D. 79 eruption.*

This arrangement could last until the young man turned thirty and retired from active service, at which time he was permitted to establish a household, called a *kleros*. He and his partner then moved in together. There was no bride price or dowry payment; no religious ceremony either. At this point, unlike other places in Greece, wives ran the household and may have handled the family finances.

Since procreative sex was the main object of marriage, a Spartan wife who remained childless was ordered to do something to remedy the impasse. To find a more fertile mate, Spartan law required her to sleep with another man straightaway! This might sound jolly—or ghastly—depending on your point of view. Being sparse in numbers, the Spartans made certain that every Spartan was paired up. No bachelors or spinsters allowed.

How did these Spartan Greek marital customs compare to the Roman style of marriage?

In the earlier Roman centuries B.C., there were three kinds of marriage, divided by social class. Nobility generally wed with a *confarreatio*, a bread-sharing ceremony, while plebians married by bride-purchase (a reverse dowry, so to speak) or by living together in mutual cohabitation.

Later, the Romans scuttled all three types in the early republic, instead going for the *manus* agreement, a one-sided affair that simply transferred the bride from the *manus* or hand of her domineering father to the hand of her bossy new husband. Fortunately for Roman women, marital agreements got more equitable around the second century B.C., under a new statute called the "free" marriage. The bride brought a dowry; but if they were divorced and no adultery was involved on her part, most of the money was given back to her.

Romans did not practice speed dating, but they did have speed remarriage—especially popular among elite families. New widows (or divorcees) could get hitched again without social condemnation or penalty, since the wedded state was considered the most desirable status for any adult, male or female. It worked out better for the woman as well, since—unlike the first time around—she had much more say in the matter of the bridegroom number two.

(You can learn more about Athenian and other Greek customs in the entries on Thargelia, adultery, divorce, and Aspasia & Pericles.)

## ADULTERY:
### The stinging price of ancient hanky-panky

Adultery was a ferociously big issue in ancient times. Merely the word *adulterer* was an insult among Greek men, and a favorite one-liner in the comedies of Aristophanes. Roman men had equally strong feelings about adultery— and many laws to prevent the act or punish it.

The most important element of Greco-Roman marriages was the legitimacy of offspring. Married men wanted to have children, particularly sons, to inherit and carry on the family name. They needed to know: Is that kid really mine? (If not, the injured party, since he considered his wife "property," felt righteous rage over property theft as well.)

Most gals, even teens whose husbands did not meet their needs or dreams, remained faithful. But some did not. If a woman slept with someone other than her husband, it was adultery—regardless of her partner's rank or marital status. Predictably, a married man who cheated only got into trouble if his co-conspirator was a freeborn married woman. Or someone else's unmarried daughter, for example. Otherwise, Greek and Roman husbands had a free pass to get intimate with slaves, concubines, prostitutes, and even sexually available adult men.

Adultery was a very dangerous game long ago. Don't judge it by the films you've seen about the ancient world; think in modern terms. Contraception and protection against STDs were a roll of the dice. There were no condoms; no diaphragms; no "morning after" tablets. Nor were affairs easy. There were no motels; no vehicles available by the hour; few if any convenient apartments to be borrowed from obliging friends. The houses of the guilty parties, where such naughty deeds would likely take place, were swarming with slaves and household members. Privacy? Forget about it. Furthermore, husbands didn't commute to work or spend long hours at the office. Adultery was even trickier for women, whose freedom of movement was often curtailed.

In the earlier era of the Roman republic, husbands sometimes claimed the "right" to kill wives caught in the act. Most of the time, though, adultery was grounds for divorce but not justification for homicide. Beginning around 18 B.C., however, Rome's first emperor made a strong attempt to legislate morality. To cut down on sexual hijinks and hanky-panky, Octavian Augustus introduced laws to punish married women who had extramarital affairs. Ironically this put the spotlight on several flagrant examples in his own family, namely his daughter and his granddaughter, both named Julia.

Another decree gave a cuckolded husband the right to legally slaughter the male adulterer as long as his rank was lowly: a slave, a freedman, or someone with a job labeled

*Greek playwright Aristophanes gained stardom for his ribald comedies, which often involved adultery and the adulterer's punishment: sodomy!*

"infamous," such as a gladiator or an actor. On the other hand, prostitutes could legally have sex with married men—and that exemption encouraged some randy, quick-thinking patrician women to register themselves as hookers to avoid prosecution!

The Augustan laws also affected the huge numbers of men in Roman military forces. Men convicted of adultery could not enlist; furthermore, if a soldier was caught in an adulterous situation, he received a dishonorable discharge.

Over in Greece, societal rules and laws against adultery remained draconian—a word that derives from Draco, the legislator whose laws included one that enraged husbands who caught adulterous wives and lovers in the act could carry out justifiable and legal homicide on both. The laws enacted by early Athenian leaders Solon and Draco were literally set in stone, word for word, upon plaques installed in public settings for anyone to consult. Furthermore, the same laws applied to men who had long-term relationships with mistresses who were free women—such as concubines or *heterae*, the highest-ranking sexual companions. Fathers whose daughters were unfaithful could kill both lovers with impunity.

All of this sounds rather grim, since humans have always been prey to temptation and sexual misadventures. But not all scenarios ended in bloodshed or murder of the in flagrante couple. For a male caught trifling with someone's wife or exclusive mate, the Greeks (and later the Romans) came up with a most humiliating punishment. The sinned-against husband was legally allowed to sodomize the adulterer! Many times, this took symbolic form. For example, in Greek comedy, the adulterer is often punished by having a radish inserted into his rear end—at times, with witnesses guffawing at the act. You might call it an ancient sting operation, since Greek radishes evidently grew to a healthy size and had a good "bite" to them.

In one bizarre, possibly jocular case mentioned by Roman writer Juvenal, a wronged husband in Rome chose to sodomize the adulterer using a fish instead of his own member.

Adultery carried other penalties. The unfaithful wife or mistress could be exiled from her home and could not be buried in the family tomb. All parties had responsibilities, even the betrayed husband; if a Roman failed to report the crime of adultery, he was guilty of being a procurer or pimp.

Given the extreme secrecy with which affairs must have been conducted, the adultery statutes must have been equally hard to enforce. In later, more lax centuries, when sexually louche emperors and empresses set the tone, attitudes softened. Infidelity—at least among the patrician smart set—became at times amusing, the subject of piquant murals, ribald poetry, and jests in plays.

## DIVORCE:
### No fault, no fees, no attorneys!

Even though marriage in those long-ago centuries could be challenging, divorce, by comparison, was a breeze. Divorce proceedings today often resemble an arena in which blood is spilled and combatants are scarred; in contrast, the Romans restricted most of their bloodshed to the gladiatorial amphitheatre.

Romans tended to be anal and legalistic in many regards, but they treated divorce in a casual, almost informal way. Although men—and a tiny handful of women—studied law, there were no lawyers (divorce attorneys or otherwise) for hire as we think of them. Marriage therapists and family counselers? Nope.

Although sources disagree on the year, the first recorded divorce in Roman history probably occurred around the year 230 B.C., when a certain Spurius Carvilius divorced his wife. The reason given? She was unable to have children. Infertility (even though it might have been the old man who was sterile) was the only legal reason for divorce given in the Twelve Tables, Rome's oldest written code of laws. The original tables, destroyed by the barbarian invasion and burning of Rome in 390 B.C., have only survived in jumbled, incomplete form.

Over time, three other "serious marital faults" besides infertility became justifications for Roman men to divorce their wives: adultery; consuming wine; and most heinous of all, making copies of the household keys.

Eventually women got to sue for divorce as well.

The actual "ceremony" was unceremonious. After a couple declared their intent to live apart in front of witnesses, they were divorced. In some cases, if the husband had initiated the divorce, he simply took away her household keys and turned her out.

The most outlandish aspect of Roman divorce? Unless the wife could prove that her hubby was worthless, he generally got to keep the kids.

From the second century B.C. on, husbands and wives kept their property separate during marriage, so "community property" became an oxymoron. Besides her dowry, a well-to-do woman or an heiress might own rental property or a business; generally, however, she didn't have a hands-on role in her investments or business transactions. Her male guardian (her father, brother, husband, or other male kin in the background) did.

The wife and her dowry (except in the case of adultery) would return to her father's household, who as *pater potestas*, all-powerful dad, had an obligation to find her a new husband. When it came to remarriage, though, Daddy's domineering hand was not the final word—hers was.

When it came to the Greeks, separation was a far likelier scenario than divorce, especially if infertility seemed to be the cause. In causes of abuse, the wife had some legal protection—although in high-status marriages, look out. (See the entry on Alkibiades for an ill-fated attempt to divorce.)

If a Greek wife committed adultery and was found out, and if upon discovering it, her husband did not murder her or her lover in so-called justifiable homicide, Athenian law prohibited the couple to continue to live together. So in essence, the couple was already divorced. If a Greek husband committed adultery, what then? Didn't count, of course.

## CROSS-DRESSERS:
### It started with Caligula's sandals

A serious student of moral turpitude, teenage Caligula studied sexual excess on the isle of Capri, mentored by his uncle Tiberius, then Roman emperor. The young man was both a voyeur and the object of his uncle's ingenious depravity. When Caligula learned that he became sexually aroused by cruelty and torture to others, he tried on every perversion he could manage.

During those formative teen years, Caligula often cross-dressed, preferring blond wigs and long robes. He adored clothes, especially the expensive, clingy garments that women wore, made of Koan silk. An army brat who'd moved often with his family, Caligula had caught sartorial mania early. While he was a wee boy living at the military outposts of his father

Germanicus, his mom had dressed him in soldier's kit, including a child-size pair of the legionary's classic footgear: sandals with hobnail-covered soles called *caligae*. Soon the bored-senseless soldiers nicknamed the kid Caligula, meaning "little boots," or (to be precise) "little hobnailed sandals."

As time went on, Caligula managed to sexually abuse his three sisters and quite a number of other innocent folks. Once he became emperor in A.D. 37, his real forte was one-upping rivals, nonrivals, and anyone else who came into his presence. With Caligula, sexual pleasure was inextricably linked with punishment, the more vicious the better.

Afflicted with mental illness that ranged from delusional to manic, the emperor often failed to sleep at night. He frequently put on extempore dramatic and musical performances during those insomniac hours, ordering his top aides and family members to be his adoring audience. Those witnesses who managed to survive the random killings and maimings that Caligula routinely dished out on a daily basis no doubt remembered the remarkable ladies' attire the emperor wore during those memorable nights.

Nero, who as a small boy spent time in Caligula's tender care, was very impressed by his uncle's style. In fact, when Nero became emperor twenty-plus years later, he emulated Caligula's fashion sense, often dressing as a woman as well. His favorite gear to wear to dinner was called a *synthesis*, the flowered gown worn by men only during the Saturnalia festival each December. Otherwise, the *synthesis* was female garb. Nero tried hard to make it a new trend in Roman fashion, but in vain, apparently.

Nevertheless, as emperors came and went, there were ardent cross-dressers among them, such as Elagabalus, whose purple gowns

*A dedicated sadist and an occasional transvestite, Emperor Caligula terrorized family, friends, and Romans throughout his four-year reign.*

and painted eyes drew much attention. A figure of fun and an object of Roman disgust, this young emperor had a real desire to be female, not just look like a dame. As emperor, he seriously explored the possibility of sex-change surgery with his doctors. A man well ahead of his time, Elagabalus asked them to create for him a prototype of a female vagina! Pretty daring stuff, given the surgical abilities and the paucity of anesthesia in those days. The doctors managed to decline without incurring imperial wrath.

In ancient times, cross-dressing occurred for multiple reasons—many times it wasn't a gender statement. For example, women occasionally had strong motives for dressing themselves as men. Greek philosopher Plato, although he disparaged the minds of women as inferior, did accept two young women named Axiothea of Phlius and Lasthenea of Mantinea as students. They wore what the other male students wore; more about them we do not know. They received a passing mention in Diogenes Laertius's *Lives of the Philosophers*.

Other women, such as Thecla, the assertive and determined sidekick of Paul of Tarsus during his wanderings on land and sea around the Greco-Roman world, adopted male garb for safety. She remained his staunchest disciple for years.

Still others cross-dressed so they could take part in activities declared taboo for women. Such was the case for Pherenike, the Rhodian mother who acted as boxing trainer for her son in the Olympic Games of 388 B.C. (You'll find her story in the entry on Pherenike of Rhodes.)

Of even more ancient vintage, Hatshepsut, the female pharaoh of Egypt during the eighteenth dynasty, ritually dressed in male regalia to legitimize her reign, even though it was through the female bloodline that pharaohs became heads of state.

In seventh century Mesopotamia, Ashurbanipal, the Assyrian ruler famed for creating the world's first great library, appears, like Elagabalus, to have been a true cross-dresser, a man with transgender longings. Although married to a redoubtable gal named Ashursharrat, he chose to wear female clothing and accoutrements. He also used a major amount of cosmetics and imitated a female voice as he spoke. All of this vastly irritated other Assyrian men, including one of his generals, who happened to walk in when Ashurbanipal was penciling his eyebrows. Pulling out his dagger, the general ran his boss through on the spot.

## GLADIATOR SEX LIVES:
### Even Commodus got lucky

Even though gladiators were officially scum of the earth, they often had female fans willing to swoon all over them. Or under them. Not just shady professional ladies or plebeian chicks, either, but women of exalted rank. Some of them hung around the barracks where the gladiators were billeted; a few even played make-believe viragos, practicing with the wooden swords that the fighters employed in training.

Other groupies expressed their feelings by posting impudent notes on walls, in public baths, and elsewhere. At Pompeii, Capua, and Ostia, graffiti such as these have been found: "Celadon the Thracian, three times victor and three times crowned, who makes the girls sigh," and "Thrax is the heart-throb of all the girls."

To get closer to the subject matter, matrons in higher tax brackets some-times hired off-duty gladiators as muscle. As Philip Matyszak, author of

*The Gladiator Manual*, notes with a twinkle, "Many a wealthy lady who hires gladiator bodyguards for the night does so in expectation of her body being guarded very closely indeed."

Gladiators were first used in Etruscan times as warriors at the funeral games for bigshots. They came to form a professional cadre in centuries to come, and by the third century A.D. there were more than 230 permanent gladiatorial arenas around the Roman Empire, from Britain and Spain to Albania and Tunisia. Like champion boxers, gladiators didn't fight that often; that kept the excitement level of the fans high, and the entry fees as well.

On the other hand, patrician sponsors of the games competed insanely, each trying to outdo the other in terms of flash and cash spent on the gladiatorial spectacles. Emperor Marcus Aurelius wasn't a fan himself, and he passed legislation that restricted the amount anyone could spend on the games. A philosopher and writer in his spare time, Marcus was one of the most decent and hardworking emperors to ever don a diadem.

He loved his wife Faustina, perhaps to excess. Within a twenty-three-year period, she gave birth to fourteen children, including twins Antoninus and Commodus in A.D. 161.

According to accounts from authors Herodian and Dio Cassius, Faustina may not have returned Marcus's devotion in equal measure. While watching gladiators on parade, Faustina got hit by Cupid's arrow, becoming inflamed with passion for one of the burly fighters. This inappropriate love gnawed at her until she became ill. Finally, she confessed to Marcus; a calm and thoughtful guy, he refrained from strangling her and instead consulted Chaldean soothsayers for their advice. They suggested that his wife have sex with the gladiator in question, who should then be killed while still

*According to some sources, Empress Faustina got the hots for
a gladiator. Instead of homicide, her understanding husband
kept her busy, bearing fourteen imperial children.*

on top of her. She should then take an immediate bath in gladiator blood, tidy up a bit, and follow that with lovemaking to her husband Marcus. She and Marcus allegedly followed that routine, and it seemed to cool her passion—or so the story goes.

The *Scriptores Historiae Augustae*, called an unreliable source by modern historians, also claims that Faustina regularly had gladiator paramours, and that son Commodus was the result of her adultery.

That boy, the sole surviving child of the fourteen she gave birth to, did grow into a monster. Commodus became emperor in A.D. 180 and for twelve years actually outdid Nero and Caligula in terms of shameful behavior, cruelty, and just plain weirdness—even by Roman imperial standards.

Although during his tenure the Roman army fought and won battles hither and yon, Commodus was never present on the battlefield. Instead, he served as the star in the lavish triumphs that were held after each victory. Dismissing imperial dignity and Roman gravitas as things of the past, Commodus enlivened the proceedings by bringing along his latest boy-toy in his parade chariot, kissing him ardently from time to time.

Sexually, however, Commodus was more often a voyeur than a doer; he kept "harems" of nubile young boys and girls and enjoyed watching as many as six hundred bodies copulate simultaneously. He also had a fascination for deformities and supersize genitalia. One of his favorites was a man he called "Ass," whose male member closely resembled that of an animal in the equine family.

The Roman public, a bit blasé after nearly two hundred years of outrageous imperial antics, was stunned when Commodus announced that he was going to pursue his two true vocations: becoming the new Hercules; and becoming a gladiator.

To make time to accomplish his passions, Commodus blew off the circle of wise advisers his father had left him and assigned the running of the government to a flunky named Perennis. Commodus's first priority was to focus on looking like his idol, Hercules. At nineteen when he began to reign, he already had a muscular body and a full head of curly blond hair. Before long, he grew a beard and put on

*Misfortune dogged Emperor Marcus Aurelius, however. His sole surviving child with Empress Faustina was Commodus, one of Rome's most notorious rulers—and a self-proclaimed gladiator.*

Herculean regalia: a lion-skin headdress and flashy purple-and-gold robes. And he carried a club. A big club.

Because of his hands-off policies regarding actual governing, Commodus was regularly confronted with plots and conspiracies, which he managed to suppress by slaughtering his enemies, real and imagined. As the years passed, he became even more paranoid, trusting no one and hating almost everyone. Except gladiators, of course.

A natural athlete, Commodus had talent as a swordsman and archer. After learning from the pros and practicing a great deal in his large private arena (in the year 2000, archaeologists excavating his villa in Rome found traces of it), Commodus declared himself ready for the big time. For the next two years, he appeared in public a number of times. He fought in front of sellout crowds, of course. No one could ever remember seeing an emperor perform *in* the arena, although everyone knew emperors who'd condemned people *to* the arena.

The sorry fact is, Emperor Commodus cheated. Although he was a terrific marksman at throwing the javelin and shooting arrows, he seldom got down and dirty in the actual arena. Instead, he had a terrace built that encircled the amphitheatre, from where he stood and fired away.

Still, if you were an average Roman, at first it might have been rather exciting to see him slaughter a hundred bears and a hundred lions in a row, along with herds of other animals, from bulls to flocks of ostriches. To make the emperor's job even easier, the arena would be partitioned off into sections where various species were penned.

To vary the program a bit, Commodus had a group of leopards mixed in with a group of condemned criminals. When a leopard made a lightning move and grabbed a man, about to take his face off, the emperor saved the day with a javelin shot to the animal's head. Thus rescued, the man was then obliged to die in some other stomach-turning fashion.

On a few exceptional occasions, Commodus did appear on the sands of the arena, barechested and bold, taking up arms like a real gladiator. His opponents, however, weren't much of a match for him. Knowing that you're obliged to fight the ruler of the entire known world does that to a guy. So does being handed a wooden sword. In one instance, Commodus's "opponent" was a handicapped fellow, "armed" with a sponge!

Roman emperor Commodus had time to write out a few more death lists and rename all the months of the year after divine aspects of himself before general disgust resulted in his assassination on December 31 of the year 192.

# Red-Letter Days &
# Red-Hot Nights

## HISPALA FECENIA:
### Wet blanket at the orgy

Heroines and villains show up in the strangest places. Take this story of two flesh-and-blood gals named Hispala and Paculla.

First, a little background. In Thrace, a lightly populated wilderness north of Athens, the female followers of the wine god Dionysus used to get together three times a year. Their rites, called *orgia* (origin of our word *orgy*), were secret. And it was a girls-only gathering. Once initiated, matrons as well as young unmarried women would decompress by hanging out together all day and night. Everyone loved the maenad gear too: ivy garlands, fawn-skin robes, a walking stick made of fennel, and an optional live snake or two.

While the sun was up, the gals confined themselves to mild mischief: binge drinking, hallucinogen intake, and raucous singing. As it grew later, the maenads ran barefoot in frenzied, torch-carrying glee on the hillsides, occasionally bringing down a victim or two (usually mammal, on occasion an unlucky higher primate) to serve as carpaccio appetizers. And so it went for ages.

Then a smarty-pants priestess named Paculla, whose turn it was to direct the Dionysian activities, made major changes. First shock: she dragged her two grown sons into it. Then she bossily decreed they should allow more men to join. Finally she insisted that the group meet monthly for five consecutive nights of "initiation." When the members groaned, she shut them up by hollering, "Dionysus the god personally told me to do it!"

In the third century B.C., the cult went mainstream, as more and more male initiates wiggled their way into the mix. And it spread from sleepy, bucolic Thrace to Greece and then to Italy. Now popularly known as

Bacchanalia after Bacchus, the Latin name for the wine god, the cult took the Etruscans—always game for late-night partying—by storm. It then captured the fancy of big-city Romans, who were reveling in the ecstatic aftermath of a successful war against Hannibal and the Carthaginians. By 186 B.C., the wild initiations and orgiastic goings-on had reached a fever pitch—the cult had over seven thousand avid adherents in Italy alone.

Living in Rome at that time was an upscale young courtesan named Hispala Fenecia, a former slave who longed to find a decent guy, settle down, and live the straight life. As it happened, she moved into a neighborhood where a good-looking fellow named Publius Aebutius lived with his mother and stepdad. Propinquity struck and sparks flew.

Although Hispala continued to turn a few tricks, she gave her new love the "on the house" intimacy discount. A generous sort, she also chipped in to help Aebutius with his finances, since he was kept on a tight leash by his parents. At length, convinced that her relationship was truly serious, Fenecia made out her will and designated her boyfriend as sole heir.

Meanwhile, the plot thickened, as plots tend to do. Aebutius's stepdad Titus, who controlled the young man's inheritance from his dead father, was a rotter. He'd played fast and loose with the funds. Fearing disclosure, he pressured his wife to compromise the boy in some fashion. "We've got to keep his trap shut," Titus threatened.

After some coaching, the mother told her son that the last time he'd been ill with the dropsy, she'd made a vow to the gods that if he recovered she would initiate him into the Bacchus cult.

Bewildered, Aebutius agreed to comply, although the prep for such a ceremony—a ten-day chastity fast—sounded awful. By this time, he and Hispala kept no secrets from each other. That night, he told her he wouldn't be around for the next couple of weeks—some religious vow the mater made while he was sick.

When Hispala learned it was the Bacchanalians, she had a meltdown, cursing and lamenting. "No way will I let you do that!" she cried. "It's an abomination and will destroy your life. I know—because when I was a slave, my mistress compelled me to take part in their hideous rites. Oh, the wine, the feasting, the loud music, the debauchery—it took me weeks to recover."

Even though it sounded suspiciously like fun to Aebutius, he solemnly swore to his girlfriend that he'd confront his parents and just say no. When he told them, they screamed, "The caresses of that serpent have made your disrespect your parents and the gods!" With the help of four slaves, they kicked Publius Aebutius out of the house.

After much travail, a terrified Hispala and Aebutius took their story to a high official, the Roman consul. Hispala reluctantly agreed to give a full deposition, naming names and revealing what went on at the Bacchanalian orgies, but insisted on being placed in a witness protection program. A flood of details began to emerge. The orgies took place in the grove of Stimula, and the agenda included a mix of homosexual and heterosexual activities, with special emphasis on defiling new members, who all had to be under the age of twenty. Uncooperative initiates were defiled anyway, then tortured and/or killed.

Once Hispala got rolling, she spilled it all. "All those shrieks you hear five nights a month? That insanely loud

*Orgies among the worshipers of wine god Dionysus, or Bacchus, often had wild initiation rites, their sordid secrets for members only.*

drum and cymbal music? Bacchanalians. You might think it's a live concert, but the noise is cover for the sounds of murder and rape," added the young stoolie.

Thanks to the courageous testimony of Hispala and Aebutius, the entire Roman senate heard the case against the Bacchanalian cult and passed a decree to reward both of them. The senators voted the young man exemption from military service and 100,000 in coins. Hispala, the key witness, received the same amount—and also the legal freedom to wed a man of honorable birth. Oh, and round-the-sundial witness protection for her safety.

Did the two marry and live happily ever after? Roman historian Livy, that old spoilsport, didn't say, although he did cover the story in vivid detail. As a postscript, however, Livy noted that the Bacchanalians were immediately restricted to holding their sacred rites in groups no larger than three women and two men—which really took the wind out of the defiling ceremonies.

By that time, enthusiasm for Bacchus bashes was flagging fast, since the authorities had rounded up everyone from the top-ranking orgiasts to the rank-and-file members of the "Bacchanalian conspiracy," imprisoning and/or executing more than five thousand men and women.

Nevertheless, like a phoenix rising from the ashes, the rockin' Bacchantes rose again. Centuries later, during the reign of Emperor Titus at the time of the Vesuvius eruption in A.D. 79, it was no longer a felony to explore the mysteries of Bacchic worship. In fact, the most stunning villa found in Pompeii, dubbed the Villa of the Mysteries, contains wraparound murals and male and female Bacchanalians carrying out their solemn (possibly felonious) rites.

# THE ISIS SEX SCANDAL:
## Anubis loves ya, baby!

In Rome during the first century B.C., the Egyptian cult of the goddess Isis took root quickly, especially among humbler folks and women of all social classes. Isis, a compassionate and loving goddess of fertility and motherhood, was often portrayed nursing her infant son Horus, a composition that would soon be echoed by the Christians and their Virgin Mary with her baby son.

Like other mystery cults, the cult of Isis required initiation and baptism and had a professional priesthood on staff. The Isis temple in Rome, built in 43 B.C., sat next to the temple of Serapis in Mars Field. Although Isis took human form, she was often worshipped in conjunction with other Egyptian deities, including Anubis, the jackal-headed god of the dead.

In Rome around A.D. 19 lived an outstanding follower of Isis called Paulina, a Roman matron described as virtuous, well-to-do, and easy on the eyes by the Jewish Roman historian Josephus, who related her story in his book called *Antiquities of the Jews*.

It seems that Paulina had an unwelcome admirer, a Roman called Decius Mundus, who peskily plied her with a great many gifts, all of which she refused. Desperately in love with Paulina, he finally offered her 200,000 Greek drachmas if she would sleep with him. (Author Josephus discreetly called his offer "for one's night lodging.")

When Paulina indignantly refused, Mundus went into a tailspin. Seeing no love in his future, he resolved to starve himself to death. Ide, a freedwoman who lived in his household, was horrified. Being a gal prone to mischief and possibly sweet on Mundus herself, she offered to help. Soon

*The Egyptian goddess Isis became very popular in Rome. A loving mother, she was often depicted with her baby son or with a sistrum, a musical rattle.*

she'd convinced the lovelorn man that she could persuade the object of his obsession to get into the sack with him. "Of course I'll need some money to make the arrangements," she said, adding, "Fifty thousand drachmas should do it."

Much heartened, Mundus started eating meals again, while Ide went about her nefarious plotting. Well aware that Paulina was not swayed by money but by her faith, Ide hit up a couple of the most dubious individuals in the Isis priesthood. At length they came to a mutually agreeable deal. They would get half the loot if they helped snare the luscious parishioner for Decius Mundus.

The older of the two Isis priests then asked for a private audience with Paulina, telling her, "I've been sent by the god Anubis, who admires your faith and who's fallen in love with you. He invites you to come to him for a private prayer session."

Paulina, whose gullibility quotient would make her a prime target for televangelists these days, went for it. Smirking with pride at her specialness, she told her husband about being singled out by the god Anubis. He might have frowned a bit when she got to the part about dining at the temple and a sleepover with the jackal-headed god, but he trusted her implicitly.

Accordingly, Paulina put on her best "virtuous but sexy" ensemble and headed for the temple of Isis. During dinner, the god Anubis remained invisible and inaudible, which obliged Paulina to make small talk with herself. Afterward, she was shown to a private chamber. The priests then left, dousing the light and closing the doors as they did so.

It wasn't long before "Anubis" made his appearance. With alacrity, Mundus closed in on Paulina and began to make love to her; she seemed equally engaged. She didn't even question his lack of a jackal's head. Before daylight, he crept away and a disheveled but serene Paulina headed for home.

She couldn't wait to tell her husband and friends about her intimate new status with the god. They were dumbfounded; knowing Paulina's innate modesty, however, they were forced to believe her story. For three days, she gloried in what she thought of as her spiritual adventure.

On day four, Decius Mundus showed up at her door. "You've saved me two hundred thousand drachmas, madam," he told her. "Even though you rebuffed my love gifts and reproached me, you liked me pretty well when I called myself Anubis." Paulina was floored. And furious. Crying, ripping at her garments, she immediately became hysterical about the wicked trick that had been played on her. "It was horrible!" she sobbed to her husband. "He came at me again and again. I want you to take my cruel deception to the highest level! To Emperor Tiberius, in fact!"

Her uxorious husband took Paulina at her word; he repeatedly nagged at the emperor, asking him to inquire into the matter. To everyone's shock, Tiberius did so. The outcome? The guilty priests and Ide, the evil little enabler, were crucified, and a large number of Isis worshipers were deported to the malarial island of Sardinia. Tiberius also ordered the temple of Isis to be razed to the ground and the goddess's statue to be thrown into the Tiber River.

But what about Decius Mundus, the secret adulterer, whose avatar-sharp portrayal of Anubis was obviously spot-on? Tiberius merely banished the man from Rome. As the emperor explained, the crime Mundus had committed was done out of the passion of love.

*The Egyptian god Anubis often accompanied the goddess Isis. Anubis had a human body and the dark head of a jackal.*

## ABDUCTION, SEDUCTION, RAPE:
### Unwilling partners

Our term *rape* looks as though it came from the Latin *raptus* but long ago the word meant kidnap, abduction, or even elopement. Greco-Roman mythology is rampant with *raptus* episodes, starting with that incessantly horny king of the gods, Zeus aka Jupiter. In addition, legends about early Roman history, such as the *raptus* of the Sabine women, generally signified the forceful takeover of one cultural group by another through mass co-mingling in marriage. (Elsewhere in this book, check out the entries on the Amazons and on marriage for other perspectives on *raptus*.)

Sometimes the assault on a woman, the violation of her sexual integrity, became a symbolic catalyst for social or political change. A classic example? The often-told tale of heroic Lucretia. She and her husband lived in Rome, in their day a small town ruled by a king and filled with Roman newcomers struggling to eliminate the original Etruscan inhabitants.

The wife of Lucius Tarquinius Collatinus, Lucretia was a model spouse and mother. One afternoon, her husband and his pals, including an Etruscan guy named Sextus, son of the very last king of Rome, were having dinner together (no wives invited, of course). They began bragging along the lines of: "My sword's bigger than yours! Well, mine's sharper than yours!" When that debate got old, they began to boast about the virtue of their wives, with Lucius maintaining that nobody could measure up to his spouse.

Before the arguments got physical, the men agreed to go together unannounced to check on what their wives were doing. Off they galloped, making the rounds. At each house, they discovered their wives yakking it up, maybe sipping a little wine while the men were out.

They ended up at Lucius's home, where they found Lucretia working away, spinning wool while barking out orders to her household slaves. By acclamation, she was declared the winner in the virtuous matron competition. Lucius beamed.

Unbeknownst to all, the provocative sight of Lucretia caressing her spindle made one of the men extremely aroused; it was that blackguard Sextus. Several days later, when he knew that Lucretia's husband was away on business, he came over. He put the moves on her and when rebuffed, assaulted her sexually.

"If you tell anyone who did this," he warned, "I'll kill you in your bed, and then I'll put the naked body of a dead slave beside you."

That threat and the rape she'd just endured left Lucretia in shock. After Sextus left, she reached a quick decision. Calling an urgent family meeting, she summoned her husband, dad, and uncle. "I've got good news and bad news," she said. "My heart is still pure but my body has been violated by that blackguard Sextus. I want all of you to swear that you'll avenge me!"

With that, she drew out a dagger, accurately stabbed herself in the heart, and died.

Galvanized by the attack on Lucretia and her actions, her husband and uncle speedily organized a revolution, nailed that blackguard Sextus, threw out the king, and founded the Roman republic in 509 B.C.

It wasn't until 184 B.C., however, that the Romans officially recognized rape as a sexual crime, which they called

*The rape of Lucretia and her suicidal method of provoking her menfolk to avenge her honor was a favorite story in Roman households.*

*raptus ad stuprum*. Both the Romans and the Greeks developed laws against rape and other assaults but the acts they legislated covered a narrow set of circumstances. The victim's lack of consent was secondary. Rape could sometimes mean sex by seduction, by coercion or threats, or by physical violence.

It became a capital crime if the victim was a citizen in good standing, a female virgin, or a freeborn child. Sexual predators of children received the death penalty and the rape of a boy was considered especially heinous. On the other hand, sexual assault or even gang rape was not a crime if the victim was a prostitute of either gender, a gladiator, an entertainer, an actor, or anyone who worked at a job defined as "infamous" by the Romans.

Sexual assault of a slave was a crime—but of property damage, not personal harm. Believe it or not, the slave's owner was the injured party and could sue the rapist!

Men and women around the Greco-Roman world may have worried more about the possibility of sexual assault during times of war. Mass rape was a standard practice when enemy forces sacked a rebellious city, or conquered an island nation. Just as dire was the treatment of war captives; sexual violence to them did not count as a crime.

Looked at in modern terms, we might even conclude that not just rape but a large percentage of sexual activity during the Greco-Roman millennium was non-consensual. Slaves male and female were used and abused by owners at their whim; wives (and sometimes children) were used and abused by their husbands or fathers when they saw fit. These are disquieting reminders of how far we've traveled from those times, when individuals—more especially women, slaves, and people considered low status—could be sexually assaulted, often with impunity.

## IMPERIAL JULIA:

### "Baby on board" was her all-clear sign

Emperor Octavian Augustus pulled a few sly sexual shenanigans in his earlier years; during the five decades of his marriage to the eagle-eyed Livia, he even managed the occasional indulgence with a concubine.

As he aged, however, Augustus grew offended at the moral laxity of Roman patricians and their increasing refusal to procreate plentifully within the bonds of marriage. With that convenient memory lapse that humans often have, he wallowed in memories of the "good old days" and what he saw as the ethical standards and marital fidelity of those times.

His most egregious lapse? His own progeny, which consisted of a single daughter by his first wife Sempronia: Julia. He and Livia had no children. Julia, who was kind, motherly, well educated, and far wittier than her dad, also had his strong sexual drive. She, however, lacked a way to sublimate it, as Augustus did, with the prerogatives of power.

Although willful, she obediently married her first cousin Marcellus, only to lose him to death in two years. A widow at eighteen, at her father's behest she married his forty-two-year-old right-hand man and general Marcus Agrippa. In classic Roman "musical chairs" fashion, he in turn had to dump his current wife.

When not traveling with her husband Agrippa on his assignments outside of Italy, or entertaining in their glorious villa near Pompeii, Julia birthed five children in nine years: three boys and two girls, all of whom survived childhood.

Julia was quite a multitasker. Although still wed to Agrippa, she began to entertain a string of witty young noblemen who better suited her lively personality and sensuous needs. When a friend asked how she managed to avoid exposure while producing children that all resembled her husband, she quipped, "Passengers are never allowed on board until the ship's hold is full."

Julia and her father, however, were on a collision course. In 18 B.C., Augustus, gung-ho about his legislative plan to reform the lackadaisical marital and childbearing habits of the upper class, introduced an elaborate suite of new laws—some of them incentives and others quite punitive. Named (ironically, as it transpired) after his own exemplar of good behavior, his daughter Julia, the Leges Iuliae offered tax breaks for people in the senatorial class who got married and got busy procreating.

Men and women between the ages of 20 and 60 who remained unmarried and childless forfeited their inheritance rights. Other Augustan laws slammed adulterers with a criminal offence. It also allowed fathers to kill married daughters who dallied outside their marriage.

Freeborn women, on the other hand, who gave birth to three surviving children earned the "three kids and you're out of bondage to male guardians!" bonus.

In 12 B.C. Julia's husband Agrippa died, and straightaway she was pushed into marriage with Tiberius, the morose thirty-year-old who was Livia's son from a previous marriage. (Again, in the patrician divorce-go-round, Tiberius was obliged to divorce Vispania, the wife he really quite adored in his own grumpy fashion, to wed the now-notorious Julia.)

The false front of their marriage soon crumbled. Five years into wedlock, Tiberius announced he was "retiring" to the island

*Octavian Augustus, Rome's first emperor, called the marital shots for his kinfolk. His only daughter, Julia, dutifully wed a string of men picked by Daddy, including Marcus Agrippa, Octavian's right-hand man.*

of Rhodes—sans Julia—supposedly stepping aside to let Julia's sons by Agrippa assume public office. This greatly angered Augustus, who saw it as desertion. The "perfect family values" of the imperials were being mocked by the hypocrisy of actual events.

When the emperor learned the sheer number of times that his own daughter Julia had broken his new morality laws, he went insane with rage. In the year 2 B.C., on the heels of an ostentatious citywide celebration of the emperor's twenty-five years as "first man in Rome," Augustus grimly announced to the Roman senate that he was disowning his treasonous daughter for committing adultery with a long list of men. The juicier statements made by them alleged that she'd even had sex on the Rostra, the platform in the forum where daddy had originally proclaimed his new laws on marital reform.

Since Augustus had made the new rules, he had to abide by them: he also announced that Julia would be exiled to the wee island of Pandateria, forbidden wine and male visitors.

After some years, Augustus allowed Julia to move exile sites, newly banishing her to the city of Regium on the toe of Italy. He never spoke to her again. Julia was disinherited and forbidden burial in the family mausoleum. When Tiberius, always one to hold a grudge, became emperor at Augustus's death in A.D. 14, he continued to punish Julia by cutting off all financial assistance to her. She died of malnutrition the same year.

In recent years, classical historians who've studied the matter feel certain there was more to Julia's banishment than sexual folly. They theorize that the adultery charges against her cloaked a more serious matter: a political plot, possibly a coup, against her father. Several of the men named (and exiled) as her co-adulterers came from high-ranking families. One, the son of Mark Antony, who'd been the young Octavian's greatest enemy, was executed.

## CATULLUS THE POET:
### Doomed love was catnip for the X-rated poet

Gaius Valerius Catullus came from a well-to-do family in Verona, Italy, and owned a villa himself near fashionable Tivoli, but as a young man soon settled into a decadent life in Rome. As a poet in training, he idled with other ink-stained scriveners and lowlifes, striving to integrate a scruffy, streetwise vibe into his work.

He succeeded. His small book, preserved within an anthology of 116 *carmina*, is still around today, thrilling new generations of college kids with its smutty verses. The amazing thing is how much loftier salacious porn sounds in Latin. Reading Catullus increases the reader's vocabulary, especially useful for conjugating difficult verb forms for unmentionable activities. Bonus points: Latin porn allows the reader to feel studious, even virtuous, reading it in a dead language.

Catullus got a great deal of his raw material (and I mean raw) from his gut-wrenching affair with Clodia Pulchra, which probably began when she was still the wife of Quintus Metellus Celer. Clodia was about thirty-five, Catullus perhaps twenty-five. He called her Lesbia in his poems.

She was bright and rebellious, an unabashed woman who liked mixing it up politically, socially, and erotically, preferably at the same time. Very much a free spirit—which was part of her attraction—Clodia refused to be confined to one husband, one lover, or even her own social rank. She insistently scandalized Rome, openly choosing cosy intimacy with her brother at times. Her husband Quintus wasn't the compliant sort, either; they had sordid screaming matches in public. Clodia abused wine and got addicted to gambling to ease her sorrows. In short, a real handful.

Although Catullus fell hopelessly in love with her, she may not have felt as deeply. At times, Clodia preferred to be his muse, or his intellectual sparring partner.

In 59 B.C. her husband died in what were described as odd circumstances. There were nasty rumors she'd poisoned him, but Clodia was never formally accused. Once she became a new widow, she promoted Catullus to full-time lover! But his joy quickly vanished. She put him through the wringer by aardvarking his best friend Marcus Caelius Rufus at the same time. Fidelity? It clearly did not suit her. She wasn't adverse to dallying with lower-ranking men, either. It was rumored that even slaves had known her intimately.

Catullus channeled his grief about his faithless woman into his poetry. His verse 70, for instance, says: "The woman I love says that there is no one whom she would rather marry than me, not if Jupiter himself were to woo her. Says; but what a woman says to her ardent lover should be written in wind and running water."

Doomed love aside, the bittersweet fact remains that Catullus himself took other lovers, including a boy of tender years named Juventius, to whom he also wrote passionate, anguished poems: "I stole a kiss from you, honey-sweet Juventius, while you were playing, a kiss sweeter than sweet ambrosia." Today he'd be likely to be hit with a child abuse charge.

In addition to his short poems, Catullus wrote a long, very loving epic to his dead brother Manius, and some traditional *hymenaios* marriage verses. He insulted Julius Caesar in another verse—and had to apologize. He admired Sappho, who by her era was out of fashion, immensely. In three of his poems he emulated her, perhaps translating directly from her (now-lost) works. In one poem to his Lesbia, he attempted to rewrite in Latin one of Sappho's most famous Greek poems. In this, he may have come away the victor.

But the unsavory fact remains that Catullus lamented his loss of love as thievery, as something valuable stolen from him. His invective or sexual verses are extremely coarse. Like the god Priapus, whose giant phallus guarded the grounds and gardens of Rome, he threatens thieves of love with rape, or worse. His morose opinion of women, including Lesbia, swung between two extremes: beloved creature or sluttish pig.

As befits a poet of what was then the modern school, Catullus died tragically young, around the age of thirty.

## CLODIUS PULCHER:
### Rome's lovable, unspeakable rogue

Mutinous army officer, political turncoat, gang leader, cross-dresser, pirate hostage, and zestful incest aficionado: Publius Clodius Pulcher jammed all that and much more into his forty-one-year lifespan. And the Roman public loved that bad boy for it.

From one of Rome's most ancient and aristocratic families, the Claudii, he, his mom, and his three sisters (all named Clodia) were left nearly destitute at their father's death.

As the Third Mithradatic War in Asia Minor heated up, the twenty-five-year-old joined the military, becoming minor brass under his brother-in-law,

General Lucullus. He immediately got into a jam by inciting mutiny among the legionaries. Tossed out of the army, Clodius wheedled another brother-in-law into letting him take command of his fleet.

On this outing, Clodius was captured by pirates. The brigands demanded a ransom from the ruler of a nearby island, who sent a miserly sum. That tickled the pirates so much, they let Clodius go.

Back in Rome, Clodius faced an army treason charge brought by Lucullus. Making things even stickier, Clodius had also been doing the wild thing with his own little sister, Lucullus's wife Clodia. When Lucullus discovered the adultery, he divorced her at the speed of light.

Expecting a death threat at any moment, Clodius hastily took shelter by marrying Fulvia, a ferociously active member of the influential Tuditani clan. They promptly set about making babies. By 62 B.C., bored with respectability, Clodius sought extracurricular diversion, hoping to find it with Pompeia, at that time the wife of Julius Caesar.

Things seemed to jell in December, when the all-nighter mystery rites of the Bona Dea goddess took place at Caesar's home. Bona Dea, goddess of chastity and fertility, had superstrict rules. Absolutely no men allowed; even tomcats and baby boys were removed from the premises.

Clodius enjoyed complicated romances and a bit of transvestite fun as well; this seemed like a perfect time to try them out. The women at Caesar's house had just sacrificed a sow and were having cocktails with the vestal virgins who ran the ceremonies when a commotion broke out. An alert servant heard a strangely deep voice coming from a person wearing female robes—and cross-dressing Clodius was busted. The Bona Dea ceremony was ruined, called off due to male sacrilege.

In the tumultuous aftermath, Caesar quickly divorced Pompeia, saying,

"The wife of Caesar must be above suspicion." Now that Pompeia was free of marital complications, Clodius lost interest.

Clodius thought it best to go hide out at his middle sister's place. Sisterly incest was such a comfort, especially with the drop-dead-beautiful Clodia. His brother-in-law Lucullus was still peeved about his incest with little sister Clodia, and now brought him up on three counts of sexual immorality.

At his trial, the evidence was solidly stacked against Clodius. At the eleventh hour, however, his rich buddy Crassus bribed all the jurors and got Clodius acquitted. His wife Fulvia even stood by him.

As Clodius reveled in his reversals, up popped Cicero, his worst political foe. Not only was the man a social climber, he'd become a boorish neighbor over a property dispute. As if that weren't hubris enough, Cicero had gone after the Cataline conspirators who'd plotted the overthrow of the government, and got some of them executed. Without due process, either.

Well, he, Clodius, was now the newly elected tribune and head of the plebeian party. And he (backed by the muscle of his own personal gang of thugs) wasn't going to stand for it. He immediately used his shiny new legislative powers to push through a law that ordered exile for anyone who'd executed a Roman citizen without a trial—which meant Cicero, his sworn enemy. In 58 B.C. he waved a smirking goodbye to Cicero, headed to exile in northern Greece. He and Fulvia had a good laugh about it. Quick as lightning, he passed another law, prohibiting Cicero to approach within four hundred miles of Italy. More fun!

Sadly, it was downhill from there for Rome's most popular rogue politico. Within two years, Clodius and his gang would be battling the rival gangs of another thuggish political aspirant named Milo.

In December of 53 B.C. Clodius' string of lucky breaks ran out. He was murdered by Milo's gang. Even after death, Clodius had maniacally devoted fans. To mourn him, the mob built his funeral pyre inside the Roman Senate house, then burned it to the ground!

If this tale of Clodius et al sounds like a novel of the American wild west, it should. This century of Roman history was plagued by lawlessness, civil war, the shift from a nominal republic to a de facto monarchy, and the protracted power struggles between the likes of Caesar, Pompey, Mark Antony, Octavian, and many others. Colorful Clodius, a better lover than a fighter, was a mere bit player in the grander scheme of things.

## MENSTRUATION:
### A flower, a curse, a bitumen remover

Until the later centuries B.C., many cultures around the Mediterranean used a lunar year, as women's bodies do, roughly correlating to the phases of the moon. The Romans had a special name for calculating time: they called it *mensuration*, which meant "knowledge of the female menses."

Women of that era probably welcomed their period, since it meant they had made it through another month without getting pregnant. Childbirth, while often longed for, was a high-risk, high-mortality activity.

Males usually respected and often feared female menses. From a feminine point of view in ancient times, "the curse" could have been a blessing. It might have represented a face-saving, welcome way to ward off unwanted sexual advances from husbands and lovers. If you were a slave, menstruating would have been especially useful to discourage your owner.

Occasionally women lost their periods for reasons other than pregnancy. Just as today's endurance-sport athletes (and anorexics) sometimes stop menstruating, so too did long-ago females. Then, however, it was largely due to the lack of high-quality food rather than to dieting. The cycle of menstrual fertility needs a certain level of stored body fat to function. Low-status girls and women in cultures from Egypt to Greece to Rome to Assyria got less to eat.

In Leviticus, the Bible referred to menstrual blood as the flower that comes before the fruit of the womb, meaning a child. But in Genesis 31, Rachel was able to steal the figurines of her father's household gods by putting them under a camel saddle, then sitting on it while telling Dad, "I really feel crappy, it's that time of the month." In the Talmud, men were warned not to approach menstruating women; if one walked between two males, one of the men would die.

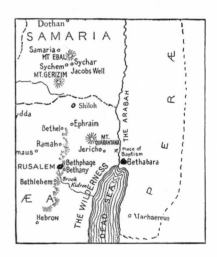

Persians also joined the "avoid them like poison" club; Persian women were ordered not to speak to men or even sit in water during menstruation. The Greeks had a similar phobia. The sixth-century poet Hesiod warned that men should never wash in water that women had already used—just in case a drop of menstrual blood had somehow found its way there. Greeks altogether avoided discussing the mechanics of monthly periods. The earliest known mention of the menstrual cycle was in a play by the out-to-shock Aristophanes, who called the cloth that women used as pads "a pigpen."

*Roman and Jewish men were terrified of menstrual periods. They did recognize one practical use for that monthly flow, however—its supposed ability to extract bitumen from the Dead Sea.*

Roman encyclopedist Pliny the Elder produced a whole laundry list of menstrual myths and taboos: gals on the rag could turn wine sour, dull knives, and chase bees away from the hive. Aristotle had this to add: "If a women who is menstruating looks into a mirror, the mirror's surface becomes bloody-dark, like a cloud." Another firmly held belief of the day: Romans with a death wish were encouraged to have sex with a menstruating woman during an eclipse. Sickness and death would inevitably follow.

There was, however, one invaluable service that the monthly effluvia from females could provide. In the Dead Sea, which in the first century A.D. was known as Asphalt Lake, large chunks of the solidified petroleum product called bitumen routinely floated to the surface. The tarry substance was used to waterproof wood, caulk boats, and even embalm bodies, but extricating it from the lake was a chore.

In one of his books, the Jewish-Roman author known to us as Josephus revealed the secret. "When they have filled the boats with bitumen, it is no easy task to detach their cargo, which owing to its tenacious and glutinous character, clings to the boat—until it is loosened by the monthly secretions of women, to which it alone yields."

Besides its practical application as a bitumen remover, menstrual flow had another purpose, according to a widely held notion of the time. When on occasion menstruation stopped, the blood appeared to remain in a woman's womb and, over a matter of months, "coagulate" into a baby!

## LUPERCALIA FESTIVAL:
### Whip it to me, wolfie!

Lupercalia, a purification festival from Rome's past, was perennially popular among females, from luscious young things bursting with hormones to marriage-ready young women and anxious-to-get-preggers matrons.

Why? Because Lupercalia, held on February 15 since only Venus knew when, was all about becoming pure: not to abstain from sex but to get ready for sex.

Even the Romans didn't agree on the top dog deity being celebrated. Although candidates for the honor included Lupercus, Pan, and Faunus, the frontrunner appeared to be a god we haven't heard much of but who would fit right into the twenty-first century. His name? Inuus, the god of sexual intercourse.

As February 15 approached, the estrogen level climbed in Rome. Women got up early to nab the best street corners. From there, they could ogle a number of spectacular young men, their skin glistening with oil and not much else, race barefoot through the streets. Unlike Greek men, who got naked in public at the drop of a loincloth, Roman males, especially high-ranking ones, usually kept their gravitas under wraps.

The Lupercalia, which began as a shepherds' festival, also honored legendary twins Romulus and Remus, who were shepherds as well as the city's first kings. For its first five centuries, only patrician males could join the cult of the Lupercii, a word that may mean wolf or possibly goat. (In later Christian times, the bar was lowered, allowing young men of humbler origins to take part, which caused a great deal of sneering and sighs about "back in the good old days . . .")

For the event, the boys gathered on the outskirts of Rome at the dingy cave of the Lupercal, where they began by sacrificing a goat and a dog to the deity. Two lads then had their foreheads dabbed with animal blood, wiped with wool and milk, followed by mandatory laughter. Ritual accomplished, they all dug in to a feast, well splashed with wine.

As if things weren't messy enough, the guys then peeled off the goat's hide and sliced it into ribbons, draping the bloody pieces around their body parts. Each gathered enough goatskin to make a nice whip, which would be used to ritually flog any females and random males they came across.

One memorable Lupercalia took place in 44 B.C. At the peak of his powers, Julius Caesar sat on a golden throne on the speakers' platform in the Roman Forum, watching the antics of the barefoot, bare-buttocked men as they raced into the open space where the public awaited. The leading Lupercus happened to be Mark Antony, who was well oiled in every sense of the word.

Clambering onto the platform, he went up to Caesar and tried to "crown" him with a laurel wreath. This gesture drew mixed boos and cheers, turning to applause when Julius pushed it away. Antony tried again—Caesar refused more strenuously. Was this a clumsy drunken homage from Antony to his commander? Or a trial run to see if Romans would tolerate a king again? The incident ended with someone else putting

*During the Lupercalia Festival, seminaked men ran through Rome, lashing women with goatskins to ensure their fertility. One celebrant was Mark Antony, who tried to "crown" Julius Caesar during the festivities.*

the crown on one of Caesar's statues, after which others tore it down, to great cheers.

Elsewhere in the Forum and around Rome, the festival roared on, the goatskin thongs hitting skin with a whistling sound. Married women and girls of marriageable age crowded in, anxious to get a ritual smack. Being whipped on the hands, back, or bottom with goatskin thongs not only chased off evil spirits, it made a gal receptive in the most basic sense to the guy in her life. The Lupercalia ritual also promised easy and uneventful pregnancy and childbirth, the dream of every fertile woman in those medically treacherous days.

As they made a circuit around the boundaries of the city, the Lupercal runners also performed a lustration or cleansing. This magical ritual, thought to repel the powers of evil and liberate the powers of good, promoted the fertility of humans as well as their animals and their crops.

Naughty songs, peeks at male equipment not normally on display, and other merrymaking took place at the Lupercalia, but it wasn't an orgy scene in the least. Notwithstanding, later Christian leaders fulminated against its "licentious" character.

## THESMOPHORIA FESTIVAL:
### Sharing secrets with girlfriends

There was nothing Greek women relished more than overnight festivals for gals only. Generally, they were BYOB and LYHD: bring your own bacchante gear and let your hair down. Back then, it was impossible to get a married woman excited over shoes, since sandals were worn 24/7. Or dinner dates, since there were none. Or husbands, since they were nonresponsive to honey-do lists, and their bedside manners often sucked.

But oh, the glory of the Thesmophoria, a multi-day campout of ritual, revelry, and female-only secrets held each fall throughout Greece. The one in Athens got all the raves, but similar outings took place for centuries in fifty different locales: from Sparta on the mainland to the island of Delos, from Thebes to Ephesus in Asia Minor. Some of them ran four or five days, and the one thrown by the Greek city-state of Syracuse on Sicily rocked on for ten.

*Thesmophoria was the glorious time of year when Greek women let down their hair in friendship and ritual—no males allowed. Their multiday festival honored the harvest goddess, Demeter.*

In Athens, every married woman got to go—and her husband was obliged to pay expenses so she could attend. Some accounts also say that mothers could bring their daughters, which seems reasonable, since the festival honored Demeter and her daughter Persephone. (See the entry "Mystery Cults" for more on another Demeter festival.)

It was more than a social gathering and a blessed chance to get away from housewifery. Thesmophoria, meaning "the carrier of the laws," was first and foremost a very emotional religious celebration. During it, the heartbreaking myth of Demeter, mourning the loss of her daughter, who had to live six months of the year in the Underworld, was retold. This poetic myth was the way in which Greeks chose to explain the natural progression of the seasons. As the deity of vegetative growth and harvest, Demeter appeared to abandon human farms and vineyards during the hot, rainless summers of Greece. By holding the Thesmophoria, women honored the goddess and ensured her return come fall.

The getaway required some serious ritual cleansing beforehand. Attendees had to remain chaste for up to a month (depending on locale), which was probably the biggest break they got all year from sex on demand from husbands. According to Pliny and other writers, before the festival, fertile women dosed themselves with a drink made from *agnos*, the chaste tree, actually a small shrub with sweet-smelling lilac flowers. The *agnos* had contraceptive potency, a fact now confirmed by modern chemists. It's likely that most women kept a stash of the stuff at home. Moreover, the chaste tree also acted as an abortifacient in the right dosage. (You can learn more about ancient abortion and contraception methods elsewhere in this book.)

The chastity aspect of this festival, by the way, dated back to earliest Greek times, when information of this sort was transmitted by women, among women—long before medical writings on the subject existed.

Because the Thesmophoria rites were "mysteries," meaning ceremonies and rituals that the initiates swore to keep secret, very little written evidence exists about the annual event, but certain facts are known.

The night before the official agenda began, the participants elected older women to preside over the festival. Business concluded, they loosened up with wine during a laughter-filled evening of foul language and vile insults. (Besides being cathartic, such language was apotropaic and kept malign spirits away. It also commemorated part of the Demeter myth, where she was cheered from her sorrow by the rough jesting of her friend Iambe.)

The first day started with a pilgrimage, a climb up to the sacred open space of the Thesmophorion, which sat on the outskirts of Athens near the hill of the Pynx. The women, who must have numbered in the thousands, set up leafy huts and slept two to a shelter.

On day two, the celebrants took off their festive garlands and mourned Demeter's loss. Everyone fasted, and no fires were lit. At some of the Thesmophoria sites, only pomegranate seeds, the attribute of Persephone, were eaten—but not those that had fallen on the ground, which were considered food for the dead. At places other than Athens, the gals consumed a little nosh consisting of sesame cakes.

Day three, called "Fair Offspring," echoed the goddess's search for her daughter Persephone with a torchlight ceremony. At this point the women sacrificed a pig to Demeter.

Another curious ritual involved recycling and a fertility rite. Months before the Thesmophoria, certain items were thrown into a pit called the *megaron*, there to rot into ritual compost. Among the items? Pine cones, sacrificed piglets, and special baked goods in the shape of male genitalia. During the festival, a couple of daring females called "the bailers" had to retrieve the now-finished compost. Their task was made more challenging because the pit was deliberately filled with snakes! After the Thesmophoria, the pungent compost would be placed on a public altar for local farmers to mix with their grain seed. In this fashion, the Greeks gave whole new meaning to the phrase "organically grown."

Athenian men did their level best to "shield" their wives, sisters, and female children from the outside world and to keep them from participating in public life. They were quite successful at it. Thus the best part of the Thesmophoria must have been the camaraderie, the shared laughter and grief, and the chance to exchange information, share stories, and renew friendships during those memorable, star-studded nights.

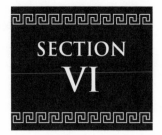

# Love Is a Many-Splendored Thing

## SEXUAL PREFERENCE:
### A rainbow of choices

Since words like *homosexual, heterosexual,* and *transgender* didn't even exist long ago, the idea of defining sexual preferences as life choices or as unnatural practices would have sounded nonsensical in Greece or Rome.

There clearly was a prodigious amount of sexual activity, from male-to-young-male flings to durable erotic relationships between adult males—the latter sometimes frowned upon. Men relished these choices and many more besides. The thing was, they didn't have to choose either-or. They could sample it all, or nearly so.

*Love and sexual attraction weren't either-or choices among the Greeks of old; many enjoyed heterosexual relationships as well as same-sex bonds.*

In centuries more puritanical than the present one, classical historians and researchers tended to view the bewildering array of Greek and Roman polysexuality as outrageous, orgiastic, even abusive. Since the twentieth century, however, specialists in the field, particularly in light of evolving ideas, began to see the sexual paradigm of those long-ago cultures as active versus passive.

And that boiled down to: Who got to penetrate? And who was penetrated? Today that idea has also been rejected as too rigid.

Therefore, regarding the Greeks and Romans of old, we're back to square one with Socrates the philosopher, who simply said, "I only know what I don't know." (At least we're in good company.)

One of America's much-read weekly columnists, Cecil Adams of The Straight Dope fame, wrote a column in 2006 that nails this issue. As he puts it: "Truth is, we don't really get what was up with the ancient Greeks. Even now there's a lot we don't know and probably won't ever know . . . The real handicap, though, is that little of what we think we know about sexuality now prepares us to understand what the Greeks thought about it then. Today we tend to regard sexual orientation as a binary proposition—most people are attracted to either men or women; relatively few are consistently attracted to both. What's more, we think of sexual identity as innate and more or less immutable. It may take awhile . . . to figure out if you're gay or straight, but once you do, you stay that way for life. None of this could confidently be said of the Greeks."

To make matters more complex, the traditions of male-to-male intimacy and the status of such couples varied greatly from Greece to Rome, and even more so within the Greek world itself. For example, male couples in the city-state of Athens were invariably free citizens, typically an adult paired with a teenager outside his immediate family. This was not viewed as pedophilia but pederasty, a bonding relationship that could have both non-sexual and erotic aspects. When the teen reached full manhood, the relationship ended; later he in turn might become the mentor (*erastes*) of an *eromenos*, a loved one twelve to seventeen. Long-term male-to-male relationships were discouraged but occurred just the same, as you'll see in the entry on bisexual playwrights Sophocles and Euripides.

Other Greek city-states followed different traditions for male-to-male relationships. On Crete, for instance, where the earliest evidence about pederasty has been found, a coming-of-age abduction took place, after which a lover and his youth spent several months hunting and feasting together.

On the Greek mainland, the city of Thebes and the region of Boeotia were famed for the frank acceptance of male couples in civilian and military life, which you can read about further in this book's entry on the Sacred Band.

Although the literary and archaeological evidence is uneven and sometimes contradictory, pederasty in its various forms was clearly embedded in Greek population centers from Ionia to Sicily, and from Corinth to Macedonia. Elsewhere in this book, you'll also encounter the glorious yet tragic love story of history's most famous Macedonian: Alexander the Great and his lifelong friend and lover, Hephaestion.

In sharp contrast to the Greeks, when a Roman of the knightly or patrician class got intimate with a boy or man, that person was either a slave, a male prostitute, a foreigner, or someone of lower social status—such as a dancer, actor, or gladiator. In imperial Roman times, elite males strove mightily to outdo one another in terms of power, influence, and level of conspicuous consumption. One way to flaunt it was by adoring (and sexually using) a *puer delicatus*, an exquisite boy, chosen for his good looks and grace, at times taken from the ranks of that person's household slaves.

What precisely did a Roman do with his delicate boy? Or a Greek with his teenage *eromenos* lover? One option was a nonpenetrative but satisfying technique also employed by couples of both genders today. Called intercrural or interfemoral coitus, the Greeks referred to it as "doing it between the thighs." It appears on Athenian Greek vases and on other objects as well. The stance shows an older male with a teenager, sometimes facing each other while standing, and at others, from behind, lying down. Another technique, today called frottage or genital-to-genital sex, involved sexual rubbing, usually face-to-face. Beyond these, of course, existed other options, from anal to oral—which are discussed elsewhere in this book.

Today, a number of worthy books on the subject of ancient sexual practices and mores vis-à-vis our own shed more light on what the Greeks and Romans really did, and what they really meant by their terminology.

These titles (representing a spectrum of views) are especially helpful: *Looking at Lovemaking*, by John R. Clarke; *Sexuality in Greek and Roman Society and Literature*, by Marguerite Johnson and Terry Ryan; *The Reign of the Phallus*, by Eva Keuls; *Love Between Women*, by Bernadette Brooten; *Pompeii: The Living City*, by Alex Butterworth and Ray Laurence; *Pederasty and Pedagogy in Archaic Greece*, by William A. Percy; and *Courtesans and Fishcakes* plus *The Greeks and Greek Love*, by James Davidson.

K. J. Dover's updated edition of *Greek Homosexuality* also contains rich visual evidence about the techniques and positions used within male-male and male-female contexts. That old adage, "A picture is worth a thousand words" certainly holds true with regard to Greco-Roman art. Studying the erotic and romantic depictions on drinking vessels, cups, mirrors, and other artifacts, including items as minute as seal rings, is revelatory. As John Clarke, author of *Looking at Lovemaking*, notes, "The artistry remains are far more democratic and catholic than the texts that have come down to us." And more honest, too, since artists of long ago felt freer to portray the authentic sensuality and tenderness of couples, as well as their complex repertoire of sexual positions; furthermore, they did so with male-to-male subjects, male-female ones, and female couples.

Clarke also points out their popularity. A wide variety of consumers commissioned or bought items with erotic themes. The objects ranged from modest lamps and accessories within the reach of almost anyone to luxury items like the Warren Cup, its exquisitely detailed scenes created in silver by a superb artisan. Since their cultures had a frank appreciation of human physicality, they were much more accepting of nudity and sexual imagery.

Put another way: Greeks and Romans, whatever their orientation or gender, liked to look at sexual portrayals—as well as take part in them.

And oh yes, what about female sexuality? Because male minds (no matter which gender, or both, aroused them) often focused on the pitcher versus catcher side of sex, they found it supremely difficult to believe that women, who conveniently enough were designed in a way that invited penetration, longed for anything other than a good poke. And pokes they got, since heterosexual intercourse (for fun or for procreation) occurred with very great frequency. So did sodomy or anal sex, which from the female point of view had contraceptive value in long-ago times.

Lastly, Greek and Roman males had a big blind spot when it came to females. Since they tended to view women as inferior versions of men, they also believed that women were empty vessels that required filling periodically—in one way only. And by males only. Could women experience erotic fulfillment with their own gender? Impossible; just look at that female plumbing.

In the next entry, you'll read more about female eroticism and the women who proved the men wrong: the gals who chose to be *tribades*, one of the earlier terms (none of them very cordial) for lesbian.

## TRIBADES:
### Friction between women? Not always a bad idea

Even before Sappho and her poetic disciples gave the term *lesbian* a whole new meaning beyond "person from the island of Lesbos," there were gals who felt erotically attracted to other women. Although Sappho lived and loved in the sixth century B.C., "lesbian" did not become common parlance until much later, when Christian writer Clement of Alexandria first used it in print in the second century A.D.

In ancient times, female lovers tended to be called *tribades* (singular *tribas*) from the Greek verb "to rub." As noted earlier regarding Greek and Roman males, we need to remember that erotic attachments in those times were not an either-or proposition. A woman like Sappho might prefer her own sex as love objects but might also have heterosexual relationships, including marriage, some of them loving as well.

In the second century A.D. an author-orator named Maximus of Tyre argued that Sappho and her fans and followers on Lesbos bonded philosophically and spiritually rather than sexually. As he put it, "What else could one call the love of the Lesbian woman than the Socratic art of love?

For they seem to have practiced love after their own fashion, she the love of women, he the love of men."

Nevertheless, most Greek guys found it easier to believe in mythical beasts than in the love life of lesbians. A substantial number of male writers scoffed in print at the whole notion; they simply could not credit that anything romantically worthwhile (much less sexually satisfying) could occur between females.

In later Roman times, only a handful of authors mentioned *tribades* in passing: the elder and young Senecas, Lucian, and Martial, in an epigram or two. They too expressed anger at the presumption of such women, finding the idea of female intimacy threatening, disgusting, illegal, or all of the above. Christian writer Tertullian later called them *fricatrices*—an even more disapproving variant of rub-a-dub-dub.

About the only clear-eyed male to comment on female proclivities lived much earlier than Tertullian. In the fifth century B.C., comic playwright Aristophanes parodied Plato and his fantasy about humankind's original three genders. Aristophanes asserted that female lovers of women existed, and he called them by various names, including *hetairistriai*. Since any word with that many vowels is going to be a loser, the term did not catch on, although Aristophanes did.

The most curious part about male views of long-ago lesbianism? As they did with all matters sexual, men defined it as sexual penetration. Since, however, both

*Although Sappho's home island of Lesbos eventually gave its name to the term* lesbian, *during the poet's own era women attracted to other women were commonly known as* tribades.

parties were female, men assumed the deed was done using a dildo or an abnormally large clitoris! In other words, if female lovers existed at all, they must be capable of penetration. Because anything else was not sex.

The Roman and Greek poets who specialized in sexual invective and X-rated epigrams, such as Juvenal and Martial, got into a real froth just contemplating the notion of women "usurping" the male role. They too insisted that one of the partners in tribadic sex must play the part of the active male, either by using a dildo, her enlarged clitoris, or another appropriately shaped instrument. (Suffering Sappho, where'd I put that cucumber?)

Although Greek and Roman men had practiced or knew about intercrural, nonpenetrative sex, they likewise scoffed at the idea of women finding delight in this manner. The whole spectrum of nonpenetrative lovemaking between women was lost on them. Nonetheless, art historians and archaeologists have found a growing amount of pictorial proof. Depictions of lesbian lovemaking adorned numerous household objects, from mural art to mirrors, from jewelry boxes to bowls.

Contemporary writers on ancient sexual mores such as Bernadette Brooten, author of *Love between Women*, point out that "the concept of female homoeroticism as unnatural runs like a thread, especially through the Greek sources, both Christian and non-Christian. [The sources] implicitly contrast unnatural sex between women with the natural roles: men 'do' or 'act,' while women 'suffer' or are 'passive.'"

So what did women in love actually do back then, and how did they lead their lives? We cannot know for certain, but what we can glean from scraps of text, passing literary remarks, letters, and graffiti, along with the richer stew offered by art and artifacts that survive from sources as diverse as walls in Ostia and Pompeii, mosaics on Sicily, and the rubbish heaps of

Greco-Roman Egypt, it's likely that lesbian couples two thousand years ago did the same things that female lovers do now, from kissing to scissoring, from full body contact to oral pleasuring.

Given the intense and often vicious masculine reactions to women taking the "male" role in long-ago lovemaking, however, it seems fairly certain that most long-ago tribades and lesbians—like unicorns—took care to remain invisible.

One impudent exception? Female pornographers. Believe it or not, talented gals who possessed a way with dirty words and a gift for salacious illustration produced a number of X-rated publications in ancient times—only scraps remain, but it's clear that the whole joyous spectrum of lovemaking was represented in these forerunners to *The Joy of Sex*. (For amusing details, see the entry on pornographers, male and female, elsewhere in this book.)

## DILDOS:
### Eco-friendly—& sometimes edible!

As the story goes, two women went shopping at a farmer's market. Spotting a display of firm, tasty-looking cucumbers, they stopped. The sign said, "Three for a dollar!" After some discussion, with a wink one gal said to the other, "Well, I suppose we could always *eat* one of them."

Although cucumbers, plastics, and K-Y Jelly weren't readily available long ago, imaginative Greeks, male and female, got along just fine in the bedroom department with the help of olive oil, wheat, and fine leather.

Being intensely phallocentric, Greek men confidently assumed that when lacking male partners, women used dildos or other phallic objects—because

sex was mostly about penetration. Comic plays such as Aristophanes'
*Lysistrata* got many of their laughs through dildo jokes. Countless drinking
cups also portrayed slaves and hookers putting leather phalluses to good use.

Greek men were partly right.

Lonely housewives in Athens, off-duty courtesans in Corinth, widows in
the wilds of Arcadia, gay couples everywhere, females seeking same gender
for soulful get-togethers, playwrights producing satyr plays that featured
comic genitalia, and event organizers for processions that featured oversize
phalluses all made use of objects that would be called sex toys today. The
Greeks slangily referred to dildos as "sliders" or "strikers."

Everywhere you looked in ancient Greece and other locales around the
Mediterranean, phallic symbols were proudly on display. Temples were
rife with rocket-shaped monuments to testosterone. Standing at every
crossroad and street corner in Athens were stone markers called herms,
each sporting the head of Hermes (the god Mercury among the Romans)
and his perky phallus, but they were sacred boundary markers, not incite-
ments to lust. Standing in gardens, temples, and other sites throughout
Rome and Italy were ferocious images of Priapus, his oversize red erection
a warning to thieves. These phallic symbols, however, were warding-off
measures, apotropaic objects to deflect the evil eye and protect humans
from malign forces. (Learn more details at the entries for Priapus, hymen,
and marriage.)

For personal lovelife aids, ancient Greek consumers turned to the experts
in the tannery industry, who obligingly took the softest leather, formed it
into a hot-dog shape, stuffed it with wool, then polished it to maximum
smoothness. Greek dildos, called *olisboi*, did not vibrate or possess any bells
and whistles. But padded leather in the shape of a male organ, lavishly

anointed with good-quality olive oil, did have a lively, humanoid feel to it (or so it was said).

Discerning shoppers knew that the best *olisboi* were made in Miletus, a prosperous Ionian city-state on the coast of Asia Minor (Turkey today). Specialty items included ones carved from ivory, wood, and marble.

From the abundant materials that have survived, including satyr plays and comedies by Herodas, along with thousands of portrayals on painted Greek pots, vases, and cups, it's clear that dildos came in all sizes. There were dildos-for-two models, some joined end-to-end, others strung together with woolen ties. Dildos could also be attached with soft leather straps to satisfy oneself or one's partner. A more expensive model, called a *baubon*, was made of red leather, as most of the dildos used in comedies were. Besides being festive and highly visible, they imitated sexual arousal.

*The inventive Greeks had surprisingly modern ideas about recycling. Around the fifth century B.C., a Greek baker invented the first biodegradable sex toy: the breadstick dildo.*

In Herodas's popular play *Mime*, a courtesan of Miletus asks where her friend got her bright red dildo made—which leads to the other gal's fury, because her new dildo was loaned out before she even got to use it. The purpose of the plot was to exaggerate excessive female lust, but it also reveals interesting details about such devices and how they were used. Or lent. And even how sex-toy manufacturers of long ago kept their enterprises secret to avoid taxes.

Somewhere in the fifth century B.C., a historic breakthrough occurred within the dildo industry—one that might resonate today as well.

It was a slow day at the bakery. An unknown Greek, a genius at baking who also happened to be an outside-the-box thinker, started fooling around with some extra bread dough. She was kneading the dough; and kneading brought to mind the Greek word for masturbation, *dephesthai*, which evolved from a word meaning "to mold" or "soften by kneading." So her mind was already in the gutter, and one thing led to another.

After a while she saw what she had wrought. And it was good.

Thus was born the *olisbo-kollix*: the breadstick dildo.

With that vivid image in mind, it's easy to fantasize further scenarios. A Greek matron serving lunch to her often-absent husband, for example. She brings him a salad and a breadbasket, remarking with a twinkle in her eye, "Nothing says lovin' like something from my oven!"

While this entry might sound fanciful, the discovery in question came about through a neat bit of research by a Greek professor named Alexander Oikonomides. In 1986 he rediscovered this remarkable, edible, easy-to-dispose-of invention of ancient times after seeing a jocular reference in an inscription to *kollix* ("breadstick" or "baguette") with *olisbos*, the Greek word for dildo. He later found the word *olisbokollix* in a lexicon of classical Greek that dated to the fifth century A.D.

Further confirmation came from pictorial evidence. Certain Greek vases bear artwork, heretofore puzzling, that depicts women with baskets filled with phallus-shaped breadsticks. One famous illustration shows a nude female taking part in a religious procession, proudly carrying a gigantic phallus (ceremonial, we hope!) clearly made from bread dough.

## OUTERCOURSE B.C.:
### Foreplay & backstabbing

Long ago near the Dead Sea, several raunchy little cities competed to see who could take the top spot as the lowest places on Earth. They already were the lowest, being 1,388 feet below sea level, but the low they were going for was depravity. Although their original sites may now be under the Dead Sea, their infamy remains. One was Gomorrah. The other, called Sodom, gave its name to a class A felony. The locals were fond of the back-door sexual approach, the rougher, the better. In time, their predilection became known as sodomy.

The Sodomites did other creepy things. In Genesis 19:5–8, when a wrathful God wants to destroy Sodom and neighboring cities for their grievous sins, the prophet Abraham offers to find some decent people worth saving—such as his nephew Lot and family. So two male angels disguised as humans show up at Lot's house, his wife and daughters fix dinner for everybody, and things seem cool. Soon, however, an ominous mob of local men surround the house, shouting, "Where are the guys who came here tonight? Bring them to us—we wanna get to know them." "Know," as in the Biblical sense: assault them sexually.

So what does Lot do? To protect his guests, he throws his young daughters to the wolves! He says, "Behold now, I have two daughters who've not known men; let me, I pray you, bring them out unto you—and do nothing to the guests [the male angels]."

Small wonder that God got disgusted and destroyed Sodom, Gomorrah, and two neighboring cites with fire and brimstone. As Jude 1:7 notes, "Sodom and Gomorrah, giving themselves over to fornication, and going after strange flesh, are set forth as an example." Scholars have wrangled over the "strange flesh" epithet, some interpreting it as illicit sex with strangers, or sex with angels, but most labeling it same-sex relations between men.

As luck would have it, almost no one in ancient Greece or Rome read the Old Testament. Or even wanted to. Thus sodomy, or *pedico* as the Romans called it, again became popular. Anal sex had quite a few loyal adherents among women: housewives who didn't want to get pregnant (again); female prostitutes and sex workers, who didn't want to get pregnant (ever); female slaves (ditto); and many a ruler's wife, who preferred her spouse to stick it

*According to the Old Testament, Sodom gave its name to sodomy,*
*a sexual practice that enraged God so much that he destroyed*
*the city as Abraham's nephew Lot and family fled.*

where the sun didn't shine—just not in hers. Once Spartan women reached age eighteen and formed intimate attachments, they routinely engaged in anal sex, to preserve virginity and to prevent pregnancy.

Sodomy also became a common practice among young Greek and Roman brides; to "spare" her from being deflowered on the wedding night, hubby put his *mentula* up her bum. How thoughtful can you get?

As Greco-Roman art illustrates, the sexual position called "the lioness" was a classic pose for rear entry; to get into position, a woman crouched, lifting up her buttocks at the same time.

Males in a variety of relationships represented another demographic who enjoyed or routinely preferred rear-end action—gay couples, male prostitutes, and other men with homoerotic bonds. Sometimes it was ritualistic, such as those grooms on their wedding night. At others, it was punitive—male adulterers who'd gotten caught, for instance. In Greece, adulterers and males known to be erotically passive were often made fun of by Aristophanes; in his comedies, he called them "wide-assed" and was fond of "roasting" local individuals, such as Athenian politician Cleisthenes. In the Roman Empire, however, sometimes the adulterer was ceremoniously sodomized by the cuckolded husband.

Plenty of slaves served as objects for sodomy—and took active roles as well. So did many Roman emperors, along with their wives, girlfriends, and boyfriends. Sexually addicted emperors such as Nero, Caligula, Tiberius, Elagabalus, and Commodus got deeply involved in sodomitic giving and receiving. Other couples outed as sodomy aficionados included Greek orator Demosthenes with Cnosion; Pompey the Great with his wife Julia; and Caesar assassin Brutus and his wife Portia.

Although the literature (and the graffiti) is contradictory, it does appear that men who preferred anal sex to the exclusion of other sex practices were called *cinaedus* in Latin, a borrowing from the Greek word *kinaidos*. A blunt term, it implied effeminacy.

Oddly enough, long-ago sodomy got much more favorable press than oral sex did. The array of actions which nowadays are often thought of as pleasurable, gender-friendly foreplay (or even considered "not sex at all" by many younger participants) were called abominations. And worse. Why? It may have been linked to a widespread custom among the upper classes in the Greco-Roman world, where men and women routinely greeted each other with a kiss on the lips, irrespective of gender.

To the Romans especially, *os impurum* or "filthy, impure mouth" was a repellent notion—and a term of abuse. Men and women rumored to be fond of fellatio or cunnilingus were never invited to dinner parties—people claimed that their perverse behavior gave them hideous bad breath.

There was a nastier side to fellatio, too. Men sometimes forced other males (slaves or free men) to fellate them, an act called *irrumatio*. In a Roman male's mind, nothing could be more degrading than to be a receptacle for oral sex. The vicious verses of Martial, Catullus, and other poets of sexual invective made that very clear. To drive home its depravity, *irrumatio* was sometimes the penalty inflicted on an adulterer, or on a male found guilty of other crimes.

Nevertheless, both practices were cheerfully on tap, as easy-to-find commercial propositions (graffiti "ads" for both services still cover walls in Pompeii and elsewhere) and as part of the personal erotic repertoire of countless sexually active persons.

## KISSING:

### Loving lips versus foul mouths

The Greeks and Romans of old could really be negative about innocent pleasures. Kissing, for example. As Greek historian Plutarch fiercely noted in his essay called *Precepts for Conjugal Life*, "It is shameful to embrace and kiss and caress each other in the presence of others."

Crusty old Senator Cato of Rome, the one who continually shrilled, "Carthage must be destroyed!" was quite a cold fish as well, when it came to marital relations. One day in the Roman senate, he ejected the man who was due to become the city's next consul—simply because the fellow had kissed his wife in broad daylight.

Not all men or women were that reserved or frigid. After Athens' famed leader Pericles got divorced, he and his philosophy-spouting girlfriend Aspasia began to live together, and their behavior scandalized the city. The scandal wasn't the presumed sex they were having. To the utter horror of the neighbors, Pericles ardently kissed Aspasia on the lips when he left each morning to attend to business. When he returned, he warmly smooched her again. And the two of them misbehaved in this revolting way, year after year! Twenty, to be exact.

Another reason for kiss phobia? An old wives' tale that suggested that old Greek wives (and possibly young ones) also imbibed to excess. Playwrights from Euripides to Aristophanes deplored the female propensity to take a nip: "O feverish women, ever ready for a drink, inventors of all kinds of schemes to get at the bottle! O great blessing for the wine merchants, and a curse in turn for us!"

Maybe those matrons had cause. Their Athenian husbands often spent a hard day socializing at the agora marketplace, followed by a lively evening at an all-male symposium, with plenty of tipple and titillation from the female entertainment. Invariably, they did kiss their wives when they finally got home. Instead of affection, however, the kiss was a breathalyzer test.

In later centuries, societal restrictions on kissing (but not on wifely wine consumption) may have eased. By good fortune, we still possess Achilles Tatius's wonderfully trashy novel *Leucippe and Clitophon*, which describes long-ago kissing in vivid, juicy detail. His novel, written in the second century A.D., was very popular.

In this excerpt, one character defends the joys of male-female kissing. "A woman's body is moist in the clinch, and her lips are soft in response to kisses. On account of this she holds the man's body in her arms, with it completely joined to her flesh, and he is surrounded with pleasure when he has intercourse with her. She stamps her kisses on his lips like seals on wax . . . and when she has experience, she can make her kisses sweeter by not only wishing to use her lips, but also her teeth, grazing round her lover's mouth and biting his kisses . . . At the height of orgasm she goes mad with pleasure and opens her mouth in passion. At this time tongues keep company with each other, and so far as possible they also make love to one another; you can make your pleasure greater by opening your mouth to her kisses."

Famed writer Ovid, a fervid lover of women, employed lots of osculation in his *Art of Love* and other poems, as in this line: "What wise man would not mingle kisses with coaxing words of endearment?"

Poets and writers also sang the praises of male-to-male kisses and, more rarely, female to female. Here is an excerpt from Lucian's *Dialogue of the Courtesans*, with two call girls discussing the party the night before.

[Clonarium]: "Did you sleep? What happened?"

*In Greco-Roman times, kissing wasn't always an innocent greeting. Upper-crust folks were phobic about "impure mouths," since oral sex was looked upon with loathing.*

[Leaena]: "At first they [two women] were kissing me just like men, not only pressing their lips but opening their mouths a little, and they were embracing me and feeling my breasts. Demonassa was also biting me while she was kissing me. I didn't know what to do with it all."

As noted in the prior entry, Romans tend to greet each other, males as well as females, with a brief kiss on the lips. That may be why they were so paranoid about foul breath—fastidious about where mouths had been, and doing what to whom. For example, after 201 B.C., when the Hispanic peninsula became a Roman province, the larger world learned about the favorite dentifrice and mouthwash of many a Spaniard: human urine. That practice provoked an *Eeeeeeeeeooooouuuuuw!* heard around the Mediterranean Sea.

Anthropologists have long suggested that kissing evolved from earlier primate behavior—either because human lips look and behave a bit like female labia when aroused; or because human mothers used to premasticate food for their young, then feed the infant mouth-to-mouth (just as birds and many animals still do).

## STRAIGHT FROM THE SOURCE:
### Love candids

In spite of the obstacles of lower literacy, a do-it-yourself postal service, and a shocking lack of Internet matchmaking sites, long-ago folks of all ages, social status, and genders did find true love. They did manage to meet their "second half," as the philosopher Plato called it. Or, alternatively, they found deep happiness in the love of siblings, of children, of grandparents, of lifelong friends.

Here's the epitaph of an eighteen-year-old, written by her husband, a humble construction worker in Roman France; they lived near the Seine River. "To the eternal memory of Blandinia Martiola, a most faultless girl, who lived 18 years, 9 months, 5 days. Pompeius Catussa, a citizen, a plasterer, dedicates [this] to his wife, who was incomparable and very kind to him, who lived with him 5 years, 6 months, 18 days without any shadow of a fault. You who read this, go bathe in the baths of Apollo, as I used to do with my wife. I wish I still could."

Here is an excerpt from a longer letter to a male friend, written by Pliny the Younger, a wealthy Roman aristocrat. He (aged about forty) is describing Calpurnia, his third wife, who would have been eighteen to twenty years old. "And she loves me, surely an indication of her virtue. She has even, because of her affection for me, taken an interest in literature. She has copies of my books, she reads them over and over again, and even learns them by heart . . . She even sets my poems to music and sings them, to the accompaniment of a lyre. No musician has taught her, but love itself, the best of instructors."

This is a graffito found on the exterior walls of what most probably was an inn, located in the Roman city of Pompeii: "Vibius Restitutus slept here, alone, and longed for his Urbana."

This letter is written from one brother to another; the writer lived in Greco-Roman Egypt in the second century A.D., and his brother was a tribune in the Roman army. Their mother was recently widowed.

*Long-ago men and women often put their loving feelings onto paper, sometimes with the help of scribes. Many touching examples are extant.*

"Sempronius to his brother Maximus very many greetings. Before everything I pray that you are well. I have been informed that you serve our mother and lady grudgingly. I beg you, sweetest brother, do not grieve her in anything. And if any of our brothers gainsay her, you ought to cuff them; for you now ought to take the name of father. I know that without my writing you are able to humor her, but do not be offended by my letter of admonition; for we ought to revere our mother as a goddess, especially one as good as ours. This I have written to you, brother, because I know how sweet a possession our revered parents are. Goodbye, brother."

From the same period, an excerpt from a letter written by a man of humble station, a Greek living in Egypt, to his wife or possibly his lover—but not necessarily his sister. "Serenus to Isadora, his sister and lady, very many greetings. Before all else I pray for your health, and every day and evening I make supplication on your behalf before Thoeris [a hippo goddess] who loves you. I would have you know that ever since you left me I have been in mourning, weeping by night and lamenting by day. Since I bathed with you Phaophi 12 I have not bathed or anointed myself until Hathur 12. You have sent me letters that could move a stone, so much have your words stirred me."

## SOCRATES OF ATHENS:
### Witty & sexy to the very last

Thanks to the adoring, high-minded verbiage of Socrates' philosophical disciples Plato and Xenophon, you might not have thought their famed teacher belonged on the "sexiest men of 450 B.C." list. Homely, chubby Socrates nevertheless attracted the ardent attentions of various men and women in the fifth century B.C. For starters, this son of a midwife and a stonemason was married twice, it appears, although no one is sure of the order. Or was it simultaneous? Several biographers assert that Socrates had both wives at the same time, making him history's earliest philosophical bigamist. Possibly it was allowed by special decree due to the scarcity of Athenians at that time. After a plague, perhaps? We just don't know.

Myrto, daughter of Aristides the Just, was the "good wife," about whom almost nothing was written—except the ghastly news to locals that she came to the marriage naked. Naked, that is, of a dowry. Most Greeks would have run the other way, but Socrates did not and the couple had two sons together.

Socrates' other wife, Xanthippe, made up for the pallid reputation of Myrto by being the saltiest-tongued woman in Athens. Her legendary irascibility led to some of Socrates' best sound-bite stories. For example, when a student asked how he dealt with his wife's shrewish temper, he responded, "When men who are fond of spirited horses master those beasts, they then find the rest easy to cope with. So too I in the society of Xanthippe learn to adapt myself to the rest of the world."

The student in question was another of Socrates' erotic connections. Brilliant, beautiful, troubled, and irresistible to both men and women, Alkibiades tried without success to seduce Socrates. The philosopher was equally taken with Alkibiades but sublimated his desires by teaching his would-be lover about a higher, noncarnal form of love.

This philosopher, called by the Pythian oracle at Delphi "the wisest of men," attracted the best and brightest in Athenian society. Among his disciples, admirers, and groupies were aristocratic writers and thinkers such as

Aristippus. But Socrates welcomed good minds wherever he found them; Aeschines the sausage-maker's son was one. Phaedo was another. Born to a noble family, Phaedo was taken as a slave when his city of Elis fell to enemy forces. Sold to a brothel of male prostitutes in Athens, he managed to become part of the philosophical circle. At Socrates' urging, a couple of his wealthy pupils ransomed Phaedo. From then on, he studied at Socrates' feet as a free man. It's possible that these two were intimate.

When not trading quips or embraces (or daydreaming about canoodling with his philosophical cadre), Socrates philosophized and flirted outrageously with any number of uppity women, including Pericles' lover Aspasia, the classy free-thinker from Miletus, and with other intellectual women who sought knowledge.

His willingness to treat men and women of dubious reputation as warmly as he did their aristocratic counterparts won Socrates mixed blessings: applause from a few, condemnation from many, and vast amounts of jealousy from men he'd criticized—including orators, poets, and politicians.

It was a trio of such men, stung by Socratic jibes and deeply offended by the philosopher's lifestyle and moral teachings as a social critic, who brought the indictment against Socrates in 399 B.C. Their charges? Impiety and corrupting youth. Ironic indeed, considering the relatively abstemious behavior of Socrates, and the lack of it in his accusers.

Anytus, Lycon, and Meletus got their death wish. About seventy years old, still sassy and spirited, Socrates went to prison and drank his hemlock brew among friends. Although in his last hours he exhibited his deepest love for his close male friends and disciples, he invited his wife Xanthippe to visit him on his deathbed. Once he felt the paralysis of the poison begin to move up his body, he sent his wife, now weeping, back home.

Then he told his friend Crito to pay a last debt for him—a rooster to Asclepius, the god of healing. Many have sought to interpret his last request. Some believe he sent this thank-you to the healing deity because death is the "cure" that frees the soul from the body. Others feel that the token for Asclepius meant that his death would help "cure" the political malaise of Athens. But there is another possibility.

Socrates had enough chutzpah for one last riposte. When he said to Crito, "We owe a rooster to Asclepius—don't forget to take care of it for me, will you?" his gallows humor was not lost on his companions. One fairly common reaction of a dying man is to get an erection. And everybody, not just the ancient Greeks, knows the everyday synonym for a male rooster.

*High-spirited and bawdy to the last, philosopher Socrates left his sorrowing followers with a piquant one-liner as he downed his hemlock cocktail.*

## SOPHOCLES & EURIPIDES:
### Brazenly bisexual playwrights

What a pair: both of them top tragedians, toasted as successes by fifth century Athenians, roasted by Aristophanes in his comic plays, and married twice. Furthermore, both of them lived their long lives as bisexuals, although that word would not have been recognized, much less used, in those days.

In her book *Bisexuality in the Ancient World*, Eva Canterella mentions, among others, these two extraordinary achievers, Euripides and Sophocles. They not only enjoyed youthful love affairs with males as teenagers but when mature, also became family men while pursuing sexual adventures with other men. As she puts it, "Faced with such evidence, how can one avoid thinking

*This open-air theater in Athens was one of many in which audiences thrilled to the tragic dramas of major-league playwrights, such as Euripides and Sophocles.*

that adult Greek males enjoyed almost untrammeled freedom, being allowed to devote time to pederastic relationships which were far more than the occasional variation?"

Older than Euripides by two decades, Sophocles came from a wealthy family that lived outside Athens. At twenty-nine he had his first triumph, taking first prize in the Dionysia theater competition. He beat Aeschylus, the man who'd reigned as king of the tragic playwrights for years.

Sophocles became famous for adding a third actor to plays and for his character development. His one-liners became bywords. Among them: "Time eases all things"; "The greatest griefs are those we cause ourselves" (both from *Oedipus Rex*); and, from his play *Antigone*, "Don't kill the messenger!"

Talented and lucky, Sophocles went on to win eighteen times at the Dionysia festivals and six times at the Lenaia annual competitions. Aristotle admired him enormously, citing his *Oedipus the King* as the highest achievement in tragedy. Invitations to visit as honored playwright came from foreign rulers, but Sophocles was a hometown boy. He turned all of them down.

Like other civic-minded Athenians, Sophocles took a very active role in his city's life; as a teen, he was chosen to lead the choral chant, celebrating the Athenian victory over the Persians. He served a term as one of the city's treasurers, and also as *strategos* or general, working with his friend Pericles.

At dinner parties, Sophocles was known for flirting, stealing kisses from the best-looking boys, and much besides. His buddy Pericles once gave him a hard time for admiring a handsome lad instead of keeping his mind on military strategy.

The best story that's come down to us about his love life involved a male assistant of Sophocles who got intimate with Nico, an older gal whose beauteous buttocks were much admired. Kidding around, the assistant asked

Nico to lend him her buttocks. Her reply: "Sure, honey—go ahead and take from me what you give to Sophocles."

The great man, despite his workload and his many erotic distractions, took care of two successive families. He was first wed to Nicostrate, with whom he had a son who grew up to become a tragic poet. With his second wife, Theoris, he had another son, Ariston. A bright, merry, well-liked fellow, Sophocles lived to be ninety-two; it was not until late in life that he lost his sexual vigor. He reportedly confided to Plato, "I'm glad to be free of that raging, savage beast."

Euripides was more somber, a reclusive chap born on Salamis Island who spent much of his life in Athens. As a youngster, his dad received an oracle prediction that Euripides would win crowns of victory. He promptly put his son into training as a pro athlete. The prediction proved true—but the victory crowns would be for five theatrical productions, among them *Medea* and *The Bacchae*.

His talents extended to painting as well, and he pioneered many innovations in the theater. His writing, by turns ironically comic and profoundly tragic, depicted ordinary people in extraordinary circumstances. He shocked Athenian audiences with his empathetic portrayals of women and other victims of society. Unfortunately, the real tragedy is that over 80 percent of his plays have been lost.

He described both of his marriages, to Melite and Choerine, as "disastrous," although he and the latter wife did collaborate to produce three sons. He had a happier long-term relationship with another tragic poet, a much younger man named Agathon whose own work wobbled from flowery to improbable. Accompanied by Agathon, in later years Euripides went to the Macedonian court of Archelaus, where he would spend his last years, dying in his mid-seventies. Macedonia is thought to be where he wrote *The Bacchae*, his psychological study into the primitive side of Greek religion.

## MANDRAKES:

### Grow your own little mannikin!

According to the Old Testament, women were generally enchanted with an erotic powerhouse of a plant that magically "cured" infertility. In Genesis 30:14–17, two sisters married to the same guy fight over the shrub—Rachel wants it because she has yet to get pregnant; Leah, because she longs for more kids than the four she has. They strike a deal—and (very) eventually, both have dates with the stork. That fabled baby-maker flora may have been the mandrake. (The biblical Song of Songs also waxes poetic about the sweet-smelling apple of love.)

Give its long-standing aphrodisiac and medicinal reputation, the mandrake was seen as a symbol of love for the Egyptians, too, who made a wine laced with it. The Greeks later recognized mandrake as the favorite food of the sex-crazed satyrs.

Over the millennia, however, it's likely that *Mandragora officinarum* caused more havoc and heartache than happy news. A member of the nightshade family, mandrake is closely related to henbane, datura, and the deadly nightshade—all of them packed with high-potency alkaloids like scopolamine, atropine, and hyoscyamine. In the proper dosage, it can be an effective anesthetic, invaluable in surgery; the scopolamine from mandrake was used into modern times, before the advent of ether. Taken for its hallucinogenic effects, mandrake in the

*Long thought to be an erotic aid, the mandrake root could kill. Its humanoid shape led alchemists to fantasize that with supernatural help, a "little man" could spring to life from the root.*

correct dosage may produce a dreamy, out-of-body experience—or delirium and coma.

Over time, mandrake took on an even more magical aura. It had a malevolent spirit, along the lines of *The Little Shop of Horrors*, and the ancients believed that once awakened, mandrake's shrill scream could kill. Thus, in the first century A.D., Roman Jewish writer Josephus advised would-be harvesters to dig a furrow around the root until its lower part was exposed, tie a dog to it, then quickly move away from the plant. The dog would try to follow the human, pulling up the root in the process—and the pooch (instead of the human harvester) would perish. At that point, the mandrake root could be handled without risk.

The root itself often had a human shape—which led to more fantastical beliefs and warnings. Around the third century A.D., a Greek alchemist named Zosimus combined some early beliefs about reproduction with the mandrake legends. The first natural scientists in ancient Greece to ponder human reproduction had suggested that, just as the bodies of hens held miniature eggs, perhaps inside the bodies of humans there might be a preformed individual called a homunculus—a "little man."

The notion of a "little man" (whether inside a human being or not) was admittedly beguiling. So Zosimus and other alchemists began to elaborate this concept further. According to them, in order to possess a little man of one's own, seekers first had to find a mandrake plant. This was not an easy task, since by now it was reputed to grow only with the help of the semen ejaculated in his final spasms by a man being hanged! That laborious mission accomplished, the seekers then had to locate a black dog, train it to dig for roots, keep their distance until the hideous shrieks of the plant had died away, etcetera.

Once dug up, the small mannikin figure of the mandrake root needed to be washed, then fed with items such as honey, milk, and blood. If all went well, the root would develop into a homunculus. Furthermore, the homunculus would act to protect its human owner, leprechaun fashion.

A little mannikin to love, and direct. It was, and is, a winning idea, much repeated in mystical writings from medieval witches' manuals to the Kabbalah. Mandrake plants are still around, their large strappy leaves and small "love apple" fruits as poisonous as ever. Need I add, do not try this at home?

## FILTHY GESTURES, IMAGES, LANGUAGE:
### What obscene really did mean

Most of the ancient cultures around the Mediterranean strongly believed that filthy words, naughty gestures, and what we might consider inappropriate or obscene images, such as erect phalluses, were necessary and effective to chase away bad luck, ill omens, ghosts, vampires, malign spirits, and the terrifying evil eye.

Despite their brio for life and their outgoing ways, long-ago Romans and Greeks had numerous fears, many of them starkly real: wars, wounds, rabid dogs, crop failures, plagues, piracy, and the obscenely high mortality rates of mothers and babies in childbirth.

Therefore, much of what we see today at archaeological sites, as museum artifacts, and in ancient art must be looked at through the prism of its period's own value system. Objects, words, and gestures that had apotropaic powers to ward off bad luck and evil eyes were valued. And they were produced in glorious quantities. The existing art alone, from paintings, murals, and mosaics to bronzes, marble sculptures, and protective amulets, fills museum displays and overflows into storerooms worldwide.

The Egyptian had similar beliefs, especially in times of great vulnerability. One of the objects they routinely produced to protect mothers and new infants was a throwing stick made of hippo ivory and carved with the images of Bes and Taweret, the deities associated with childbirth.

Women's jewelry and belts often included the decorative knot of Hercules on them, another apotropaic symbol. Greek and Roman brides wore the knot of Hercules on their marriage day, and their new husbands got to untie it on the wedding night. In both cultures, dirty jokes, scatological songs, and humorous sexual language were also protective parts of the wedding celebrations.

During childhood, Roman girls and boys did not go anywhere without their *bullas*, round or half-moon-shaped pendants of gold or leather worn for protection against spells or malignant glances. The young were thought to be particularly vulnerable to such things; babies, for example, from birth wore amulets and used teething rings of pink coral, carved in the shape of a phallus.

Moreover, if children (or brides, for that matter) were complimented, the remarks would be quickly dismissed and a protective gesture made, sometimes involving spit. In daily life, and throughout their waking hours, men and women routinely used obscene words while making warding-off gestures. Typical gestures included the *mano fico* (the "fig hand," imitating the female genitals), the *corna* or horns, and that still-perennial favorite, the *digitus impudicus*—the middle finger.

A large number of annual festivals in Italy, Greece, and elsewhere rein-
forced these homely personal methods of protection against malice, evil
eye, and bad luck. One such festival celebrated the fertility god Liber, who
boasted an important cult following in Rome. During his March festival,
protective phallus displays were everywhere—stationed at crossroads,
lugged around in carts throughout the countryside, and in the city itself. In
some parts of Italy, Liber got a month-long observance, during which arti-
ficial phalluses big and small were publicly paraded and obscenities ritually
uttered. Each March also, the festival of Anna Perenna, the goddess who
personified the year, took place. While sacrifices were made to her, naughty
songs were traditionally sung with gusto by young girls.

The quantity, variety, ubiquity, and geographic reach of such apotropaic
festivals, with open sexuality in the form of phallic display and lots of sexual
jokes and obscenities, apparently did much to soothe ancient fears about
such dangers.

Like that of some of the biggest businesses in the United States today,
the Greco-Roman philosophy was: You can never have too much insurance.
For additional protection from the evil eye and other ills, phallic symbols
were painted on walls, posted over business doorways, erected at street corners, embedded in roadways, posted at doors, planted in gardens, worn as
jewelry, and carried as amulets. These long-ago measures still have potency
among some Mediterranean populations. If you spend any time in Greece
or Turkey, you might learn that schoolgirls still pin tiny blue evil-eye deflec-
tors to their bras, and the corner pharmacy sells similar charms next to the
cold remedies.

# For the Love of It—
Pure Passions

## CALLIPYGIA WORSHIP:
### Rear end fixation

Oh, to live in ancient Greece and never have to say: Do you think my butt looks too big in this tunic?

Greek males, especially the Athenians, adored the booty beautiful. Greeks even had a special word for it: *callipygian*, "with beautiful buttocks." For those girls cursed with too-slender tushes, the Greeks invented posterior enhancers, apparently a padded number that lifted and tightened the rear view.

Long-ago Greeks had exacting standards but open-minded tastes. The buttocks in question could be female. Or male. They could belong to a teen working out in an all-male gymnasium, or to an exquisite nude statue of Aphrodite, goddess of love.

In fact, some of the major artistic hullaballoo that occurred in the third century B.C. can be chalked up to a stylistic breakthrough moment in sculpture. That is when an unknown master created a bronze of the love goddess, carrying loads of sexily folded draperies while looking over her shoulder at her shapely bare tush. The original has disappeared, but a very good first century B.C. Roman copy in marble called the Kallipygean Venus can be ogled at Naples' marvelous museum.

Speaking of gorgeous behinds, the Greek city of Syracuse on the island of Sicily seems to have had well-endowed citizens. A famous story in Athenaeus's *Sages at Dinner* tells of an island farmer who had two daughters. They began quarreling as to which had the more handsome hiney—and took their dispute into the street. A young man (the kind with a rich old father) just happened to be cruising by, and they persuaded him to vote. Back then, you could do things like that and not get arrested.

He chose the buttocks of the older sister, falling in love with the rest of her at the same time. Naturally there was a younger brother; when he heard his bro rhapsodize about the shapely derrieres, he had to see. Straightaway he fell in love with the body parts of the younger sister. Daddy, being rich, tried to get his sons to marry some upper-class dames, arguing that there must be some good-looking tushes in that crowd. The love-smitten brothers remained adamant, and their dad eventually gave in, marrying his sons to their callipygian true loves.

And the sisters? Endowed with brains as well as fine hindquarters, they quickly commissioned a temple to the Fair-buttocked Aphrodite, in which stood a cult statue—possibly the original of the one still seen in the Naples Museum. The religious cult of the Fair Buttocked in Syracuse had staying power, too; centuries later, Christian author Clement of Alexandria put it on his "shamefully erotic examples of pagan religious art" list.

Around 350 B.C., famed Athenian sculptor Praxiteles created a staggeringly beautiful, completely nude Aphrodite—the first ever seen. He'd done it as a commission for the Greek islanders on Kos; they, however, got huffy about the nudity and refused it. Unperturbed, Praxiteles took it back and sold it to the eager citizens of Knidos. He'd also made a clothed Aphrodite—which the folks on Kos received. The model for both statues was Phryne, a saucy *hetera* whose rich curves made her the Marilyn Monroe of her day.

On Knidos, the locals built a special temple to house the sculpture; soon, the novel beauty of a nude goddess of love became a tourist attraction. And a sexual attraction, according to one account. One young fan became so entranced that one night he hid himself within

*To create statues of the love goddess, Greek sculptors used live models, such as the* hetera *Phryne. The Marilyn Monroe of her day, her lush figure included beautiful buttocks—always a crowd-pleaser with the Greeks.*

the temple, later manfully attempting to make love to the naked Aphrodite. Evidently he had a buttock fixation as well, since a stain allegedly appeared on the statue's luscious rear thigh, where it remained ever after.

## ETRUSCAN *AMORE*:
### Open affection, Etruscan style

Way back in 590 B.C. or so, an Etruscan married couple named Tanaquil and Tarquin rolled into the two-bit town that was Rome at that time. As they gazed at their new home, an eagle swooped, removed Tarquin's hat, then returned it to his head. His wife Tanaquil kissed him. "It's a sign from the gods! You're going to rule this joint, honey!" Those may not have been her exact words, but her demonstrative love—and her ability to read omens and bird signs, called augury—were typical traits and skills of Etruscan women. Although a man of humble origins, Tarquin did become Rome's fifth king, ruling with his queen for thirty-seven years.

Researchers still argue over the origins of the Etruscans and their still-enigmatic language. What's no longer an enigma, though, is the status of women in their culture and the wonderfully warm nature of male-female personal relations. Visual evidence of it glows from the astonishing murals found in Etruscan tombs, as well as on grave goods, bronze sculpture, mirrors, jewelry, and other artifacts.

Etruscan men and women from all walks of life, not just the elite, enjoyed the social mixing of the sexes and expected to have marriages of equals. They also had unembarrassed views about nudity and a frank appreciation of tenderness and love.

What a contrast the Etruscan pictorial evidence and these views were to those of the Greek and Romans! Although the latter two cultures had a keen interest in erotic pleasures, sought love, and experienced it, all too seldom was plain old garden-variety tenderness shown or written about.

Unsurprisingly, they expressed horror at the "decadent" doings of the Etruscans. Greek author Theopompus got quite lathered up about the Etruscan lifestyle. His rumor-based ranting is by turns hysterical and openly envious. The inclusion of women at parties! The wild dancing! The nudity! The promiscuity! Much of what he said is probably pure fiction, but his terror about the autonomy of Etruscan women is real. An excerpt: "Sharing wives is an Etruscan custom. The women take particular

*Although Greeks, Romans, and other cultures engaged in a stunning array of sexual activities, the Etruscans of Italy were nearly unique in demonstrating tenderness and affection as well.*

care of their bodies and exercise often, sometimes along with the men
. . . It is not a disgrace for them to be seen naked. They do not share their
[dining] couches with their husbands but with other men who happen to
be present, and they propose toasts to anyone they choose. They are expert
drinkers and very attractive."

Other authors added their own spurious assertions. In his comic plays
of the second century B.C., Roman playwright Plautus claimed that before
marriage, Etruscan women sold their bodies in order to collect a dowry.

Around A.D. 40, Roman emperor Claudius wed his first wife, a woman
with Etruscan antecedents; later he wrote a long history of the Etruscans
which did not survive. If it ever turns up, the work of Claudius might prove
a balanced look at a long-ago culture both passionate and dispassionate.

Etruscan women may have been the first truly emancipated females in
early history. They routinely dined with their men (and guests), socialized
with their friends, moved about in public, and freely offered their opinions
(and sometimes their favors). On bronze sculpture and other art, married
couples are portrayed as gently caressing and touching the faces of their loved
ones. In addition, they appeared to be very caring mothers, judging by the
multiplicity of art objects depicted a mom tenderly breast-feeding her child.

The autonomy and freedom of movement of Etruscan women was
extraordinary; so was the local custom of giving and receiving hands-on
affection. It is hard to reconcile these beautifully depicted gestures of love
and affection with the hard reality of other Etruscan traditions—such
as gladiatorial matches, which originated in the funeral games held for
Etruscan nobles.

## PERPETUA, CHRISTIAN MARTYR:
### Blood lovingly shed

Once Rome's most feared enemy, the city of Carthage on the North African coast had a fighting force and a love of violence second to none. At length, the Roman army defeated these powerful Phoenicians. To make sure Carthage would never pose a problem again, in 146 B.C. they razed the city to the ground, salting the earth so that nothing would grow.

Three centuries later, however, Roman emperor Hadrian reconstituted the city, and by A.D. 200 Carthage was again a thriving metropolis. In addition, it became the setting for an unusual story of love, courage, and martyrdom.

As a youngster, Perpetua got a good education and a tender upbringing from her doting Carthaginian parents. They lived in swanky comfort, enjoying the amenities of a typical Roman city, as Carthage now was, and pledging allegiance to the emperor, as all citizens of the empire now did.

After Perpetua married, she became part of the young matrons' circle. Somewhere along the line, though, she fell in love with the Christian movement. Not only that, she persuaded her African servant Felicity to convert. Her husband and parents could have tolerated this aberration but for one thing: hard-core Christians refused to pay even lip service to the emperor. (Here's a prime example of how words change meaning over time: this refusal was labeled "atheism," which back then meant "denial of the [pagan] gods.")

At that time, Septimius Severus of Lepta Magna on the North African coast was emperor. Unlike some Caesars we could name, Severus wasn't a bad guy. He loved his wife Julia Domna and doted on his two sons, counting on them to follow him in office. Geta, the elder by one year, was his special pet.

As had earlier emperors, Severus worried about the growing Christian movement and the audacious behavior of some of its adherents. To quell it, in 202 he passed a law that forbid Christians to openly promote their faith.

By now Perpetua was a very vocal activist, proselytizing on the streets of Carthage. Conflict with the authorities was inevitable. When the twenty-two-year-old got arrested for religious agitation, she was a new mother, breast-feeding an infant. The authorities also arrested four male activists and Perpetua's maid, a now heavily pregnant Felicity.

A number of women became early Christian martyrs, but only Perpetua documented her ordeal. While imprisoned for eight months, she kept a diary; on her day of execution, she handed it off to a fellow Christian, who recorded the grisly details of Perpetua's martyrdom.

The original meaning of the word *martyr* is "witness," and that is what Perpetua and others like her set out to do: to suffer and possibly die rather than give up their faith. And to do it publicly, so that others would in turn be witnesses. Christian activists were routinely sentenced to be thrown to the wild beasts in the gladiatorial arena. Their willingness to undergo such torture showed the strength of their belief.

In the dank, overcrowded Carthage prison, Perpetua and her Christian companions received word of their sentence date. They were joyous but stressed out over Felicity, who would not be able to appear in public (and thus miss out on martyrdom) if she were still pregnant. After an intense group prayer session, Felicity finally went into labor and gave birth to a little girl in their cell, three days before their arena date.

On a clear March day, this small band of Christians marched into the amphitheatre of Carthage. All wore brave smiles, and Perpetua was singing. (Neither infant was present, having been taken in by relatives or friends.)

The true horribleness of death by wild beasts was that most carnivores will not attack humans on demand; thus the Romans resorted to starving and/or abusing the animals. At times, they simply trussed the human victim to the wild animal—itself a victim, since no animals ever left the arena alive.

First, several of the men in Perpetua's group were dispatched by a fierce leopard and an aggressive bear. But when Perpetua and new mother Felicity came into the center of the arena, members of the audience were sickened at the sight of milk leaking from the breasts of the lactating women, both of them naked. After the crowd protested, the two young mothers were taken out of the arena, given tunics to wear, and returned.

A wild heifer entered the arena, and tossed Perpetua into the air. She was unhurt. The heifer then attacked Felicity and knocked her savagely. More animals were released, but failed to kill the two women and one man remaining.

At length, all three were made to climb upon a platform where a gladiator waited to dispatch them. His sword missed with the first stroke; Perpetua cried out, then positioned his sword on her neck for the final blow.

She died with extraordinary courage, expressing her love for her god and her joy at going to meet other martyrs in heaven.

As this sanguinary event unfolded, the emperor who had set it in motion was busy celebrating. It was the fourteenth birthday of his well-loved son Geta. As was the custom, the executions of both the beasts and the martyrs represented a sacrifice, made on the boy's birthday, to

*A Roman citizen, Perpetua loved Christianity and longed for martyrdom. She left behind a journal documenting her activism and death in the gladiatorial arena of Carthage.*

ensure his health and prosperity. It was in vain. Emperor Severus would pass away in six years. And that same year, Geta would die at the hands of his own brother.

## OCTAVIA & MARK ANTONY:
### Mother love trumps the rest

What happens when the mother of the century meets the world most flagrant, testosterone-filled lover and fighter? If it's Rome in the first century B.C., they marry. But first, a little background.

Talk about male virility and fertility—over the course of fifty-six vigorous years, Mark Antony married (and/or formed serious relationships) with five women, several of them simultaneously. It couldn't have been easy to please them or maintain a regular visitation schedule, given the sailing times and road distances between Rome, Greece, and Egypt. Not one to shirk his responsibilities, multitasker Mark also conducted business on the move (he would have adored cell phones) and took care of his aged mother by dragging Mom along.

And these five simply represented his legal wives and key lovers! In his youth, Mark made love to a spectacular variety of ladies. One special squeeze was a singer-hoofer-mime-actress named Lycoris. With her, he traveled by litter throughout Italy, in a procession of wine-quaffing, music-playing disreputable characters carousing together.

To warm up nuptially, he wed a freedwoman named Fabia about whom little is known—solely a mention in Cicero's letters. Mark was also fooling around with Fulvia Flacca Bambula (yes, that really was her name), at that time married to a scandalous patrician named Clodius Pulcher.

At age thirty-nine, Mark Antony married his first cousin Antonia, which lasted just two years until he caught her in an affair with his best friend and kicked her out. They had a daughter together.

A year later, Mark entered into marriage number three with Fulvia, now widowed and a mother of three. Their blended family included four kids. Theirs was a tempestuous relationship; Fulvia possessed political moxie, sexual desire, and wealth in abundance; so did Mark, although he ran through his money much faster than she did. In short order, the couple produced two sons. After Caesar's assassination rocked Italy, Mark and Fulvia became even more powerful, thanks largely to the generous terms of Julius Caesar's will.

At the same time Queen Cleopatra VII, who'd been in Rome as a guest of Julius Caesar, was anxious to return home. Before she scuttled back to Egypt, however, Cleo decided to get into Mark's good graces by loaning him money. It was partly a bribe to shore up her position as queen of an independent Egypt, and partly because she thought it wise to bankroll one of the likeliest male contenders to rule Rome in the future.

Three years later, she and Mark Antony rendezvoused again, in Asia Minor, ostensibly to discuss the status of her land as a client state. Chemistry took over, and Mark became besotted with Cleopatra. He bedded her, the result of which was the birth of twins in due course.

Once Fulvia caught wind of all this, she exploded with anger. While she was frantically fighting a small war against Octavian on Mark's behalf, there he was, sleeping with some hussy! Irate, Fulvia died of an illness in May of 40 B.C., at which time Mark Antony and Octavian sat down to an informal bull session to see if they could come to terms before all-out war.

Mark ungallantly blamed the recent hostilities on his newly dead wife, but found it hard to brush away his sexual alliance with the queen of Egypt. (Secretly, Octavian was probably delighted, since most of Rome already hated Cleopatra, and she made a perfect pretext to go to war.)

Octavian himself had his own weighty family problems, which the ever-ready Mark agreed to solve. He had a sister, Octavia, who was moping around, newly widowed, heavily pregnant, and mourning her husband of fifteen years. The obliging Mark married Octavia in the fall of that same year. With her three children, the household now numbered at least nine youngsters from a variety of connubial events.

*Octavia, the emperor's sister, had five children and two husbands, the second being Mark Antony. After the Cleopatra debacle, this compassionate woman also adopted all of Mark's kids from prior marriages.*

Things went swimmingly for three years, at least from Octavia's point of view. She loved children, producing two more, and loved Mark, even though he was pushing fifty by now.

But Mark suffered from a chronic itch. And now only Cleopatra could scratch it. He began to commute to Egypt, resulting in another young'un on the way for Cleo— and demands from the Egyptian queen for a more permanent relationship.

After a hurtful divorce from Octavia in 36 B.C., Mark Antony settled in with his fifth wife (not recognized as such by the Romans, of course) in Egypt. Their fateful challenge to Rome met with failure and humiliating defeat in 31 B.C. The two lovers

(Mark aged fifty-six, Cleopatra at thirty-nine) committed suicide and were buried together.

In the aftermath of the Mark/Cleopatra suicides, in 30 B.C. Octavia showed her most compassionate side. Although her brother Octavian (now Rome's first emperor) fought her on this issue, Octavia stepped up to become the sole caretaker of her children with husbands one and two, plus all of Antony's children with Fulvia. Not only that, this deeply forgiving and maternal woman volunteered to become the guardian of the three surviving progeny of Mark and Cleopatra; toddler Ptolemy Philadelphus and the ten-year-old twins Cleopatra Selene and Alexander Helios.

Octavia took great care that all of her children, whether adoptive or blood kin, married well; they became the patrician backbone, an imperial dynasty of sorts, for the next generation of Julio-Claudians.

One standout was Cleopatra Selene, who blossomed under Octavia's care, growing up smart and emotionally stable. Her marriage to Juba II, king of Mauritania, was a long-lived success on both sides.

The greatest tragedy to befall maternal Octavia? The unexpected and sorely lamented death of her oldest son, Marcellus, at that time the golden boy and heir apparent to her brother, Octavian Augustus.

## VESTAL VIRGINS:
### Cut to the chaste

The vestal virgins of Rome, aged six to ten when they took on the thirty-year obligation of the position, were always very much in the public eye. They led ritual cleansings of the city, opened solemn ceremonies, and graced official state banquets and religious festivals. They had secular tasks, too. Their lives were neatly divided into thirds: the first decade, learning to be a vestal; the second, doing duties as one; the last, teaching newly selected young vestals.

Along with other secret sacred obligations, they had the crucial task of maintaining, night and day, the sacred fire of Vesta, the virginal patron goddess of Rome. Their priestess order might sound quaint to modern ears, but the morality and stability they represented were the lucky rabbit's foot of Rome, a city of a million people. As a result, they were well loved. During the thousand years in which their institution held sway, almost all the vestals led exemplary lives and did much for the city.

In several ways, being a vestal was a rare opportunity for a female, once mature, to use her intellect and make important decisions free of male interference. The post was in essence the best job a woman could hold in Roman times. And hold it they did, for an entire millennium.

Occia, for example, began as a youngster in 38 B.C., and worked as a Vestal for fifty-seven years, though she was only required to serve thirty. She won a reputation for her dedication, even during the civil war decades in Italy.

Another standout was Junia Torquata, who later became head of the order, a post called Virgo Maximo— Maximum Virgin. The vestals had powers that extended to special pleadings to the Roman senate and emperor. They also had the power to intercede and extend mercy to any condemned person who happened to cross their path. During Junia's tenure, she had ample opportunity

*The vestal virgins were Rome's lucky rabbit's foot, guarding the safety and moral stability of the city through their sacred duties and their own exemplary behavior.*

to test her powers, since two of her brothers got into trouble with the law. One, accused of extortion and treason, got exiled to a crummy uninhabited island off Italy. After she pled his case to Emperor Tiberius, he wasn't freed—but was upgraded to a nicer island. Her other brother had gotten himself into really hot water; his crime was adultery with Julia, the sexually voracious granddaughter of Emperor Octavian Augustus, no less. He quickly fled into voluntary exile, but it took fourteen years and all of Junia's persuasive abilities with the emperor to get her brother back to Rome. She was an old woman by that time, having served the goddess Vesta for sixty-four years.

Not only did the vestal virgins have the respect of society, political influence, and independence from male guardians, they also gained financial independence when they retired. The parents of new vestals had to hand over dowries when they were accepted, just as though they were getting married. After thirty years of service, a vestal could retire with a generous pension. (Or she could, as many did, remain in vestal quarters, semiretired for the balance of her life.) The record shows that a vestal named Cornelia did extremely well in the investment department. When she took her post in A.D. 23, she received a dowry of two million sesterces. When she retired, still fairly young, it was as a very wealthy woman.

## IMPERIAL BRANDING:
### Gotta love that emperor—he's everywhere

So much ink (to say nothing of blood) has already been spilled over Octavian Augustus, Rome's first real emperor-CEO, there would seem to be little left to say. But this young man—a general at eighteen, and Rome's leader and "restorer of the republic" at nineteen—was astute at more than war and politics. He foresaw the power of imperial branding and even the value of mass production, ideas that seem far-fetched and too "modern" for the first century B.C.

In 44 B.C., a short time after the assassination of Julius Caesar, Octavian's adoptive father, a huge comet appeared over Rome. Priests immediately identified it as Caesar's soul in heaven, and called it *sidus Iulium*, "the Julian star."

About eighteen months later, with the full consent of the Roman senate and the people of Rome, Octavian put on a solemn and extravagant apotheosis for Caesar, officially making him a god—*divus Iulius*. Octavian's next brilliant move? On the very site of Caesar's cremation, he dedicated a temple to Julius the god. As a result, he was then able to call himself *divi filius*, "son of the god." What cunning modesty! And what a lineage to point to.

When Octavian defeated Antony and Cleopatra in 31 B.C., and now in sole command, he began his diplomatic, low-key transformation of Rome's "republic." Instead of calling himself a dictator and/or imperator (as his adoptive father Julius Caesar had done), he insisted on being called *princeps*, a vague and soothing term meaning "first man" or "leading man."

After the bloody decades of power struggles following Caesar's assassination, Octavian wanted a return to law and a senatorial framework in which to exert his influence. Accordingly, he made the big decisions but almost humbly presented them to the Roman senate for their approval. That adoring body soon voted him a new title: Augustus, the majestic, awe-inspiring one. (Well-behaved empresses would later get to be called Augusta.)

In other parts of the Roman Empire, in places where kings traditionally had been given godlike attributes, people clamored to deify the man who still refused to call himself emperor. Although Octavian and his wife and political adviser Livia publicly protested and stoutly refused all efforts to deify them, little by little they allowed provinces from Greece to Asia Minor to have their fun and hold apotheosis ceremonies.

This fit in quite well with Octavian's long-term plans for an imperial brand, one that extended to his entire family. He wanted all of them to become well-loved; adored. In an age without printing presses, photography, or photocopy capabilities, he engineered various ways to replicate, replicate, replicate his image and theirs.

Coins bearing Octavian's name and face were the perfect propaganda tool. During his forty-one-year tenure, tens of millions of coins with his portrait were issued. Not simply in Rome, either, but from a variety of mints established throughout the growing empire. Each new batch told another story: of Rome rebuilt in marble; of new lands conquered; of army veterans given land, and the hungry fed. All of his good deeds and qualities were immortalized on coinage, the most important advertising medium of his day.

Some might argue that an even more ingenious marketing plan fed Octavian's imperial love cult. During his long lifetime, more than 20,000 bronze statues of "the son of god" poured out of workshops around the empire. In addition, there were cheap plaster casts as well as larger-than-life-size marble statues of Augustus in heroic poses.

The creation of elegant yet visually accurate images in such huge numbers was a difficult trick. How was it solved?

*During his forty-one-year reign, Emperor Octavian Augustus distributed thousands of his statues and millions of his coinage portraits throughout his far-flung empire.*

Art historians and archaeologists knew it must have been done via mass production techniques that maintained the quality and standardized the likeness of the originals. They finally solved the mystery when some unfinished marble statues turned up. On the heads of each piece, they found twenty-four or more wart-like protuberances. After consultations with working sculptors, they realized these were *puntelli* or checkpoints. Using calipers and the puntelli, a sculptor two thousand years ago could achieve startling accuracy in the copying of an original bust or statue.

Thus statues, busts, and other imagery of Emperor Octavian Augustus remained uniform and readily identifiable throughout the empire. Art featuring Augustus and his family members was everywhere—near theaters, in the forum of each town and city, and, as the years went by, in growing numbers of temples where the cult of imperial worship was held. The busts and statues were also a fixture in every one of the Roman army camps, where legionaries could daily behold their commander-in-chief even while on bivouac or at war.

Besides his other astonishing accomplishments, Octavian knew how to play the unassuming man of the people while imposing his brand on the marketplace. Becoming the literal love object for millions of people may have contributed to his long and largely peaceful reign. He certainly kick-started the cult of emperor worship, which after Augustus grew to obscene levels. It served a good purpose, however. Perhaps the Romans, always happy to add to the plethora of gods and goddesses, also needed a flesh-and-blood figure to admire, love, and lean on as their godlike protector.

*Even without photography, Rome's first emperor made his face instantly recognizable. How? Clever mass production of his image.*

## DIVAS LIVIA & THE JULIAS:
### Not easy, becoming a goddess

There's a modern trend regarding popular female singers. Even if they aren't opera stars, the ones who feel the love of millions are often called divas. An Italian term meaning "prima donna" (literally, first or lead singer), diva is closely related to the words divine and divinity.

Several thousand years, however, if you wanted to become a real diva—a goddess worshipped and loved by everyone—you generally had to be dead. Still worth it, most gals would argue, as the apotheosis of a woman did not happen all that often.

In the first century B.C., one extraordinary woman, queenly in manner, razor-sharp in intellect, and expert in manipulation, managed to gain apotheosis—goddesshood—in her lifetime. Her name? Livia. Like many modern celebrities, she was known by one name. She was the wife of Rome's first emperor, Octavian Augustus, and saw him out of his long life.

One especially memorable scene in the classic *I, Claudius* series on BBC television years ago featured Roman empress Livia as an old woman, pleading with her slimy young grandson Caligula, "I want to be a goddess—promise me that when I die, you'll make me a goddess!"

Caligula responded as you might expect, with spite: "You're a disgusting, smelly, wicked harridan! Why would I do that? You murderous old bag, you belong with Hades!"

In spite of Caligula's scoffing, Livia got her wish. And she didn't have to die to get it. She had the most splendid luck; by A.D. 14, she'd become a goddess with cults in cities around the empire: on Lesbos, on the island of Cyprus, in the city of Pergamum in Asia Minor, even in Athens. Not only was she worshipped there, coins were issued from various mints with the words *Thea Livia*—Goddess Livia—on them, with her profile. What could be more heavenly? When she died a decade later, in A.D. 29, she also received apotheosis from Emperor Claudius and the Roman senate. Modern diva-hood just can't measure up to that.

Livia was the first but not the last lady of Rome to be deified.

When Julia Drusilla, the favorite sister of Caligula, died at age twenty-two, he deified her, adding *panthea*, or "all goddess," to her title, and mourning in highly dramatic fashion. Was it love? Or guilt? Probably both, since Caligula was thought to have molested all three of his sisters from childhood.

Another Julia, this one a Flavia, the daughter of Emperor Titus, was married to one man and ostentatiously sleeping with another—that sick puppy known as Emperor Domitian. Julia, dead at twenty-three, may have expired from an abortion forced on her by the emperor. Domitian had her deified; later, for his treatment of Julia and other crimes and cruelties, he was murdered.

The wildest quartet of diva-loving Julias hailed from Roman Syria. After they hit Rome around 218 A.D., the city was never the same. Julia Domna and Julia Maesa were sisters from a family of wealth and importance in Syria; the former married Septimius Severus and became empress. When Julia Domna's "bad apple" son Caracalla murdered the other apple, lovable son Geta—in her arms, no less—Julia had to suck it up. To survive, she became co-regent and handled Caracalla's paperwork, including all that hate mail about brotherly slaughter. When he in turn was assassinated while taking off his pants, she took it hard—following him in death within a few weeks.

Her sister Julia Maesa had grand plans to restore the luster of the dynasty—and who better to do it than her darling fourteen-year-old grandson Elagabalus? After paying a grotesque sum to bribe the Roman legions, she and her daughters, Julia Soaemias and Julia Mamaea, left Syria and headed for Rome with the teen in tow. At first he was no trouble, too busy with his flowery gowns and his jeweled shoes and touching up his eyepaint. They entered Rome to cheering crowds that soon were scratching their heads at this goofy kid, running in front of a four-horse chariot pulling a large black stone, symbol of the Syrian sun god.

Soaemias, his mother, soon tired of her son's bizarre activities: getting up at dawn to sacrifice a herd of cattle to the sun god. His insistence on marrying one of the vestal virgins—what a stink that raised! His nightly outings, too, sometimes in drag, sometimes playing a whore. She and her mom Julia Maesa tried to reason with him, but it was hopeless. She never knew if he was dating a girl or a fellow or an orangutan, for that matter. Once Elagabalus fell for a Carian slave and played the female—even encouraged the fellow to abuse him physically.

Luckily, Julian Soaemias and her mom had gotten some nice honors in Rome; they were given honorific Augusta titles. They even got invited to attend meetings of the Roman senate. Until they'd sat in the Senate once, they didn't realize how dull this governing business was. Just for giggles, she and her mom put together a Senate of Women, but stuffy Romans looked cross-eyed at it as well.

Before long Romans from senators to plebeians were completely steamed at the antics, sexual and otherwise, of the teenage Elagabalus. The Julias, mother and daughter, agreed he was troubled, but they were sure he'd grow out of it. Just in case, they

*During his reign as emperor, this transvestite teen demanded sexual reassignment surgery. Unfortunately his medicos lacked vagina-building skills.*

forced Elagabalus to "adopt" his twelve-year-old cousin, Severus Alexander, and name him the heir.

A good thing too, because within two years Elagabalus and his mother Julia Soaemias were brutally rubbed out by irate Roman soldiers. Young Alexander, with his mother Julia Mamaea and his grandmother Julia Maesa as co-regents, wasn't nearly as outrageous as the late unlamented Julia Soaemias and her son. Romans breathed a grateful collective sigh of relief. Thus in A.D. 223, when Maesa the matriarch died, she was given diva goddess status. She joined her older sister Julia Domna, who'd been made a goddess by Elagabalus—the one almost normal "deed" he'd accomplished in his short reign.

Now the last Julia standing, Julia Mamaea set out to restore order and moderation to the regime. Since acting as regent for young Severus Alexander took no time at all, she had ample opportunity to dream up and then assume the most grandiose titles ever given to a Roman woman. She began with "mother of the emperor, the army, the senate, and the homeland" but finally settled on the pithy and less cumbersome "mother of the whole human race." (It sounds even better in Latin: *mater universi generic humani*.)

Keeping in mind the fates of her Julia kinfolk, Mamaea picked some wise advisers, amassed an indecent amount of wealth, kept a tight leash on son Alexander's sex life, and—wisest move of all—without fanfare of any sort, sent Elagabalus's detested sungod and his shiny black stone back to Syria. Nevertheless, she and son Alexander were not fated to live long and prosper; assassination by soldiers also awaited them in 235.

# ANIMAL WORSHIP:
## Fishy love stories & feline tales

We live in a pet-worshipping, animal-venerating world, from the astonishing amount of supermarket square footage devoted to dog and cat food to television programs extolling the high-priced wisdom of horse and parakeet whisperers. We support environmental causes to save whales and songbirds. We even have a national bird that we've managed not to extirpate.

But we weren't the first when it came to serious animal adoration.

Take the she-wolf of Rome, legendary mother of the city who suckled those crazy human twins, Remus and Romulus. Early in Rome's history, she was immortalized in bronze by an Etruscan master sculptor. A symbol of fierceness and intelligence, the wolf was also sacred to Mars, Apollo, and Silvanus and worshipped accordingly. The Lupercalia festival, described elsewhere in this book, had the wolf as its totem. In the Roman army, special troops called *signifers* wore wolf's heads and pelts as part of their uniform while carrying the battle standards of the legion.

Although lizards, parrots, snakes, and tropical fish have their ardent followers today, few modern pet lovers share the Roman fetish for large eels of the lamprey and murena species. Although some were kept for consumption (eel flesh being high-status gourmet seafood), many were treated like members of the family. Living in elaborate man-made ponds along the Bay of Naples, feeding on delicacies and at times wearing gold jewelry, such eels were unlikely love objects. When his lamprey died, a Roman senator named Lucius Crassus wasted

*Ancient Greeks favored pet dogs;*
*Romans fawned over giant eels; and*
*Egyptians went mad over kitties.*
*Their cat worship cult had countless*
*followers humble and highborn.*

no time in putting on full mourning. As one writer put it, "He grieved for it as though for a daughter."

Among the Romans and the Greeks, dogs large and small were bred for hunting and guarding livestock, especially Cretan hounds, Laconian sheepdogs, and the Umbrian and Etruscan breeds. Folks also cherished small lapdogs as pets. A favorite breed was the long-haired silky Maltese; Emperor Claudius had one. Canine pets got pampered, and when they died they were buried with care, often memorialized with poignant, poetry-filled headstones.

The pussycat, however, never made the Greco-Roman list of popular domestic animals. Thus when Greek and Roman writer-historians such as Herodotus and Diodorus of Sicily visited Egypt on different occasions, they were flabbergasted to discover the idolization of felines.

Pharoahs and royals weren't the only one to worship cats. In humbler households, cat owners would shave off their eyebrows in mourning after the death of the family tabby. The cat goddess Bumastis or Pasht represented a major cult, with numerous temples and countless worshippers. Archaeologists have found whole cemeteries filled with feline mummies, nicely embalmed in cedar oil and wrapped in linen.

From time to time in our era, hard-core kitty fans and saviors of strays make the headlines, but it would be hard to top the passion the Egyptians felt for their felines. About halfway through the first century B.C., a Roman diplomat, newly stationed in Alexandria, Egypt, accidentally killed a cat. At that sensitive time, Egyptian top officials were trying to placate the Romans in order to prevent a war. Despite their best efforts to calm the public, a mob of outraged Alexandrians made mincemeat of the unfortunate man.

## CETACEAN ADORATION:
### Nearly divine dolphin rescues

The Greeks (and to a lesser extent, the Romans) were as soppily enamored with the cutest member of the cetacean family as any Flipper fan today. The literature of writers from Aulus Gellius to Oppian is crammed with "awwww" stories about dolphins scooping up drowning humans and long-term relationships between boys and greathearted cetaceans.

The Greeks were seagoing folks, and, like all ancient sailors, superstitious. Ever since early Minoan times on the big island of Crete, dolphins had pride of place in Greek mythology and art, and were often associated with the wine god Dionysus.

One of the myths relates the story of Dionysus, who boarded a pirate ship while traveling in human disguise. The crew, hard up for drinking money, decided to sell what appeared to be an ordinary fellow into slavery rather than deliver him to his destination. Getting wind of the plot, the wine god drove the sailors insane by giving them hallucinations. They jumped into the sea and were drowning when Dionysus called out, "Do you repent your evil plan?"

When they screamed, "Yes!" the deity turned them into dolphins.

This myth and many others kept Greeks from harming dolphins, believing that these social animals that tenderly care for their young were once human (even if some of them were formerly bad guys and pirates). To

*The ancient world adored dolphins, considering them true protectors of humans. Legends of their rescues and friendliness filled the pages of Greek and Roman writers.*

kill a dolphin was considered a serious crime in ancient Greece.

Another great story involved Arion, a famous singer and lyre player from Corinth, Greece. When he was on his way home from a lucrative concert tour of Italy, his boat crew turned traitorous, demanding all his money before they put out his lights. To buy a little time, Arion asked if he might sing one last song, and the crew—being big music fans and not all bad—said yes.

The musician carefully dressed himself in his performance robes, then began to sing the lovely ode to the Pythian Apollo. The musical piece he chose was a lengthy sucker, and the crew grew restive. When Arion saw them pull their knives, he jumped into the sea.

As he sank, he was swept up and borne above the waves by a school of dolphins that had enjoyed his performance even more than the boat crew. Greeks also believed that dolphins were charmed by human singing. Swimming well into the starry night, the brainy cetaceans gently carried him to the shore, where some amazed humans witnessed the dolphins encircling Arion for a group hug. As they left, the dolphins frolicked near the promontory, leaping a joyous farewell.

Soon Arion hotfooted it back to Corinth to tattle on the mutinous crew. When the boat crew finally arrived, they got what they richly deserved from Periander, the testy tyrant of Corinth.

Dolphin legend-spinning grew in several directions. The marine mammal was believed to guide human souls to the Isles of the Blessed—or to the underworld, if that was your final destination. Folks were convinced that dolphins, also long thought to be friendly and helpful to humans, had a sense of honor. Borrowing a page from such mythologizing, the early Christian church boasted nearly half a dozen saints who claimed to have been rescued by dolphins.

Plutarch, Greek historian and author, once wrote something that reveals how deeply the Greeks felt about these animals. "To the dolphin alone, beyond all others, nature has given what the best philosophers seek: friendship for no advantage. Though it has no need of man, yet it is a friend to all men and has given them great aid."

## HYPATIA OF ALEXANDRIA:
### Taught the truth, loved it to death

There aren't very many sixteen-hundred-year-old fan letters still in existence, much less ones from grateful students of esoteric philosophy to a female teacher.

The recipient in this case? The exceptional Hypatia, daughter of Theon, thinker and teacher par excellence. Although misconceptions muddle her story, and some accounts of her are romanticized, substantial evidence of her genuine life and works remains, beginning with her fan mail.

Born around A.D. 355 in Alexandria, Egypt, Hypatia was the apple of her father's eye, and his intellectual protégé as well. As a leading professor at the Great Museum and Library of Alexandria, Theon taught his classes—and his daughter—a wide range of subjects, from the latest advances in astronomy to the deepest investigations into Greek philosophy, including Neoplatonism.

The words "museum and library" don't fully describe the place where Theon taught and Hypatia learned, and later lectured professionally. Funded by generations of Ptolemies—the Macedonian leaders who ran Egypt from Alexander the Great's demise through the Cleopatra VII period—the edifice and its resources comprised the first university of higher learning as well as the world's biggest library of the time. Besides the schools of specific inquiry within the museum, this well-endowed entity also offered residential facilities for visiting scholars and scientists, enabling them to do fruitful long-term research.

In this milieu, alternatively pushed and encouraged by her parent mentor, Hypatia grew to maturity. Early on, she came to realize that the demands of a wife and mother would sorely inhibit the life of a scholar, and she chose celibacy. Later on, her status as an independent woman in an Alexandria roiling with religious and political controversy would have big implications.

But in the beginning, Hypatia saw knowledge as her personal playground. Her thirst for deeper meanings found in logic, mathematics, astronomy, and other sciences soon outstripped her father's ability to teach her. Although numerous works are often attributed to Hypatia alone, it seems likely that she and her father collaborated on such projects as editing Ptolemy's *Almagest* and writing learned commentaries on the Conics of Apollonius and the thirteen-volume *Arithmetica* by Diophantus. She also chalked up credits for editing her father's commentary of Euclid's *Elements*. A whiz at charting celestial bodies, she wrote an astronomical canon, the text of which may have been a new edition of Ptolemy's *Handy Tables*.

She is also credited with perfecting the prototypes of the astrolabe and the hydrometer, which is used to determine specific gravity of liquids.

But these achievements pale when compared to her value as a teacher. From Theon, she'd learned the secrets of clarity as an orator and lecturer. Students loved her lectures, and as she took a more prominent role at the museum, she gained an enthusiastic following. Hypatia herself was neither a Christian nor a practicing pagan; her students, however, came from all walks of life. They were Christians, future converts, pagan sympathizers, and still others, like their teacher, who "declined to state."

Her fan mail illuminates those inspired by her lucid insights and mode of teaching. One longtime student, Socrates Scholasticus, counted her as a dear friend as well as teacher. In one of his seven extant letters, he writes, "Your student feels the presence of your divine spirit." At times, his letters were simply addressed to "Hypatia, the philosopher." Synesius, another disciple who became a bishop, corresponded with her throughout his life. His collection of 156 letters, to Hypatia and to other members of their philosophical circle survived, along with other writings that include mention of her.

A third extant source is her student Damascius, who recounted this telling story about her. Hypatia always wore the classic long robes of a male scholar. Nevertheless, it was inevitable that male students would fall in love with her, and when a certain student dared to declare his adoration, Hypatia did not respond. Later, in front of the other students, she presented him with a wrapped gift. In it—to his shocked embarrassment—were bloody towels from her menstrual period. "This is what you really love, my young man, but you do not love beauty for its own sake." Carnality had no place in her life.

That student was not one of her inner circle, Hypatia's group of about six that began to coalesce when she was in her mid-twenties. This tightly knit group resembled that of Alexander the Great and

*A celebrity in Alexandria, Hypatia taught philosophy and science to devoted students from pagans to Christian bishops. Her forthright love of the truth made her the target of extremists in later life.*

his inner circle, who called each other *hetairoi*, "companions." Hypatia's circle, however, focused on wisdom and the philosophical life—and only to them did she impart the inner mysteries of such a discipline.

What she had to offer was more than knowledge. With her sexual abstinence, her levelheaded courage, and her love of the unvarnished truth, Hypatia represented moral authority. She lived by the sage advice inscribed at the oracle of Delphi: Nothing in excess, everything in moderation.

As time went on, unfortunately, the religious groups in Alexandria became more strident, more extreme. When Hypatia reached her fifties, the adolescent Christian faith had splintered into various rabid factions. She neither backed nor opposed any of them. City officials, such as Orestes, the governor of Alexandria, and Cyril, the top religious official, quarreled bitterly. Periodically torn by riots, the whole city polarized, developing a "which side are you on" mentality.

Hypatia continued her normal life—teaching, driving her chariot, making her opinions known, being a friend to Orestes, and backing him politically. Meanwhile, Cyril inflamed his followers by insisting that Hypatia taught "sorcery," claiming that she "beguiled many people through her satanic wiles." This female philosopher made a point of being prudent and discreet—qualities that the Greeks called *sophrosyne*. Nevertheless, as an independent women, a non-Christian, and an intellectual, she made a tempting target.

In March of A.D. 415, this sixtyish, still vigorous woman was attacked by a mob of black-robed *parabalani* while driving her chariot. Often described as monks, most *parabalani* were male fanatics who acted as a quasi-military strike force for Cyril. They dragged her from her vehicle into the church that had once been the Serapeum, the temple of Serapis. Stripping her naked, they tore Hypatia to pieces, at length quartering and burning what remained of her ruined body in a place called Kinaron.

There was no criminal investigation, no trial, and no blame assessed, although Cyril, who would become a bishop in the aftermath, clearly had a hand in her assassination. The companions in Hypatia's inner circle spoke out; some wrote accounts, still around today, describing the savagery that took the life of Hypatia, philosopher and lover of truth.

# Demon Lovers &
# Gods Dark & Light

# THE GREAT GOD PAN:
## Not dead, just poorly translated

A homely, squatty, horned god who never made the Olympic deity lineup, Pan is often confused with Greek satyrs and fauns—when not being accused of being the devil. (For the latter label, you can thank later Christians, who transformed Pan into the Satan familiar to modern eyes.)

Without a doubt, Pan was a hybrid. Besides ram's horns and bad hair, he boasted the hindquarters and cloven hooves of a goat. He's gotten an even more rancid reputation in today's world. That's what comes from being caught in mid-coitus with a large male goat—and then having your private bestiality interlude captured as an X-rated marble sculpture that tourists giggle over at the National Archaeological Museum in Naples. When that sculpture went on exhibit in 2001, an Italian priest called it a temptation that could "corrupt the morals of the chastest." It was almost as bad as being immortalized on YouTube.

Anthropologists now believe that Pan, a fertility deity, god of spring festivals, and rustic lord of the wilderness, was far more ancient than the Olympian gods. In Greece, Pan called Arcadia home, where he was worshipped in caves and grottoes by mountain people and shepherds.

Even though he invented a flute and played a mean panpipe, Pan's brutish looks and behavior never played well with the ladies. He did manage to seduce the moon goddess Selene once by wrapping himself in a sheepskin, but had an unsavory way of turning nymphs and other chicks he fancied into trees or tearing them into little bits. Pan's habit of uncouth yelling and making other eerie sound effects often caused fear among humans—a reaction still called "panic" in remembrance of the god.

Unlike other deities, who by definition are immortal, Pan was believed to have died. As written up by Greek historian Plutarch, Pan's alleged death occurred in the reign of Roman Emperor Tiberius (A.D. 14–37). As the story goes, an Egyptian sailor named Thamus was en route to Italy when a voice described as "divine" hailed the sailor across the water, saying, "The Great God Pan is dead!"

When Christianity got rolling, the faith's spokespeople were delighted to pass this tale along, since it seemed to sound the death knell of paganism and the coming of the new order. Eusebius of Caesarea was the first Christian writer to relate the anecdote, adding juicy details of his own devising.

Interestingly enough, subsequent study of Pan's death by author and mythology expert Robert Graves and newer genera-tions of mythologists has revealed a "lost in transla-tion" aspect to the whole matter. *Thamus Panmegas tethneke*, "The all-great Tammuz is dead!" sounds a great deal like *Thamous Pan ho megas techneke*, "Thamus, Great Pan is dead!"

So who or what was Tammuz, as opposed to Thamus the sailor? Known as a shepherd god as early as 2500 B.C. by the ancient Sumerians, he was the con-sort of Inanna or Ishtar, goddess of love. The myth of Tammuz and Inanna has him going through a life-death-rebirth cycle to save his lover each year. When Tammuz goes to spend six months in the underworld, he is deeply mourned by his worshippers, especially the women. The Old Testament Ezekiel also mentions the women weeping for Tammuz.

*The goat-human hybrid called Pan cavorted with his own fan club of fauns and satyrs but was a fertility deity in his own right.*

A century after Plutarch wrote of Pan's putative death, an early travel writer named Pausanias visited a great many sites around Greece where shrines to the Great God Pan were still drawing crowds. As Mark Twain would say centuries later, "The reports of my death have been greatly exaggerated."

## SATYR PLAYS:
### Satyrists made Athens laugh

When the Greek playwrights of the classical age—Aeschylus, Sophocles, Euripides, and others we know less about—competed in the annual drama contests in Athens, they were required to write a cycle of three tragedies, plus a shorter piece called a satyr play.

Most of us got a somewhat dreary dose of Greek tragedy in high school, but little was ever said about satyr plays. What a pity. As it happens, this form was a playful invention dating back to the sixth century B.C. and brought to Athens by a writer named Pratinas. In his homeland of Phlius, they were very big on the *dithyramb*, a wild poetic hymn to the wine god Dionysus that included a chorus filled with satyrs. Pratinas felt that the cheeky jokes, obscene gestures, and slapstick provided by the irrepressible satyrs would provide a lighthearted balance to the tragic drama that had been developed by Thespis in Athens.

Athenian audiences had a lot of stamina. They needed it. At their annual dramatic competitions during the Dionysia and Lenaia festivals, playgoers sat on the stone seats for hours. And hours. And hours, thrilling (and perhaps dozing off) to the tragedies of Aeschylus, Sophocles, and Euripides.

The plays took place during the day, not at night. The broiling hot sunny days of Athens.

What probably helped keep Greek audiences awake and in their seats for the long haul was the clever introduction of satyr plays. These pieces, half the length of a tragedy and a mix of sight gags, slapstick, drunken protagonists, and coarse merriment, were also dramas of a sort. The main setting and the theme of the play came from an epic or a myth, and the actors wore serious costumes and spoke dignified lines.

*Greek drama got a lighthearted break in the sixth century B.C., when an interval called the satyr play was introduced. The satyrs did song and dance numbers wearing hairy shorts and perky leather phalluses.*

The uproarious counterpoint was provided by the chorus, made up of twelve to fifteen men dressed as satyrs, wearing scary, hairy masks and animal skins over their naked bodies. Fore and aft, they wore perky, over-size leather phalluses and horsetails attached to a hairy pair of shorts. Throughout the play, they sang and danced, a saucy, bouncy, show-stealing hip-hop number called the *sicinnis*.

In Sparta and other Doric city-states, satyrs were half men, half goats, wearing goat horns. Later satyrs followed the Ionian mythical tradition, being horse deities. Both types were traditional companions of the god Dionysus.

Once Athenian playwrights got accustomed to the addition of the satyr play, they plunged into the spirit of the thing. A full satyr play by Euripides, called *Cyclops*, survives, and pieces of others do too, including Sophocles' *Tracing Satyrs*. The material could get quite blue at times, although maybe the earthy Greek audiences, male and female, didn't see it that way. Aeschylus, who helped develop and "refine" the satyr play, wrote one in which the action includes a curious or confused baby Perseus who masturbates the male organ of a satyr.

With their prominent phallic component and their musicality, the satyr plays underlined the fact that they were celebrations of the god of wine and excess, Dionysus. As companions to the tragedies, the satyr plays furnished comic relief, a jolt of surprise and mirth to the gloomy, fateful dramas—and some terrific, toe-tapping, carthartic laughs besides.

## VESTAL VIRGINS:
### Scapegoats in dire straits

During its thousand-year run, ancient Rome had more than a few imperfect rulers, to say nothing of deranged, despotic, and deeply disturbed ones. The city also suffered ghastly defeats in war. But over that millennium, the city was kept from harm spiritually by the offices of the six vestal virgins and their devotion to Vesta, the patron of the city—or so most Romans ardently believed. There were a few tragic incidents, however.

One occurred in 216 B.C., when the huge Roman army was badly defeated at Cannae by Carthaginian general Hannibal. Rome's citizenry was in a state of panic, and its leaders resorted to scapegoating. Who better to blame for Rome's ills than girls whose chastity must have been compromised? Vestals Opimia and Floronia were accused of licentious behavior and buried alive, while Floronia's accused lover was clubbed to death. Were they innocent or guilty? Historian Livy claimed they'd been unchaste, but he lived two centuries after they did.

Another instance of scapegoating and human sacrifice happened just two years later, when Rome suffered another agonizing defeat. This time, because of testimony from a slave, three vestals were put on trial for illicit behavior. All three lost their lives.

At least a few vestal virgins seemed to have been framed for political reasons. The reign of Emperor Domitian, whose iron-fisted rule and bizarre personal behavior was the stuff of legend, provided several infamous examples. In

*Although Rome's vestals protected the city for a millennium through their chastity, accidents did happen. A few vestals broke their vows; others were scapegoated or molested by unscrupulous emperors.*

A.D. 83, three vestals were charged with *incestum*, which in Latin specifically meant "an act that violated religious purity." Instead of being buried alive, the usual punishment, the trio were forced to commit suicide, while their supposed lovers merely got sent into exile.

The years A.D. 213 through 220 were again dire for the current crop of vestal virgins, largely due to two rotten emperors: Caracalla and Elagabalus. Caracalla wreaked havoc on Roman peace of mind by accusing four young vestals of sexual misconduct—a charge no one dared to challenge, given the emperor's vicious temper. The accused vociferously protested but got nowhere. Convicted vestals Aurelia Severa, Clodia Laeta, and Pomponia Rufina were buried alive, while Cannutia Crescentina managed to commit suicide before that happened by leaping from the roof of her family's house. A few years later, to general rejoicing, Emperor Caracalla was dispatched by his mistresses and a gladiator.

Rome got a brief respite until a flamboyant, cross-dressing young teen named Elagabalus became Rome's new emperor. In A.D. 219 he chose a vestal by the name of Julia Aquilia Severa to be his new bride, so that, as he boasted, "Godlike children could be produced from the two of us." The longsuffering Aquilia put up with Elagabalus for several years, during which time the polysexual teenage emperor carried on various affairs with men and women.

She wasn't the only vestal virgin to be molested by a Roman emperor, sad to say. About two centuries later, among his many infamies, Nero brutally assaulted a vestal named Rubria, a crime hastily covered up by imperial family members.

# NYMPHOMANIA & SATYRIASIS:
## Uterine fury & sex addiction

You may be relieved (or perhaps disappointed) to learn that nymphomaniacs never roamed the streets of ancient Athens or Corinth or anywhere in long-ago Greece. The term was coined about two hundred years ago, when a French doctor named Bienville tried to describe female hypersexuality. The word *mania* originally came from the Greek for fury or frenzy; and *nymph* could refer to maidens, brides, and/or junior-grade nature goddesses.

Galen, a hyperactive doctor and author of the second century A.D., did discuss the nymphomania affliction in one of his million-word write-ups. He just knew that women, especially young widows, had an insatiable desire for semen, and that lack of it would lead to madness. Or, at the very least, what he dubbed uterine fury, or *furor uterinus*. (It sounds more dignified in Latin.)

The cause of their female fury? According to Galen, a big believer in balancing the four bodily humours, and several other medical writers of ancient times, the humours of women's bodies were cool and wet. Therefore, sexually mature gals needed intercourse and lots of it to heat the blood and open their wombs. If thwarted, wombs back then had a tendency to create havoc by wandering around inside the body. (Elsewhere in this book you can read more astounding medical beliefs about these womb wanderers.)

The whole matter might sound laughable nowadays; nevertheless, ladies in prior centuries who exhibited forthright sexuality often got labeled as "abnormal." From there, they might find themselves locked into asylums, cast out as witches or prostitutes, or on the operating table, getting an unwanted surgical makeover of their sex organs.

As late as 1951 the American Psychiatric Association's official guide to madness, the *Diagnostic and Statistical Manual of Mental Disorders* (DSM), listed nymphomania as a "sexual deviation," years later modifying it to "psychosexual disorder." Thankfully, by 1994 it had dropped the whole specious label of sexual addiction. The term, however, is still a breathless byword and a frequent topic on daytime TV.

In today's world, the male equivalent of nymphomania, called satyriasis, garners sympathy and smirks in equal measure—along with book contracts. There appears to be quite a cottage industry standing by to attend to today's male sufferers of satyriasis, mostly referred to as sex addiction these days. Not so in ancient times; you'd be hard pressed to find a human male who would admit to it.

The term comes from the Greek word *satyr*, referring to a lustful woodland sprite, half human and half animal (usually goat), who was a raucous drunken follower of the wine god Dionysus. Satyrs had ugly faces, smelly, hairy bodies, and coarse genitals that were considered grotesquely large. Satyrs almost never got the girl, although they constantly chased women, goddesses, and animals and raped them when they could. They were often the sidekicks of Pan, the ancient goat god, who had similar problems getting dates.

This might sound naive, but Greek and Roman men had so many sexual outlets to meet their needs that it's hard to imagine they were ever sexually frustrated enough to behave like satyrs.

# NERO'S CAREER DEFILEMENT:
## Penetrating news update

Emperor Nero, who reigned (if you can call it that) from A.D. 54 until his suicide in 68, committed a shocking number of crimes, from matricide to fiery persecution of Christian scapegoats. These acts appalled and frightened his subjects.

But they paled next to his sex life. Addicted to perverse acts, terrified of becoming bored, given full rein by his imperial status, Nero pursued fetishes with single-minded gusto.

None of it was kept secret. But what most shocked everyone was his frank admission that he enjoyed being penetrated as well as doing the penetrating. For elite Roman and Greek males, this was a staggering message. To some, it indicated that the emperor was not a regular male at all but what the Romans called a *cinaedus*, an effeminate man who invited anal sex. The Greek and Latin languages had nearly a dozen synonyms for *cinaedus*, all of them abusive.

Today we might be more repelled by Nero's other proclivities, including a form of bestiality. Writing six decades after Nero's death, biographer Suetonius described his sexual hungers in this fashion: "He so prostituted his own chastity that after defiling almost every part of his body, he at last devised a kind of game, in which, covered with the skin of some wild animal, Nero was let loose from a cage. He then attacked the private parts of men and women, who were bound to stakes and when he had sated his mad lust, he was dispatched [i.e., given sexual release by anal penetration] by his freedman Doryphorus. For he was even married to this man in the same way he himself had married Sporus, going so far as to imitate the cries and lamentations of a maiden being deflowered. I have heard from some men that it was Nero's unshaken conviction that no man was chaste or pure in any part of his body, but that most concealed their vices and cleverly drew a veil over them."

Judging by the testimony of numerous writers, Nero played out every fantasy that occurred to him. And didn't care who saw it, took part in it, or objected to it.

Around A.D. 65, just after Nero had kicked his third wife Poppaea Sabina (and their unborn child) to death in a rage, the still-mourning emperor happened to glimpse a handsome young freedman named Sporus. The poor man had the huge misfortune to resemble Nero's late wife. Quicker than you can say "falsetto," Nero had Sporus castrated and took him to Greece, where he "married" the boy and the couple honeymooned. Sporus had to don a wardrobe of empress wear and endure frequent public kissing sprees with the salacious emperor.

The sad aftermath: Sporus outlived Nero, but notoriety followed him like a cheap perfume. He was forced to become the lover of a subsequent emperor, then another. When the put-upon eunuch was told he'd be playing the part of a maiden being ravished in an upcoming public spectacle, Sporus had had enough. He committed suicide.

Even during Nero's more conventional marriages, he sought heterosexual liaisons, the more outré and distasteful the better. As mentioned earlier, halfway through his reign, he abducted and raped one of Rome's vestal virgins. Needless to say, in the cowed political climate of that time, the emperor was never accused, much less punished, for any of these crimes.

During Nero's tenure, ancient Rome experienced its own "swinging 60s." During that period, a growing number of male prostitutes called themselves *niironas* in emulation of Nero's favored positions and sexual acts.

Nero was not the only emperor to engage in a wide variety of sexual perversions, but he was unique in proclaiming that "anything goes" and anyone could be penetrated, including himself. When Nero was born, his unsavory father, a patrician named Domitius Ahenobarbus, famously said to those who congratulated him: "Any child born of Agrippina and of me will be a disaster and an abomination." He wasn't far from wrong.

## EMPEROR TIBERIUS, VOYEUR:
### The arcane lusts of Tiberius

Judging by his *Lives of the Twelve Caesars*, which luckily has survived nearly intact, Suetonius was a keen observer and an avid collector of the personal idiosyncrasies, favorite sayings, personality quirks, and habits both virtuous and embarrassing of the imperial rulers and their families. He also had access to imperial files and primary source documents, and included what was said about a given emperor, dishing the dirt with brevity and eloquence but without taking sides. The end result: despite the gossipy, unsavory nature of many anecdotes, Suetonius comes across as strangely impartial, with no particular ax to grind.

Here is a jaw-dropping excerpt from Suetonius's entry on Emperor Tiberius: "In his retreat at Capri there was a room devised by him dedicated to the most arcane lusts. Here he assembled from all quarters girls and perverts, whom he called *spintriae* (the term comes from the Greek word *sphinkter*), who invented monstrous feats of lubricity, and defiled one another before him, interlaced in series of threes, in order to inflame his feeble appetite. He also had several other rooms adapted to his lusts, decorated with paintings and bas reliefs depicting scenes of the most lascivious character, and supplied with the books of Elephantis [a female pornographer who did an illustrated book on sex postures—see the entry elsewhere in this book], that no one should lack a model for the execution of any lustful act he was ordered to perform."

So—what precisely were those "monstrous feats of lubricity"? *Spintriae* were young sex workers, females and effeminate males, who performed daisy-chain group sex, each submitting to different ways and places of penetration. In his late sixties, Tiberius was much more of a voyeur than an active participant.

His other fetish, however, was a great deal more repugnant. It's described by Suetonius in a later paragraph: "Still more flagrant and brazen was another sort of infamy which he practiced . . . He taught children of the most tender years, whom he called his 'little fishes,' to play between his legs while he was in his bath. Those which had not yet been weaned, but were strong and hearty, he set at fellatio, the sort of sports best adapted to his inclination and age."

Occasionally this sixty-eight-year-old child abuser had enough energy to actively chase youngsters on land. As Suetonius notes, "One day during a [religious] sacrifice, he was so smitten by the beauty of a boy who swung a censer [the incense burner] that he was hardly able to wait until the rites were over before taking him aside and abusing him as well as his brother, who was playing the flute; and that soon afterwards he had the legs of both of them broken because they were reproaching each other with the disgrace."

There was a chilling aftermath to Tiberius's child perversion

*Tiberius had crummy luck in most of his marriages, but that didn't justify his perversity. As emperor, he set up a rancid sex retreat on Capri, where he abused youngsters for years.*

activities. One of his *spintriae*, a young boy from Rome, spent his boyhood and early youth on Capri as a student of depravity. He may have been at Tiberius's service from age eleven to eighteen or so. According to Suetonius, he may have even become the old man's plaything to advance his father's career.

Decades after Tiberius died, that young man—now in his fifties—became Roman emperor. Called Vitellinus, he was one of the three who wore Caesar's crown, ever so briefly, during A.D. 68–69, the year of the revolving emperors.

## EROS, THE GOD OF SEXUAL PASSION:
### Under the rose, anything goes

Those rascally Greek gods and goddesses were a love-maddened, incestuous, philandering bunch. Take the love goddess Aphrodite, for instance. With Mercury or maybe Mars, possibly Hephaestus or even with her dad Zeus, she had a son called Eros (Cupid to the Romans), who became the demi-god of sexual passion. A wild boy, he never broke into the Olympian elite but remained a delinquent, firing barbed arrows at random and setting unauthorized fires to unsuspecting hearts.

As her son matured, Aphrodite asked her nosy, never-miss-a-trick offspring to keep mum about her own sexual indiscretions. As a reminder, she gave Eros a rose, a Greek symbol of secrecy. As teens will do, Eros promptly looked around for someone else to do the job, and handed off the rose to another deity the Greeks called Harpocrates. The supposed god of silence, Harpocrates was virtually unknown. And for good reason. He represented the Egyptian god Horus as a child, and "child" is what his finger-to-mouth gesture meant—in Egyptian hieroglyphs, of course.

The Greeks, however, read that gesture as "silence" or "secrecy." This whole borrowing business was further tweaked by another error from a historian named Varro. Thanks to all these misunderstandings, the rose and the finger-to-mouth gesture, meaning silence, became a widespread symbol among the Greeks.

Later the Romans took it up. In Latin, they called it *sub rosa*, "beneath the rose," which meant secrecy, discretion, and confidentiality. Thus Roman banquet rooms, palace dining halls, and other sites where elite partygoers gathered often featured ceilings painted with roses. They were there to remind everyone that while *sub vino*, "under the influence," revelers needed to keep it *sub rosa*. We might call it an earlier, more poetic version of "What happens in Vegas, stays in Vegas."

There were occasional "oops" moments. Nero, Elagabalus, and other fun-loving emperors held orgiastic free-for-alls in which masses of real rose petals were hung in nets above the partygoers. At times (perhaps deliberately) the netting broke, literally smothering the humans below. Online and in museums you can catch a wonderful portrayal of a Roman "death by roses" orgy, painted by famed Dutch artist Lawrence Alma-Tadema, who specialized in such subject matter from the late 1800s on.

Aphrodite, who sprang from the ancient mother goddess tradition of Ishtar and Astarte, may have also had a progenitor in the sea goddess of Minoan Crete. Once the Romans took her into their bosoms as their love queen Venus, her popularity rose even further.

*The god of love, Eros to the Greeks and Cupid to the Romans, was the lead deity of sexual passion. His names live on in words like "erotic." Or "cupidity," originally meaning "strong desire" but now signifying "desire for wealth."*

Eros, on the other hand, was a tangle of contradictions. Called a love god by Hesiod and the earliest Greek poets, Eros was thought be among the oldest of deities. When spoken of by mystics and philosophers, Eros and the uniting power of love became one of the fundamental causes of the formation of the world. Later poets, especially the ones scribbling erotic and epigrammatic verse, described Eros as a boy-god, the youngest of deities.

When the Romans popularized him as Cupid, the god infantilized further, becoming a rosy toddler, equipped with wings, bow, and arrows, and often accompanied by his "love posse," the *erotes*, described in the next entry.

At a certain point in the first few centuries A.D., cupid images became commonplace on coffins as a symbol of life after death. That notion was eagerly adopted by early Christians, who preferred to call them cherubs instead.

## THE EROTES:

### Love posse to the sex goddess

Naughty boy Eros had his own entourage of godlings or godlets, called the Erotes. The Greeks, who always made room for another deity, identified them as the additional progeny of Ares and Aphrodite, the gods of war and love, respectively. (No clue as to why the children of a Greek war god would pursue a "make love, not war" philosophy.)

There was a strong family resemblance between Eros and his brothers. They all had wings, hot youthful bodies, and ran around naked. Like big brother, they carried bow and arrows as weapons. They first showed up on sculptured friezes in Hellenistic times, after Alexander the Great died.

Originally there were luscious young maidens with wings depicted with the Erotes, but apparently they did not make the cut.

Because of their pinchable cuteness, Erotes became very popular subject matter for sculptors, potters, vase painters, and the creators of bronze jewelry, lamps, and household knickknacks.

Although Eros seemed to have the bases covered on love, lust, beauty, and sexual intercourse, he was later burdened with additional chores. He became the god of athleticism and a backup deity for fertility. He also shouldered the job of guarding male-to-male sexuality.

Nevertheless, it was felt by a higher Olympian authority that some areas of romantic love and biology were not being addressed. In addition, Eros had complained of being lonely. Thus an Erote called Antero became the god of love returned, that is, requited love. A charming fellow, he wore his hair long and had wings resembling a butterfly. He also carried a golden club, apparently to enforce that "love 'em or else" idea—and to avenge those rebels who refused to commit.

After Antero, another offspring of Ares and Aphrodite came into being. Named Himeros, he became the deity of unrequited love. He also backed up Eros on sexual desire issues. To distinguish him from the other Erotes, he carried a fashionable *taenia* or headband, like the colorful ones that Greek athletes wore. It looked more dopey than sexy to carry the taenia instead of wearing it, but that was the burden Himero had to bear.

The Erotes sibling that attracted the most attention,

*Venus, or Aphrodite, the love goddess, had an entourage of godlings called the* Erotes. *Usually portrayed as winged babies, they were sought for such issues as sexual yearning.*

however, especially from the love-gone-wrong crowd, was Pothos, who represented sexual longing or yearning. From time to time Ares and Aphrodite disavowed him as a son, insisting that Zephyrus the wind god and Iris the rainbow-maker were his parents. To humans in pain, it didn't matter what his parentage was, they were simply glad to have a deity to moan to about their rotten love life.

Just as Anteros and Himeros represented the opposing aspects of unrequited and requited love, another pair of Erotes covered the bases of persuasive seduction versus sweet-talk and flattery. Peitho personified the art of romantic seduction, while Hedylogos was the deity to consult for the best opening lines and charming patter.

Greco-Roman artists were delighted to have the Erotes as subject matter, as they enlivened murals and lent a mischievous air to otherwise dull paintings. They also became important symbols in art; when they appeared in a portrait of two women, for instance, the wink-wink Erotes provided a sexual subtext.

These godlets might have seemed a charming afterthought, a trivial matter, but they were a splendid idea. Since long-ago cultures had to get along without any human therapists, much less any self-pitying country-music lyrics to sing along with, the Erotes lent a listening ear to our mortal obsession with love.

## ALKIBIADES OF ATHENS:

### Number-one hottie among women—& men

Scion of a famous and wealthy family of aristocrats, possessing the charisma and keen intellect to become Socrates' pet disciple as well as the athletic courage to be a much-admired warrior, bisexual pretty boy Alkibiades had it all during the Athenian golden age.

Well, almost all. From Plato's writings we learn that young Alkibiades, to his utter chagrin, could not seduce his mentor Socrates. An excerpt reads: "I allowed myself to be alone with [Socrates] and naturally supposed he would embark on conversation that a lover usually addresses to his darling. Nothing of the kind; he spent the day with me in the sort of talk habitual to him, then left. Next I invited him to train with me in the gym, and accompanied him there, believing I should succeed with him now. He took exercise and wrestled with me frequently, with no one else present, but I need hardly say that I was no nearer my goal . . . so I invited him to dine with me, behaving just like a lover who has designs on his favorite . . . when the light was out and the servants had withdrawn . . . I nudged him and said, 'Are you asleep, Socrates?' 'Far from it,' he answered. I said, 'I think that you are the only lover I've ever had who is worthy of me but you are afraid to mention your passion to me.'" (Alkibiades continues in this self-indulgent vein but gets no further.)

He then says, "Finally, I got up and covered him with my own clothes—for it was winter—and then laid myself down under his worn cloak, and threw my arms round this truly superhuman and wonderful man, and remained thus the whole night long . . . but in spite of all my efforts . . . I swear by all the gods that after sleeping with Socrates, I might as well have been sleeping with my father or elder brother."

This story is attested elsewhere, as is the genuine astonishment Alkibiades demonstrates at being turned down.

When it came to lovers male or female, however, Socrates was probably the only holdout. Due to Alkibiades' extraordinary physical beauty,

*Greek philosopher Plato wrote admiringly (perhaps enviously) about Alkibiades, the brilliant bad boy of Athens, who was sexually pursued by men and women alike.*

his orator's way with words, and his charming impudence, he had a long string of male suitors.

He had female alliances as well. He delighted the richest man in Athens, who gave him his daughter Hipparete; Alkibiades then treated her shamefully, bringing hookers home and forcing her to endure other abuses. When she tried to file divorce papers, Alkibiades swept her away from the magistrate and then imprisoned her at home. Hipparete died in childbirth in 417 B.C.

In addition, this arrogant risktaker had a string of reckless affairs with supposedly untouchable women. The most notorious? His fling with Spartan queen Timaea while her husband, King Agis II, was off doing battle. Their interlude produced that awkward byproduct, a love child. Later, the baby boy that Timaea and Alkibiades collaborated on got passed over for Spartan kingship, but the adulterers emerged unscathed.

Another sexcapade involved his pal and fellow philanderer Axiochus. The two went to Abydos in Asia Minor, somehow achieving the extraordinary feat of marrying the same woman. When she gave birth to a daughter, neither man claimed to know whose it was; as the girl reached puberty, they both cohabited with her. When Alkibiades was intimate with his offspring, he'd say, "Oh, she's the daughter of Axiochus," and vice versa.

Exceedingly nimble at erotic triumphs with both genders, this man was equally adept at switching political sides and carrying out criminal acts without paying the price.

An active politician as well as a part-time general, Alkibiades pushed for several disastrous moves. He led a huge Athenian armada to conquer Sicily's rich Greek cities, a defeat that lost thousands of men and the entire fleet, crippling his home city-state. After the Sicily debacle, with Athenians calling for his blood, he fled to live in Sparta (bitter enemy of his home city). Despite his despicable moves, Alkibiades easily won back the esteem and love of the Athenians when he defected *back* to them in 412!

In a few years, when it became clear that he couldn't keep his current crop of false promises, Alkibiades once more ran for it. He was killed shortly after Athens surrendered to the Persians in 404 B.C.

As comic playwright Aristophanes once said of Alkibiades, the most insolent native son of Athens, "They love, and hate, and cannot do without him."

## AMAZONS:
### Warriors who loved their freedom— & their boobs

It's surprising to learn how many places in the world claim to have been founded by the Amazons of old. To name a few: Ephesus, Sinope, Cyme, Amasia, Themiscrya, Mytilene, Smyrna, Priene, Pitana, and Thyatira. One gets a vicarious, atavistic thrill of delight at the thought of women warriors strong and savvy enough to fight their way from the Black Sea and onto the acropolis of Athens. Or going *mano a mano* with Trojan warriors.

Herodotus, one of few historians of old to do extensive field research, spent time in Scythian country around the Black Sea. His detailed account describes a legendary time when Greek forces (in retaliation for a brazen Amazon raid on Athens) went to the south shores of the Black Sea and battled the Amazons at the Thermodon River. The Greeks won and jammed their female prisoners aboard their three ships. In midstream the intrepid gals managed to free themselves, then massacred the Greeks. Now what?

they asked each other, none of them being sailors. Luckily the ship drifted to shore in Scythian country, where the women grabbed up the dead guys' weapons, disembarked, and quickly stole horses.

Delightfully soon, a battle with local Scythians ensued, which went so badly for the locals that they laid down their arms, then opened their arms to the Amazons. Joining forces in the most intimate way, the Scythians and their newfound mates produced a batch of children, which the men got to babysit. Amazon women did the breast-feeding, however—and they possessed the female equipment to feed twins if needed. As ancient Greek art clearly shows, the "one breasted" Amazon myth is ancient malarkey, as is the etymology of the word.

Calling themselves the Sauromatians, they roamed a huge area of present-day Russia, Ukraine, and Kazakhstan. And, according to Herodotus, the younger generations of Amazons maintained their ancient traditions of hunting, plundering, and not marrying until each had killed an enemy. Herodotus's account had the ring of truth but still fell in the realm of legend, it was thought until recently.

In Adrienne Mayor's book *The Poison King*, however, she describes the year of 66–65 B.C., when the very real King Mithradates VI toyed with Roman general Pompey for months—then led him right into an ambush laid by his tribal allies of the Caucasus. As she writes,

> While the Romans were celebrating Saturnalia, a jolly winter holiday of role reversals and heavy drinking, the Iberi, Albanoi, and allied bands ambushed the camp. The skirmishes were described by Appian, Plutarch, Strabo, and Cassius Dio. The barbarians numbered 60,000 on foot and 12,000 mounted. To the Romans, these tall handsome

people appeared "wretchedly armed, wearing the skin of wild beasts." They were formidable guerrilla fighters who attacked, then took cover in the forest.

Pompey methodically set the forest on fire, to drive them out. After the battle, stripping the nearly 9,000 dead bodies, the Romans discovered many women warriors with typical Amazon weapons and clothing, exactly as depicted on Greek vase paintings. Their wounds showed that their bravery matched that of the men. Female fighters were also found among the thousands of captives. According to Strabo, Amazons inhabited these mountains and the steppes beyond. In detailing the Amazon lifestyle, Strabo stated that his information came from the writings (now lost) of Mithradates' old friend, the philosopher Metrodorus, and from someone by the name of Hypsicrates who was 'quite familiar' with this region.

"Hypsicrates" quite possibly may have been Hypsicratea, the female fighter and last lover of Mithradates, who fought alongside the king during the last six years of his life—and was perfectly capable of taking on a male persona. (Read more about her elsewhere in the book.)

As late as A.D. 350, a Roman historian called Ammianus Marcellinus asserted that Amazons still lived between the Don River and the Caspian Sea. After that came more than a millennium of silence.

Then in the 1950s Russian archaeologists found the first of many Sauromatian burial sites in this area of vast steppes and mountainous terrain. A large percentage of these graves contained female bodies buried with high-status grave goods, including arrowheads, armor, horse gear, and weapons, dating from the sixth to the fourth centuries B.C.

Additional archaeological finds later showed that the Sauromatians gave way to another people called the Sarmatians, who thrived from the fourth to the second centuries B.C. Again, their burial sites contained many females with richer artifacts of greater variety than those of the males. Although the contents of some graves included more feminine items, such as spindles and bronze mirrors, a significant percentage of Sarmatian women were clearly warriors as well. Besides iron swords, daggers, and whetstones in their graves, researchers found skeletons with bowed legbones (indicating an active life on horseback); hunting trophies, such as a boar's tusk; and evidence of death in battle.

Historians have argued that the Greeks invented the Amazons as a way to explain the struggle between early matriarchal cultures and the victorious Dorian invaders. But there was no need for fantasy. Groups or clans of Amazons—fierce, independent, and able to handle both male and female roles with ease—spread across a huge swath of wild Eurasian terrain and thrived for centuries.

*Modern archaeology continues to amass more evidence that the once-mythical Amazons thrived for centuries as female warriors across the wild terrain of Eurasia.*

# Love Dilemmas &
# Lust at the Crossroads

## FAMILY AFFAIRS:

### Incest, three ways

There was more than one type of incest in the ancient world.

One was the well-known Oedipus Rex scenario, now thought by some historians to represent a very ancient tradition of sacred kingship, in which the king was slain by his successor, who became the queen's new bridegroom. It was discussed thoroughly in Sir James George Frazer's *Golden Bough*.

Another was religious: *incestum*, which meant loss of religious chastity. This generally referred to priestesses or Rome's vestal virgins.

But the most familiar form of incest to Greeks and Romans was dynastic incest, where brothers and sisters, uncles and nieces, mothers and sons, and fathers and daughters had intimate relations and/or openly married in order to preserve bloodlines and the right to rule within the family.

The eighteenth dynasty in Egypt, with famous names like Nefertiti, is the most spectacular and well-known example; it's covered in the entry following this one.

Equally famed is the Ptolemy dynasty and its headliner, Cleopatra VII, the last of her line. True to form, she briefly married her two younger brothers, coolly arranging for their executions later.

The first Ptolemy, a Macedonian Greek and not Egyptian at all, took Egypt as his "prize" in the land-grab sweepstakes after Alexander the Great's death. By 322 B.C., Ptolemy had kidnapped the mellified corpse of his former boss and brought it to Egypt for display and worship. (During his brief visit to Egypt, Alexander had been declared a pharaoh and thus a god.)

To make his own pharoahship more secure, Ptolemy I tied the knot with the daughter of the last Egyptian pharaoh. In a year or so, he shoved her aside to marry the Macedonian daughter of Antipater, one of his former enemies but now pals. Swapping female relatives for matrimony soon became a standard practice among the generals from Alex the Great's inner circle.

Not until the reign of Ptolemy III were male rulers forced to make incestuous marriages within their family. (Students of Ptolemaic history are often subject to migraines, since this dynasty routinely gave its elite females one of only three names: Arsinoe, Berenice, or Cleopatra.)

And yes, to answer your burning question: the number of incestuous links during the three centuries of Ptolemies did seem to have led to an inordinate number of grossly obese male rulers. The women in the dynasty, however, were noteworthy for being lean, mean, shrewd, and often murderous.

In Asia Minor on the eastern coast of the Mediterranean, royal marriages between brothers and sisters became common within the Hecatomnid dynasty. These Greeks ran Caria and tried to keep it out of Persian hands during the fourth and third centuries B.C. The founder, Hecatomnus, had daughters Ada and Artemisia, who happily wed their brothers Idrieus and Mausolus. Artemisia in particular was anguished at the early death of her brother-husband Mausolus and she set about completing a gigantic temple-tomb complex that became one of the seven wonders of the ancient world. That wonder is no more but we still use the term mausoleum, named after that incestuous king of long ago.

In mainland Greece, the Spartans also engaged in royal incest; King Leonidas I, who led the heroic Spartan band at the battle of Thermopylae, took his niece Gorgo as wife.

*Queen Nefertiti, the most recognized face in Egypt's eighteenth dynasty, was of nonroyal blood. Nevertheless, her marriage to Akhenaten triggered a wave of dynastic incest.*

Romans frowned on incest, considering it unacceptable and against the laws of gods and humans, but it wasn't until A.D. 295 that they got around to passing a pair of laws making it illegal; one that applied to Roman citizens, and another for non-Romans in the empire. (In the entry on Emperor Titus and Berenice, you can also learn more about incest in the Herodian clan of Judaea.)

In the interim, various members of the imperial families may have dabbled (some might call it "waded") in incestuous activity. Already mentioned elsewhere in this book are Caligula's relationships with his sisters. Nero too was accused of intimacy with his mother Agrippina, the main power behind the throne during much of Nero's reign. Agrippina also married her uncle Claudius—an act that required the Roman senate to pass a law allowing it.

The law wasn't just for fancy folk. From that time on, any Roman could legally marry his brother's daughter (which Agrippina was). It was, however, still a crime for Romans to marry their sister's daughter.

## ANKHESENAMUN OF EGYPT:
### Loved her family, not sure about Grandpa

It's not often that the quiet heroics of a woman, overshadowed by her too-famous kin, get recognized. It's even less likely when the person in question lived approximately 3,359 years ago.

If you've heard of Ankhesenamun at all, it's probably as the wife of household name Pharoah Tutankhamun, or as the daughter of Egypt's only iconoclastic pharaoh, Akhenaten, and his dazzling queen with the blue turban, Nefertiti.

She was the middle sister in a family of six daughters—a circumstance that would soon lead to heartbreak. At her birth around 1348 B.C. she was called Ankhesenpaaten, "Living for Aten." Aten was the sun god, the deity her dad and mom decided to worship after junking the rest of Egypt's lineup of gods and goddesses.

As a toddler, she had a sunny childhood, growing up in the sparkling new city her parents had built along the banks of the Nile. Vibrant, almost casual bas-relief portraits of her close-knit family exist, very unlike the stiff and solemn presentations of other pharaohs and their families.

Being an Egyptian princess, however, meant being a royal breeder—especially if there were no princes. The right to rule ran through the female bloodline; all too soon, Ankhesenpaaten learned about "keeping it in the family." Somewhere around her twelfth year, her mother vanished and she was obliged to marry her own father; a year or two later when her dad passed away, she wed her uncle Smenkhkare. These marriages were starkly real; she gave birth to an Ankhesenpaaten Junior, the baby's paternity unknown as yet but probably sired by her own dad.

While a teen, still struggling from the losses of her father, mother, uncle, and at least one sister, Ankhesenpaaten now wed her half-brother Tutankhaten, who'd stepped up as pharaoh. He was about three years younger than she, but at least she had a spouse of her own generation. As a couple, they moved back to Thebes, diligently restoring the ancient religion their parents had tossed aside. As part of that process, they changed their names, deleting the reference to Aten worship. Tut became Tutankhamun, and she became Ankhesenamun—"Living for Amun."

She had nearly ten years to love her boyish husband. Then once again, death came to the golden palace. Ankhesenamun might have been

*Ankhesenamun endured Egyptian dynastic incest with successive marriages to her father, uncle, and half-brother. Finally she heroically rebelled against wedlock—this time with her own grandfather!*

privileged, but she'd seen far too much death in her twenty-one years. Her brother-husband Tut died suddenly, barely eighteen or nineteen. Together, they had already shared the heartbreak of two baby girls, both stillborn.

The marriages and deaths she'd had to endure haunted her, but the grieving widow feared the future even more. There was no one else, no male of the Amarna royal bloodline, to take the throne. But someone wanted it badly:

*The glittering objects in Tutankhamun's tomb have made the name "King Tut" famous although he was still a teen, married to his half-sister, when he died.*

Ay, her maternal grandfather. More than once, it crossed her mind that he may have had a hand in Tut's death. A skulking figure, Ay had served as chief minister to the royal family for years. And he had a wife. But to legitimize his claim, he'd need the royal blood of Ankhesenamun.

In desperation, the young queen put aside her bereavement. She told herself, "Do something! You only have seventy days!" That was the time it would take to embalm her dead husband and prepare him for the afterlife. In attempting to break the stranglehold of consanguinity, of familial incest, she did a most astonishing and valiant thing. In her own way, she was as iconoclastic as her father, Akhenaten.

Quickly and secretly she prepared a letter, sending it off with a personal servant she could trust. He delivered it to one of Egypt's long-standing enemies, the Hittite king Suppiluliuma I, who read its lines with astonishment: "My husband died, and I have no sons. They say that your sons are plentiful. If you send me one of your sons, then he would become my husband. I do not wish to be forced to marry a servant. I am afraid."

King Suppiluliuma was rendered speechless by the offer; his second reaction was wariness. Was she really the Great Royal Wife? What were the Egyptians trying to pull? Instead of answering immediately, he sent an ambassador to smoke out the truth; he came back from Egypt, saying that indeed the offer—and Ankhesenamun—were genuine. With him, he brought back a tablet with another letter from the queen, saying, "If a son existed for me, would I have written about the shame of myself and of my land to another land? You did not trust me. He who was my husband died. I have not written to any other land, I wrote to you! Give me one of your sons! To me he will be husband, but in the land of Egypt he will be king!"

By now Ankhesenamun was frantic.

Finally convinced, the Hittite king sprang into action, choosing his son Prince Zannaza and hastily throwing together wedding gifts and an elaborate entourage for their sendoff.

Too late: the sands in the hourglass of the young queen's time ran out. Perhaps it was Ay's men who murdered the young Hittite prince en route, or perhaps he met his death via the troops of Commander Horemheb, another aspirant to the pharoah's throne.

By the time Tutankhamun was properly mummified, Ankhesenamun had been pushed against her will into marriage with her grandfather, Ay. He gave her a ring with their names on it, and then officiated at Tutankhamun's funeral.

Ay would rule Egypt for four years, but Ankhesenamun soon disappeared from the records. When Ay died of old age, Horemheb, the nonroyal head of the army, promply declared himself king (not pharaoh) in 1321 B.C.

And King Suppiluliuma? Outraged over the murder of his son, the Hittite king sent his armies against several of Egypt's territories. He captured many Egyptian prisoners, who carried a deadly weapon: the plague. It tore into Hittite country, eventually killing Suppiluliuma and his successor.

The particulars of Ankhesenamun's amazing story are now confirmed via unearthed documents and artifacts. The letters she sent to the Hittite king were preserved in the Deeds of Suppiluliuma, a compendium of primary source documents. The ring Ay gave her at their wedding has been discovered. A well-preserved mural in an Egyptian tomb shows the upstart Ay performing the "Opening of the Mouth" ceremony for Tutankhamun, needed to ensure his happy afterlife.

There are still many what-ifs in Ankhesenamun's tale; neither her burial site nor her mummy have been confirmed yet, although there are several candidates whose exact identities are still being sorted out.

Talk about things coming back to haunt us: the issue of consanguinity, once looked upon as an ancient strategy whereby rulers of Egypt and more recent regimes sought to retain their thrones, has become a modern moral dilemma. Children born from sperm and egg donors are now a significant percentage of the population. Each year in the United States alone, between 30,000 and 60,000 are born from sperm donors. As the first wave of these children have become adults, the chances of them meeting and mating become greater and greater. To date, there has not been complete transparency or reporting by either sperm banks, donors, or recipients.

And, as a 2011 article in the *Wall Street Journal* noted, "The cost of fibbing about fertility is going up. When the science isn't straightforward, people have to be."

# SNAKE ADORATION:
## Healers, prophets, & bunkmates

Decade after decade, serpent phobia (along with fear of spiders) ranks in the top five fears and loathings of Americans. This is noteworthy, since we've modified our surroundings to the extent that the chances of running across an actual snake—other than one pancaked on the freeway—are exceedingly rare.

Greeks and Romans, on the other hand, thought highly of serpents. They had more relaxed attitudes about scaly wildlife and housekeeping styles, too. In those days, the temples, public buildings, and houses of everyone, including the most lah-di-dah, were easily accessible by members of the reptilian family.

Whenever a snake happened to glide into the kitchen of a Greek housewife, she was pleased by her "good luck" visitor and set out a saucer of milk. Sometimes she invited the snake in; snakes were and still are excellent predators of vermin, so there was common sense in this positive attitude.

Romans were even more effusive, painting a large snake as the guardian of the hearth on each family *lararium* or altar. The snake was a stand-in for the male head of household's "genius," which back then didn't define dad's IQ, merely his powers of procreation.

Beyond their roles as mousers, symbols of fatherly potency, and less cuddly substitutes for rabbit's feet, snakes carried additional meaning. Serpents had prophetic qualities and healing powers. For instance, when Rome was afflicted by a plague in 293 B.C., the city got help fast when a good-sized specimen of *Elaphe longissima longissima* crawled off a ship and onto an island in the Tiber River. The helpful staff at the healing sanctuary in Epidaurus, Greece, had sent the six-foot-long serpent as a physician's assistant of their healing god, Asclepius. In no time the snake had settled in, the plague had abated, and builders were at work, constructing a new temple for the Asclepius deity in herpetic form.

The city of Athens had similar heartwarming tales of a guardian snake at the Acropolis that was fed on honey cakes and was sage enough to skedaddle when everyone else did during the Persian invasion.

Other healing cults around Italy copied the success of Asclepius; at the temple of Bona Dea Subsaxana, for instance, female worshippers could hardly move without stepping on one of the harmless serpents underfoot.

About A.D. 150 the god Asclepius, clearly tired of all the attention lavished on his serpent stand-ins, changed from a deity in human form into a large snake with shaggy hair and primate ears. The only person to witness this transformation was a glib, good-looking, out-of-work prophet named Alex in the Black Sea town of Abonutichus. In short order, Alex founded an oracle, won an audience, and got credulous souls to chip in for a shrine and a daybed for the snake god, who wanted to be known as Glykon.

Alex and Glykon carried on oracling for thirty years, scoring several important prophetic hits. Although the cult had detractors, Alex had the goods to carry off the role. As he "channeled" Glykon's messages, he often had seizures and drooled—excess saliva being a sure sign of divinity. Decades after the demise of both the snake and Alex, the oracle was still in operation. Even Emperor Marcus Aurelius sought oracle answers from the Glykon cult.

Two thousand years ago almost every man, woman, and child was savvy enough to distinguish poisonous serpents from harmless ones—called *dracos* or *dracones*—which often served as household pets. An elderly snake was a favorite of Emperor Tiberius, who fed it with his own hands until the aging slinky got so weak it was destroyed by ants. Dracos were often brought in to enliven smart dinner parties, slithering about amid the dining couches of fashionable ladies.

Given their remarkable acceptance in Greco-Roman society, it's easy to see why long-ago snakes played a leading role in dreams, portents, legend building, and salacious celebrity gossip. The life story of Olympias, the fiery mom of Alexander the Great, is a case in point. She and her future husband Philip II of Macedon met at a mystery religion orgy on the Greek island of Samothrace. A cult priestess, Olympias handled serpents and wore them on her body as she danced by torchlight. Despite the involuntary retch this inspired in Philip, he fell for her. They made love, wed, and made a baby.

One evening, as Philip fondly peeked in on his new wife, he saw an immense snake lying next to Olympias as she slept. Instant libido loss on his part. Being a Macedonian ruler with multiple wife-visitation options, Philip kept mum but scratched Olympias off his nocturnal visit list.

In due course, Queen Olympias gave birth to Alexander, who from the get-go was a clearly superior boy. The marriage got stormier. Olympias took to drinking too much wine at dinner and had a regrettable tendency to impugn Philip's paternal role by telling everyone about the night that Zeus took the form of a serpent and fathered her child.

*Ancient cultures weren't phobic about snakes. To them, certain reptiles had healing powers; that's why Asclepius, god of healing, had a serpent companion.*

Meanwhile, Philip sought counseling from the prophetic Pythia of the oracle at Delphi. The oracle warned that someday Philip would lose the eye with which he'd spied on his wife doing the nasty with a major god in snake form. And of course that is what transpired; in one of his endless battles, Philip caught an arrow in the face.

The Greeks and Romans' awe of snakes is perhaps why one of their most powerful symbols for infinity was the *ourobouros*, a snake that held its tail in its own mouth. Serpents also representing healing and wisdom to the ancients, and we see traces of that today in the serpent-twined caduceus, the familiar medical symbol.

## TEIRESIAS THE SEER:
### Gender-bender & orgasm expert

The Greeks had unusual views about male and female sexuality, at times seeming indifferent to female orgasm—or at least avoiding such discussion. One orgasmic anecdote does appear in the delightful, thought-provoking stories about the enigmatic, shape-changing seer of long ago, Teiresias.

Greek poet Hesiod was one of many who told and retold the interlocking tales of this prophet-clairvoyant of Arcadia, a bucolic wooded region of Greece. As one of the tales went, young Teiresias happened to observe some snakes copulating and couldn't resist teasing them. After wounding one snake with his walking staff, he found himself changed into a woman. (It was the goddess Hera's doing; she was displeased by his Peeping Tom act regarding serpent sex.)

Well, this is interesting, Teiresias thought; before long he started dating, and eventually, making love with a man. Pretty soon he became a priestess, got married, had some kids. One of them, Manto, promised to be a darned good prophesy-spinner, like Teiresias himself.

After his transformation into a woman, seven years passed. Then Teiresias heard from Apollo himself, who said, "You know, if you want to return to your original gender, you just need to watch for more snakes copulating. Injure one of them, as before, and I promise, you'll be a man again, my son."

Teiresias followed Apollo's advice, and sure enough, his transformation occurred just as the god said. He was wondering what on earth to say to his husband and children (who would no doubt be bewildered by his new manliness) when a racket erupted. It was that dysfunctional husband-and-wife team, Zeus and Hera, beginning one of their ferocious arguments.

Zeus claimed that women got a larger share of pleasure from lovemaking than men did, while Hera took the opposite tack. Since they couldn't agree, they turned to the seer, since he'd now experienced both sides of the man/woman divide.

"So, Teiresias—which is it?" demanded Hera, who seemed to have a lot of ego on the line.

Teiresias thought she'd be tickled with his answer. "Women enjoy nine-tenths of the pleasure," he said, "and mortal men must be content with one-tenth."

The queen of the gods dived at him, gouging out

*According to one of the tales about Teiresias, when he saw snakes copulating he couldn't resist teasing and wounding them. That ticked off the goddess Hera, who changed him into a woman.*

both of his eyes. Then she flounced off; at least, that's what it sounded like to Teiresias.

Zeus hung his head. "I feel terrible," he said.

Grimacing, Teiresias said, "You feel terrible? Try getting your eyes gouged out, and then get back to me."

"I'm going to give you the gift of prophecy," Zeus said. "It's the least I can do. Oh, and instead of one lifetime, you can have seven."

"What about my eyesight?" Teiresias asked.

"No can undo," Zeus said, looking nervously over his shoulder for Hera.

"Tell me this. Why did Hera get so angry at my answer?"

Zeus shrugged. "You are mortal, and you just revealed one of our exclusive godly secrets. Can't have everybody knowing about all that sexual pleasure that women are getting, can we now? Cheer up! You're a clairvoyant with insight into the souls of men and women."

That is merely one version of the story; another one has the seer blinded when he stumbles on a naked Athena, bathing.

Greeks myths often raise more questions than they answer. (Maybe that is their purpose.) But what I personally wonder is: Why didn't Teiresias ask to be female again, if they truly do get the lion's share of sexual pleasure?

We'll never know. Teiresias, however, gained such popularity in ancient times that he ended up with his own series, as a recurring character in Greek tragedies by Euripides and Sophocles, and in Homer's *Odyssey* as well. He hasn't done badly in modern times, either, being cast in everything from Dante's *Inferno* to one of Frank Herbert's Dune novels.

# STRAIGHT FROM THE SOURCE:
## Love gone wrong

Some of the remedies used by the ancients for a broken heart are still in use: alcoholic oblivion, I'll-show-'em sexual flings, drugs, overwork, overeating, oversleeping, and that only reliable strategy, the passage of time.

But our predecessors in love, those long-ago men and women, also had other ways of dealing with heartbreak, many of them involving a ritual or sorcery of some sort. There were no shrinks or pills for the lovelorn then, but a rich network of superstitions, myths, and magical thinking permeated daily life. Tapping into that cathartic, sometimes dark world might bring a love object back into one's life—or would make him or her sorry. If love had turned to hate, such a ritual could even harm or kill the once-adored individual.

For the most common malevolent ritual, the sorcery-seeker wrote his or her curse on a thin sheet of soft lead (or on bronze, for the spare-no-expense crowd). Called the *defixio*, the curse was folded or tightly rolled up, then hidden in tombs, or down wells, or affixed to trees. Another ritual required the participant to stick needles into wax or clay figures—a spell still seen today in voodoo circles.

There were also distinctions, not always clear to us today, between *eros* spells that induced passion and *philia* magic that induced affection. People also commissioned gemstones and rings with Aphrodite and Eros images; hidden on them were magic words and binding spells.

This excerpt comes from an elaborate erotic spell made by a woman named Sophia, who wanted to attract another woman named Gorgonia. Her oval tablet, written on both sides, contains sixty-six lines of text.

Fundament of the gloomy darkness, jagged-tooth dog, covered with coiling snakes, turning three heads, traveler in the recesses of the underworld, spirit-driver, with the Erinyes [the Furies] savage with their stinging whips, holy serpents, maenads, frightful maidens, come to my wroth incantations. Before I persuade by force this one and you, render him immediately a fire-breathing demon. Listen and do everything quickly, in no way opposing me in the performance of this action, for you are the governors of the earth. [Three lines of magical gibberish follow.] By means of the corpse-daemon inflame the heart, the liver, the spirit of Gorgonia, whom Nilogenia bore, with love and affection for Sophia, whom Isara bore. Constrain Gorgonia to cast herself into the bath-house for the sake of Sophia; and you, become a bath-room. Burn, set on fire, inflame her soul, heart, liver, spirit with love for Sophia.

Here is a Greek spell written on papyrus in late antiquity, in which a man named Apalo wished to attract a woman named Karosa for sex. The mention of love torture is typical.

Aye, lord demon, attract, inflame, destroy, burn, cause her to swoon from love as she is being burnt, inflamed. Goad the tortured soul, the heart of Karosa, whom Thelo bore, until she leaps forth and comes to Apalo, whom Theonilla bore, out of passion and love, in this very hour, quickly, quickly . . . do not allow Karosa, whom Thelo bore, to think of her [own] husband, her child, drink, food, but let her come melting for passion and love and intercourse, especially yearning for the intercourse of Apalo, whom Theonilla bore, in this very hour, quickly, quickly.

Another curse tablet found in the Etruscan territory of Italy offers a graphic example of love turned to hatred:

> Spirits of the netherworld, I consecrate and hand over to you, if you
> have any power, Ticene of Carisius. Whatever she does, may it all turn
> out wrong. Spirits of the netherworld, I consecrate to you her limbs,
> her complexion, her figure, her head, her hair, her shadow, her brain,
> her forehead, her breath, her liver, her shoulders, her heart, her lungs,
> her intestines, her fingers, her hands, her navel, her thighs, her calves,
> her soles, her toes. Spirits of the netherworld, if I see her wasting away,
> I swear that I will be delighted to offer a sacrifice to you every year.

In both Mesopotamia and Greece, men and women cast binding spells using special rings, not so much for love affairs as to win admiration and affection from superiors, such as kings and masters. In addition, both the Assyrians and the Greeks favored special stones, precious and semi-precious, that promised a similar effect, replacing anger with friendship. An example of these binding spells: "Over a copper ring chant the spell three times. You place it on your finger, and when you enter the presence of the prince, he will welcome you." "A little ring for success and charm and victory . . . when you have it with you, you will always get whatever you ask from anybody. Besides, it calms the angers of kings and masters. Wearing it, whatever you may say to anyone, you will be believed, and you will be pleasing to everybody."

# OVID THE LOVE POET:
## Life in the *Fasti* lane

In the year 2 B.C. a heavy-breathing love poet named Publius Ovidius Naso had just survived a political squeaker with Rome's ruler for the past quarter century, Octavian Augustus. An unfortunate coincidence involving Ovid's sexy new book on the art of love and the adultery scandal of the emperor's only daughter Julia. The slut had promptly been banished by her father to a rocky islet off Naples.

Neither Ovid nor his book had met her fate. So far.

Lucky that you weren't on her reading list or her kiss-and-tell list, he told himself. Stick to your wife and your girlfriends, all of them thankfully unrelated to the imperial family.

*Ovid loved women and knew how they liked to be aroused. In his poetry and his life, he honored females with foreplay.*

This was Ovid's third literary attempt. His five-volume book *Amores* had won raves back in 15 B.C. but fulsome praise didn't pay the bills. If his just-published *Art of Love* and its erotic companion *Remedies for Love* didn't hit big, he'd be forced to grovel at the knee of his stingy father for a bigger allowance.

Focus, Ovid told himself. Focus on winning the right kind of attention from Octavian, that lecherous old hypocrite with his constant calls for morality and family values. Try to win his approval for a high-minded commission of some sort.

After years of fawning and lobbying, the poet's efforts paid off. The emperor commissioned him to write a marvelous new work. Apparently Octavian craved a long poem in verse about the Roman calendar, its zodiac signs, and its time-hallowed holidays.

Ovid was still cranking away on his unfinished epic *Metamorphoses* but it would have to wait. His poetic career was back on track. Just think: the emperor as literary patron!

Seven months later, Ovid had written five thousand lines of verse but completed just six months of his twelve-month calendar book. The topic fascinated him: the zodiac signs that determined the fate of humans; the *nefasti* days when business activity and assemblies were not permitted: the *dies feraie*, when holidays and festivals were held; the *fasti*, the days on which the courts and stores were open for business; and the unlucky days of the calendar. His book would be a celebration; a mix of myth and history, legend and sacred rite, the past linked to the present.

Right in the middle of this period of intense creativity and Ovid's third marriage, this time to a woman he really cared about, the unluckiest day of his life occurred. A professional accuser went to Emperor Octavian Augustus, and straightaway the poet was arrested for treason against the emperor.

He knew he'd been framed; despite his protestations, the fifty-year-old Ovid was convicted. On a chilly December day in the year A.D. 8, he was banished to the forlorn little outpost of Tomis (now in Romania) on the shores of the Black Sea.

Since Ovid's earlier work, sexy and outrageous as it was, had been in print for a number of years, his denunciation at this late date seemed misplaced. Puzzled fellow poets and friends, along with girlfriends and wives both past and present, were in anguish over the decision.

That same year, however, Emperor Augustus also exiled his grand-daughter, also named Julia, indicting her for adultery as he'd done to her mother. And banishing her to another of Italy's miserably small islands off the mainland.

Was there a connection, at least in the emperor's mind, between the actions of the two Julias and the writings of Ovid the poet? In his letters from exile, Ovid complained and hinted as much but never revealed any details. Despite his talent, he never saw his beloved Rome or his cherished wife again, dying in Tomis at about sixty years of age.

Historians have chewed on this mystery from centuries. Today it's thought that the lurid sex scandals of the imperial daughter and the granddaughter were cover-ups for conspiracies and aborted coups against the emperor. In both cases, key men involved in them were executed or exiled.

If these were attempts to overthrow, Ovid's crime was probably one of omission. The crowd he hung out with included politically ambitious aristocrats. If he'd overheard rumblings of a plot, and done nothing about it, Roman law would label that treason.

Poor Ovid never completed *Fasti*, his calendar book. But the half-finished manuscript survived, more precious now than Ovid ever dreamed, the sole existing work about the wonderfully elaborate ways in which the Romans kept track of their lucky and unlucky days.

## SAPPHO'S BANE:
### Remembering odious Rosycheeks

If the spirits of 2,600-year-old Greek poets could wring their hands, I'm betting that the ghost of famed Sappho of Lesbos would still be doing just that. Why? Three words: her sister-in-law Rosycheeks. She was the sexy fly in the ointment of Sappho's happiness.

It all began with Sappho's brother Charaxus. In the sixth century B.C., their home island of Lesbos was very prosperous, thanks to close trading ties with Egypt and one of its major port cities, Naucratis. Among other cash crops, Lesbos produced sweet dark wine—a big seller throughout Greece and neighboring lands.

Equally affluent was Sappho's snooty, possibly aristocratic family. She had three brothers, but her favorite was Charaxus.

Sappho was slightly dismayed when her brother became a wine merchant, a traveling salesman for the superb vintages of Lesbos, instead of something classier. But dismay turned to horror when on a wine-peddling junket

*Lionized and world famous even in her own day and age, Sappho the love poet had everything. Or did she? Enter the outrageous sister-in-law.*

to Naucratis, Charaxus fell insanely in love with a women who peddled a cheekier sort of merchandise.

When Charaxus met Rosycheeks, she'd already achieved top-tier courtesan status. Born in the wilds of Thrace in northern Greece, then sold into slavery, rumor had it that she'd worked in the household where Aesop the fable-teller was a fellow slave. Ill-suited to household drudgery, Rosycheeks finally got noticed by her owner, who put her to work, propositioning for pay in Naucratis.

By now Sappho herself was recognized as a top-tier poet and lyricist. She'd even won accolades from Solon, the prominent leader of Athens at that time. When his nephew happened to sing one of Sappho's songs, Solon asked him to teach him the tune. When the nephew asked, "What for?" Solon responded, "So I can learn it and die."

In 598 B.C., Sappho, along with her family, was exiled to Sicily for political reasons unknown to us. When the political climate changed, she returned to Lesbos and renewed her devotion to poetry, music, and dance. Other female poets joined her. Some came from Asia Minor, Egypt, the other Greek islands. Some became part of Sappho's circle of intimate friends. Rivals started poetry groups, trying to compete with her. Life was good.

But Sappho found she couldn't gloat to the fullest because of that dratted brother of hers and his sleazy affair. It was beginning to interfere seriously with her creativity. She had to drag herself to pick up the lyre and kick out the verses for her latest commission, another gorgeous *hymenaios*, or marriage song.

Then came another blow. It was dreadful enough that her brother kept this mistress—now his latest stunt was to pay an absurd sum to free Rosycheeks! The next cruel development almost killed her. "Married? You married that trollop, the one whose body anyone can buy?" she screamed at Charaxus.

"Hey, sis—I adore this woman. And I didn't want to time-share," he responded.

On fire with loathing, Sappho sought therapy in the only way she knew how. She sat down to write. The golden words flew from her stylus onto papyrus. Impassioned words, in her distinctive Aeolian style, pure poetry and anguish.

Because her creative life spanned some forty years, Sappho must have produced a huge body of poetic work. Most of the time she wrote about her feelings, her erotic friendships with her own gender, her hits and misses in love, and her sensual enjoyment of life. When she and her brother parted ways, Sappho in her sorrow and anger unknowingly gave immortality to the woman he loved and she despised. Only a few precious shreds of her work survive today; ironically, among them are the wonderful, partially restored poems about Rosycheeks and brother Charaxus.

## HYPSICRATEA:

### Amazon turned historian? A love story

Ringing the Black Sea like a charm-studded bracelet, two dozen thriving cities once stood, founded by Greek colonists beginning in the seventh century B.C. On the northeast shore was Phanagoria. Once a coastal metropolis, its shorelines had moved over the centuries. The city's structures had suffered terrible damage during a massive fire in 63 B.C.; thus archaeologists had found little of note on land.

During underwater excavations at Phanagoria in 2010, however, a Russian archaeological team headed by Vladimir Kuznetsov found what he called a remarkable grave marker. Who did it memorialize? Hypsicratea, history's most overlooked Amazon. (More on her and the Amazons in entries elsewhere in this book.)

Her fond lover preferred to call her by the masculine form of her name as a compliment to her strength, endurance, and courage. In fact, the inscription on the marble headstone reads: "Hypsikrates, wife of Mithradates VI." (The king, whose name means "sent by Mithra the sun god," was also called Mithridates by the Romans.)

The man who called himself her husband, King Mithradates VI of Pontus, was Rome's most bitter and long-lived enemy, fighting three successive wars against them. The story of his last wife and lover Hysicratea was once thought to be a somewhat fanciful tale of "outlaw love," embroidered on by that old romantic Boccaccio, an Italian writer of the fourteenth century A.D.

*King Mithradates VI of Pontus liked to be depicted in the heroic rebel mode on his coinage. But the real hero might have been a heroine, his warrior companion and last lover, Hypsicratea.*

Although she was barely mentioned by ancient writers Plutarch, Strabo, and Appian, the brief details they offered about Hypsicratea have been found to be largely true. In addition, this woman did much more than she's been given credit for, deeds meticulously documented in *The Poison King*, the 2010 biography by esteemed historical researcher and author Adrienne Mayor.

In 69 B.C., along with thousands of others, Hypsicratea was recruited by the king to join his nomadic forces. She belonged to one of the fierce tribes whose women fought and lived on horseback just as the men did. They roamed the steppes and thought nothing of navigating the Caucausus, those nearly impassable white-toothed mountains that link the Black Sea and the Caspian.

Hypsicratea was selected as one of the king's grooms, but her warrior skills soon brought her to Mithradates' personal attention. (A virile man who maintained a harem while marrying a series of wives, Mithradates connected to her physically as well.) A fit, well-muscled woman with long flowing hair, she was in her mid-thirties when she met the king. Although close to sixty-five, he remained a vigorous, cunning warlord who'd already trounced Roman generals various times.

Hypsicratea and Mithradates had six years together, during which she fought by his side, on horseback and on foot, in battle sites from Pontus to Armenia. She was there when he gave a humiliating defeat to Roman general Lucullus. With her deep knowledge of the treacherous vertical terrain and the guerrilla tactics she'd learned during a lifetime of nomad raids, she had his back, time after time. It wasn't easy. Mithradates not only fought the Romans and a great many others, he also battled his five sons and some of his daughters, most of whom wanted him dead.

By 64 B.C. the now-ailing king recognized that his military endgame was near, although his "Hypsicrates" refused to concede such a thing. Nevertheless, Mithradates gave her a vial of poison to swallow in case she was captured, just as he did for his top officers. Mithradates himself could not commit suicide by ingesting poison, since he'd taken low doses of a variety of toxins, including arsenic, throughout his lifetime.

The Roman army, now led by General Pompey, closed in on Mithradates, Hypsicratea, and their army at Phanagoria, helped by the king's treacherous fifth son.

After her mate's death, Hypsicratea disappeared. Even though that marble monument is inscribed with her name, it's possible her remains were never buried under it. Author Adrienne Mayor has suggested a plausible alternative: given the masculine name she was routinely and publicly called by King Mithradates, this vibrant, still-young fighter might have survived by passing as a male.

Mayor points to a series of intriguing coincidences: in his books, author and geographer Strabo, who hailed from Pontus on the Black Sea himself, mentions one of his valued sources as a certain Hypsicrates—after the supposed death of Hypsicratea.

Equally fascinating are the other facts Mayor has assembled. Sixteen years after Mithradates' death, Julius Caesar came to the Black Sea region. At the coastal city of Amisus in Pontus, he supposedly freed a prisoner of war named Hypsicrates, who, as the *Oxford Classical Dictionary* says, "may have served Caesar . . . as Theophanes served Pompey." As a historian, in other words.

This man Hypsicrates was alleged to have written various works on Pontus and the kingdom of the Bosporus. So far the works haven't turned up, but Hypsicrates is quoted by various historians, including Strabo, Josephus, and Lucian of Samosata.

As a piquant P.S., in a work attributed to Lucian, called *Macrobii* (Long Lives), is a sentence that reads: "Hypsicrates of Amisenum, the historian, who mastered many sciences, lived to be ninety-two."

## EMPRESS MESSALINA:
### Lost her head over excess husbands

On both sides of her family tree she was a Julian—that was the blue-blooded claim that eventually gained Valeria Messalina the title of Roman empress in the first century A.D. It didn't hurt that she possessed a hot little tush and a way to look seductive and adoring by turns. Fertile Valeria had luck in her pregnancies, too, first giving birth to a girl and, a year later, to a healthy boy—a result eagerly desired in royal circles.

In A.D. 39, Messalina, all of fourteen or fifteen years old, had married the man thought to be a stuttering, drooling fool by almost everyone, including his closest relatives: Claudius, a Julio-Claudian and a grandson of Livia, Rome's first empress.

Just a few months before Messalina gave birth to her son, another stroke of luck occurred: Caligula, the nephew of Claudius, was bloodily assassinated. Afterward, the Praetorian Guard found Uncle Claudius hiding behind the drapes in the palace, and acclaimed him their emperor. Everyone was stupefied—but everyone went along with it, Messalina as well.

The now-elated third wife of Claudius, a gray-haired man in his mid-forties, Messalina had to admit that he actually seemed brilliant some days. Two years after his accession, Claudius and his army invaded Britain and conquered it—something that the sainted Julius Caesar had been unable to do, despite strenuous efforts. Since expectations for Claudius had been so low, his feats as emperor were praised all the more.

It deeply pleased Messalina that Claudius spent so much time meeting with senators or conferring with his advisers, most of them freedmen and eunuchs, or fussing about, writing his excruciatingly long history of the Etruscans. That gave her plenty of time for self-expression. Messalina loved sex and exploring the naked truth about her own desires. Claudius went to bed early, allowing her ample time

*Messalina, whose ambition and sex drive matched her beauty, became a mother and later an empress by marrying Claudius.*

to select one of her golden wigs, gild her nipples, and put on a wanton outfit to hit Rome's brothels as "the she-wolf."

She cosied up to her husband's own confidential freedmen, eventually using them to arrange her assignations. One night, she might command them to organize an orgy; another, to bring her an actor or two to warm her bed. Once she ordered them to identify the most infamous whore in Rome. Messalina then challenged her to a contest of sexual acts. Which wanton woman could service the most men in a twenty-four-hour period? Messalina beat the professional, having sex with twenty-five men.

Then something untoward occurred: she genuinely fell in love with someone. His name was Gaius Silius, a nobleman next in line to become consul of Rome.

*Emperor Claudius gamely married four women, unlucky matches all. Pictured on the cameo above are Claudius and Agrippina the Younger, the spouse who would see to his fatal demise.*

In the fall of A.D. 48, she did the most outrageous thing she had yet dared: she forced her lover to divorce his own wife, then publicly married the man while Claudius was out of town. As she and the members of her drunken wedding party whirled in bacchant frenzy, the watchful freedmen who up until then had concealed her lascivious ways sold her out. They informed the emperor of her actions—and provided a list of her sexual partners.

Claudius, more frightened of conspiracies than enraged at his pretty young wife, immediately asked, "Am I still emperor?"

Messalina thought it would be child's play to once again win Claudius over; she'd done it so many times already. But the emperor's top freedmen were having none of it. They kept her from Claudius and sent executioners, who cut off her lovely head in her beautiful gardens that very night.

The name of this imperial orgy queen received a *damnatio memoriae* from the Roman senate, an official act that meant that the words "Valeria Messalina" would be immediately chiseled off all her statues and inscriptions in the realm.

Her promiscuity was bad enough. But her downfall was the illicit marriage and the political coup it could have represented. Her faithless behavior represented a failure of control on Claudius's part. An emperor who could not keep his own house in order would surely fail to keep his empire in order.

Poor luckless Claudius; despite his stature as a ruler and as a fairly decent human being, he would have four wives in his life, none of them his comfort and joy.

## ORGASMS:
### The climax of the mating game—& life

Greek and Roman mythology can be disheartening. What terrible role models most of the ancient deities were! Whether goddess or mortal, the women in those early soap operas were often subjected to bestiality, rape, infidelity, and incest, with little say-so about their own bodies.

But then we encounter Teiresias the Greek soothsayer (more on him in a prior entry), who becomes a woman as well as a man during the course of his mythical life. As such, he learns firsthand that mortal females have been granted an extraordinary gift: the lion's share of sensual pleasure, so potent that it measures nine times that which mortal males feel.

As we now know, this lovely tale is no myth. Scientists in the twenty-first century have discovered that female orgasms have shock-and-awe Olympian powers. Besides the ability to reach the heights multiple times, a woman with the right partner may experience what's called sustained orgasm, her body contracting pleasurably for many seconds.

Despite the encouraging example of Teiresias, at first glance it appears that neither Greek nor Roman mortals got the message about fully pleasuring their women. As the entries in this book reveal, most females had restricted freedom, zero sexual initiation, and romance-free arranged marriages. Other entries reveal the mind-boggling male ignorance of female biology—plus masculine insistence on penetrative intercourse as the only road to satisfying sex.

This brutish trend was exacerbated by any number of Greek and Roman writers who specialized in invective and sexual aggression to engage their readers, a gratuitous nastiness that reduced the private parts of men and women to acts of degradation.

But there are clues to the more satisfying, loving side of Greco-Roman life if we look carefully enough.

In researching this book, I've found evidence of abiding adoration in countless marriages. I've stumbled on the fierce fidelity and passion that kindled many a relationship between males, and learned of lesbian couples who bonded and loved long-term, just as they do today.

Good fortune has left us with written evidence as to how certain men felt about their wives, from the touching inscriptions on the tombs of long-wedded partners to the words of ones cruelly separated by a mate's early death.

For instance, the words of Pliny the Younger, an aristocratic orator and author, in a letter to his wife, Cornelia: "I am seized by an unbelievable longing for you. The reason is above all my love, but secondarily the fact that we are not used to being apart."

Another example, a humble graffito left on a Pompeian wall: "Methe of Atella, slave of Cominia, is in love with Chrestus. May Venus of Pompeii [patron goddess of the city] be propitious to them with all her heart, and may they live in concord."

Males in cultures around the Mediterranean had (and still have) a sensual appreciation for life. At times they erotically admired masculine youth, the epitome of what they used to be. They also had a special gleam in their eyes for that glorious creature, the female of the species.

Thus love and orgasmic fulfillment could be found in other relationships besides marriage. Take the example of Ovid, often called the last and greatest of Roman love poets. He pursued erotic rapport as wholeheartedly as he pursued poetry. And wrote about the happy result. Married three times while giving the conquest-a-night playboys of Rome a run for their money, he put the highest priority on the feminine right to derive pleasure from acts of intimacy.

He knew, as did the ancient Egyptians, that orgasm was the source of life, a sacred act that also allowed men and women to experience life, and love, in a more stunning and complete way. As he put it, "Let the woman feel the sexual urgency, released from the very depths of her marrow, and let that be equally pleasing to both."

Another clue I've run across regarding long-ago beliefs in sexual completion comes from the

*The Romans had a Latin word for it: delecto, the pleasure that a woman reached when her lover delivered sweet release to her.*

Latin language itself. Rather than one word, the Romans had two beautiful terms for orgasm. They called it *delecto* for the pleasure a woman experienced when her lover delivered that gift to her. And they used the word *voluptas* (from which comes our word voluptuous) to describe the explosion of joy felt by the man at his climax.

Ovid also had bisexual relationships but evidently preferred women, as his extant writings show. His loving advice about sharing the joy of orgasm, however, could just as easily been aimed at same-sex couples. Being a man of his time—that is, a regular at the circus racetrack and athletic competitions—he couched his words in sports metaphors: "But don't you fail your lady, hoisting bigger sails, and don't let her get ahead of you on the track either. Race to the finish together; that's when pleasure is full, when man and woman lie there, equally vanquished."

# ACKNOWLEDGMENTS & DEDICATION

This book is dedicated to my darling sister, Mary Davis; my treasured daughter, Valerie Conroy; and my mother, Carol, whose earthy humor and Zorba spirit I honor every day.

Special thanks to my agent, David Forrer, and to InkWell Management; and to my publisher, George Gibson, and Walker/Bloomsbury for their patience and support in helping to shape this book.

My gratitude also to the friends and writing colleagues who kept me motivated and satiated to the finish line, including *hortator* Bill Morem, William Henry Crew III, Jeri Remley, Jim Hayes, Maria Lorca, Wilma Smith, Elizabeth Spurr, and Sherry Shahan, Irene Hahn and the Roman history book group, and the talented members of my own Cambria Writers Workshop.

That number includes ace author-researcher Adrienne Mayor, whose groundbreaking book, *The Poison King*, was inspirational, and Caroline Lawrence, whose deeply researched books and literary output are equally inspiring.

I'm also grateful for the encouragement and generous hospitality given to me while researching by fellow writers Judith Harris, David Willey, Joyce Wyels, and Kate Hovey.

Thanks also to Alan Hirshfeld, Dan Krieger, and Alex Comfort, whose contributions sparked the *Joy of Sexus* title.

And lastly, a passionate thanks to Paul Ogren, whose loving interest, sense of fun, and thirst to learn more about the juice and joy of long-ago love and sexuality finally persuaded me to return from the never-never land of research rapture and bring this book to fruition.

# BIBLIOGRAPHY & ONLINE RESOURCES

Curious history buffs, be forewarned: A vast haystack of material from ancient times has survived, with more coming to light periodically. The sheer size and geographic disarray of this historical haystack is daunting. The study needed to understand the context of what you're reading as well as get a rough sense of its trustworthiness is equally challenging. Nevertheless, the quest is worth the eyestrain.

Primary sources for this book include Aristophanes; Arrian; Athenaeus; Aulus Gellius; Cicero, especially his letters; Diogenes Laertius's *Lives of Eminent Philosophers*; Dio Cassius; Diodorus Siculus; Euripides; Galen; Herodian; Herodotus; Hesiod; Josephus; Juvenal; Livy; Lucian; Lucretius; Martial; Ovid; Pausanias' *Description of Greece*; Petronius; Phlegon's *Book of Marvels*; Plato; the works and letters of Pliny the Elder and Pliny the Younger; Plutarch's *Lives* and *Moralia*; Seneca; Strabo's *Geography*; Suetonius's *Lives of the Twelve Caesars*; Tacitus; Xenophon; playwrights and poets Aesop, Alcaeus, Anacreon, Apuleius, Catullus, Hesiod, Horace, Menandar, Pindar, Plautus, Sappho, and Sophocles. These works and more can be found in the Loeb Classical Library collection published by Harvard University Press. In recent years, Pantheon Books has begun publishing its Landmark editions of Herodotus, Xenophon, and Thucydides, with others in the pipeline. Highly recommended.

Other priceless material comes from ancient coins, period artwork, and a cornucopia of archaeological sources; from primary and secondary sources online, as noted elsewhere in this section; and from letters, inscriptions, and primary-source compilations found in books such as Shelton's *As the Romans*

*Did, Pompeii's Erotic Songbook,* and the Loeb Library two-volume set called *Select Papyri,* translated by Hunt and Edgar.

The following resources (most of them secondary) offer a variety of facts, theories, perspectives, and visuals on love, lust, and longing and the stories of long-ago men and women who felt those emotions. Since sexual subject matter is often a high-voltage topic, what is presented as fact in a given book may at times be rife with prejudice and opinion. Whether you're examining primary or secondary sources, keep in mind what noted author and distinguished historian Michael Grant had to say in his 1995 book, *Greek & Roman Historians, Information and Misinformation*: "The one thing certain about history is that what we are told is by no means always true."

Ackerman, Diane. *A Natural History of Love.* (Random House, 1994.)

Adams, Cecil. *The Straight Dope* (and half a dozen sequels). (Ballantine Books, 1988–1999.)

Adams, J. N. *The Latin Sexual Vocabulary.* (Johns Hopkins University Press, 1993.)

Adkins, Lesley and Roy. *Dictionary of Roman Religion.* (Oxford University Press, 1996.)

_____. *Handbook to Life in Ancient Greece.* (Facts on File, 1997.)

_____. *Handbook to Life in Ancient Rome.* (Facts on File, 1994.)

Barrett, Anthony. *Livia, First Lady of Imperial Rome.* (Yale University Press, 2002.)

_____. *Caligula, the Corruption of Power.* (Yale University Press, 1990.)

_____. *Agrippina, Sex, Power and Politics in the Early Empire.* (Yale University Press, 1996.)

Brooten, Bernadette J. *Love Between Women*. (University of Chicago Press, 1996.)

Cantarella, Eva. *Bisexuality in the Ancient World*. (Yale University Press, 1992.)

Cawthorne, Nigel. *Sex Lives of the Roman Emperors*. (Metro/Prion Books, 2006.)

Clarke, John R. *Looking at Lovemaking*. (University of California Press, 2001.)

Cruse, Audrey. *Roman Medicine*. (Tempus Ltd., 2004.)

Davidson, James. *Courtesans and Fishcakes*. (St. Martin's Press, 1997.)

————. *The Greeks and Greek Love*. (Random House, 2007.)

Dover, K. J. *Greek Homosexuality*. (Harvard University Press, 1989.)

Dress, Ludwig. *Olympia: Gods, Artists, and Athletes*. (Praeger, 1968.)

Dupont, Florence. *Daily Life in Ancient Rome*. (Blackwell Ltd., 1992.)

Edelstein, Ludwig. *Ancient Medicine*. (Johns Hopkins Press, 1967.)

Faraone, Christopher. *Ancient Greek Love Magic*. (Harvard University Press, 2001.)

Feinberg, Leslie. *Transgender Warriors*. (Beacon Press, 1996.)

Flaceliere, Robert. *Love in Ancient Greece*. (Crown Publishers, 1962.)

Griffin, Miriam. *Nero, the End of a Dynasty*. (Yale University Press, 1985.)

Grant, Michael. *Cleopatra, a Biography*. (Barnes & Noble, 1972.)

Grmek, Mirko. *Diseases in the Ancient Greek World*. (Johns Hopkins Press, 1989.)

Groneman, Carol. *Nymphomania*. (W. W. Norton, 2000.)

Himes, Norman. *Medical History of Contraception*. (Schocken Books, 1970.)

James, Peter and Thorpe, Nick. *Ancient Inventions*. (Ballantine Books, 1994.)

Johnson, Marguerite, and Ryan, Terry. *Sexuality in Greek and Roman Society and Literature*. (Routledge, 2005.)

Kiefer, Otto. *Sexual Life in Ancient Rome.* (Dorset Press, 1993.)

Keuls, Eva. *The Reign of the Phallus.* (Harper & Row, 1985.)

Kraemer, Ross, ed. *Maenads, Martyrs, Matrons, Monastics.* (Fortress Press, 1988.)

Lewis, Naphtali. *The Interpretation of Dreams & Portents in Antiquity.*
(Bolchazy-Carducci Publishing, 1996 reprint.)

Licht, Hans. *Sexual Life in Ancient Greece.* (Covici Friede Publishers, 1932.)

Longrigg, James. *Greek Medicine from the Heroic to the Hellenistic Age: A Source
Book.* (Routledge, 1998.)

Luck, Georg. *Arcana Mundi.* (Johns Hopkins University Press, 2006.)

Maines, Rachel. *The Technology of Orgasm.* (Johns Hopkins University
Press, 1999.)

Majno, Guido. *The Healing Hand: Man and Wound in the Ancient World.*
(Harvard University Press, 1975.)

Matyszak, Philip. *Gladiator, the Roman Fighters' (Unofficial) Guide.* (Thames
& Hudson, 2011.)

————. *Ancient Rome on Five Denarii a Day.* (Thames & Hudson,
2008.)

————. *Ancient Athens on Five Drachmas a Day.* (Thames & Hudson,
2008.)

Mayor, Adrienne. *The Poison King.* (Princeton University Press, 2010.)

————. *Greek Fire, Poison Arrows, and Scorpion Bombs.* (Overlook
Duckworth London, 2004.)

Percy, William A. *Pederasty and Pedagogy in Archaic Greece.* (University of
Illinois Press, 1996.)

Richlin, Amy. *The Garden of Priapus.* (Oxford University Press, 1992.)

————. Richlin, ed. *Pornography and Representation in Greece and Rome.*
(Oxford University Press, 1992.)

Riddle, John. *Contraception and Abortion from the Ancient World to the Renaissance*. (Harvard University Press, 1992.)

Roach, Mary. *Bonk: The Curious Coupling of Science and Sex*. (W. W. Norton, 2008.)

Salmonson, Jessica A. *The Encyclopedia of Amazons*. (Anchor/Doubleday, 1991.)

Scholz, Piotr. *Eunuchs and Castrati*. (Markus Weiner Publishers, 2001.)

Shelton, Joanne. *As the Romans Did: a Sourcebook in Roman Social History*. (Oxford University Press, 1988.)

Smith, William. *Dictionary of Greek and Roman Antiquities*, second ed. (Little, Brown, 1859.) Most of the Roman entries are also available, searchable, and annotated with acerbic wit online at Bill Thayer's LacusCurtius website. Another by Smith, also recommended: *A New Classical Dictionary of Greek and Roman Biography, Mythology, and Geography*. (Harper & Brothers, 1888.)

Speller, Elizabeth. *Following Hadrian*. (Oxford University Press, 2003.)

Stengers, Jean, and Anne Van Neck. *Masturbation: The History of a Great Terror*. (Palgrave Macmillan, 2001.)

Tannahill, Reay. *Sex in History*. (Stein and Day, 1980.)

Vivolo, F. Paolo. *Pompeii's Erotic Songbook*. (Plurigraf, 2001.)

Walker, Barbara G. *The Woman's Encyclopedia of Myths and Secrets*. (Castle Books, 1996.)

Zanker, P. *The Power of Images in the Age of Augustus*. (University of Michigan Press, 2001.)

Lastly, get yourself a superlative guide to place-names in the ancient world, from what they were called originally as well as what they're called now: *Webster's New Geographical Dictionary* (new or used).

# ONLINE RESOURCES:

Fans of the ancient world, from beginner fanatics to serious long-term addicts, are in luck online. Here are some of my favorites: and these gloriously wide-ranging, well-researched websites on ancient Roman, Greek, and other cultures around or near the Mediterranean Sea truly deserve that much-abused adjective "awesome."

William Thayer's massive site, LacusCurtius. Besides excellent online translations of over forty Roman and Greek writers, Thayer includes detailed notes and subject matter indices. Other felicities: a Roman gazetteer, a treasure trove of public domain articles written by experts in prior centuries, detailed topographical data, and much of Smith's *Dictionary of Roman and Greek Antiquities.*

Jona Lendering's huge site, livius.org. This bonanza, accessible and well-written (most by Lendering) has over 3,600 pages and countless articles on ancient world figures, events, places, monuments, and more. Beautifully organized into geographic and topic subheads from Anatolia to the Great Flood.

Thayer and Lendering also write rambambashi.wordpress.org, a worthwhile blog with website updates plus unflinching reviews of everything from the Vatican "museum" to time-worn tour guide myths.

Andrew Smith's attalus.org is a bright look at the ancient world, with an invaluable history overview, large sections on papyri and inscriptions, 25,000 links to relevant topics, and what must have been a labor of love: detailed timelines from the fourth century B.C. through the first century B.C.

For those seeking visual sources on the ancient world: Popular historical fiction author Steven Saylor has a fascinating section on his website, www.stevensaylor.com, that's a detailed guide to all films, television pro-grams, and TV series past and present on Greco-Roman and ancient world themes. Extremely useful, since Saylor gives direct links to acquire these visual delights. His recommended book list is also wonderful.

Romanmysteries.com is another winner, the brainchild of another prolific writer: Caroline Lawrence, author of the Roman Mysteries series for younger readers. On it, she provides a staggering array of links to the ancient world; I'm especially fond of her links to ancient Ostia—Pompeii's often overlooked rival in terms of on-site interest.

If you enjoyed my entries on long-ago beliefs about wandering wombs and hysteria, be sure to see the 2012 Sony film *Hysteria*. In comic detail, it shows to what lengths women have gone through to get an orgasm—and how long those myths about female biology have persisted.

# Central Mediterranean: Greece, Macedonia, the Greek islands, and Asia Minor

## Mediterranean: Asia Minor, the Middle East, and the Holy Land

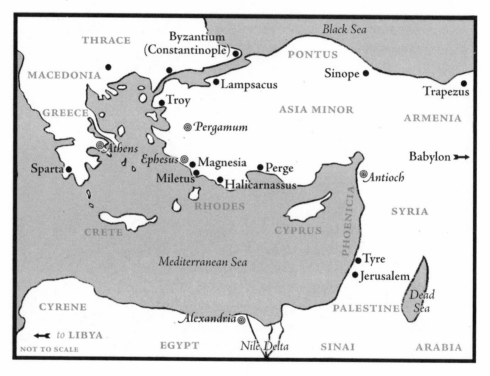

# Western Mediterranean: Italy, Carthage, and Provinces of the Roman Empire

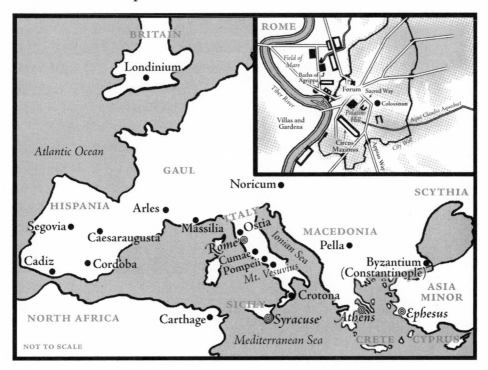

Rome, capital of the Roman Empire

## Southern Mediterranean: Egypt, North Africa, Arabia, and Mesopotamia

# INDEX

For ease of use, all the main entries are boldface in this index, including their page numbers. In addition, you will find the many cross-references mentioned in the text here (identified as SEE also). Third, most of the men and women referred to in this book are identified by hometown or geographical locale. By using the maps to the various regions around the Mediterranean in this book, you can easily pinpoint where all of them lived and worked.

Index

# A NOTE ON THE AUTHOR

Vicki León calls the central coast of California home but returns often to her Mediterranean sources. Having honed her research skills by unearthing nine hundred achievers for her Uppity Women series, including her latest book, *4,000 Years of Uppity Women*, she's also delved deeper into the ancient world with *Working IX to V* and *How to Mellify a Corpse*.